Essays on Western Hi

Lewis Gwynne Thomas

Essays on Western History

In honour of
Lewis Gwynne Thomas

Edited by
Lewis H. Thomas

The University of Alberta Press 1976

First published by
The University of Alberta Press
Edmonton, Alberta, Canada
1976

Copyright © 1976 The University of Alberta Press
Canadian Shared Cataloguing in Publication Data
Main entry under title:
Essays on Western History
ISBN 0-88864-013-7
1. The West, Canadian — History — Addresses,
essays, lectures. I. Thomas, Lewis Gwynne,
1914-   . II. Thomas, Lewis H., 1917-
FC3206.E87   971.2
F1060.E

Printed in Canada by
Printing Services of The University of Alberta

Contents

Preface

The production of this volume of essays in honour of Dr. Lewis Gwynne Thomas, Professor Emeritus of the University of Alberta, has been made possible by the enthusiasm and ready cooperation of eleven of his former students. The high standard of scholarship which their articles demonstrate, reflects the quality of his teaching over a period of thirty-six years.

Dr. Thomas inaugurated a history of Western Canada in 1949, and both lecture and seminar courses in this field have been taught by him and several of his colleagues ever since, marked by a notable growth in enrolment. But these courses in regional history have always been taught by him in the context of national history. Dr. Thomas' occasional tart comments have been reserved for those writers who have treated a theme or personality from a narrow or parochial standpoint.

The contributors to this volume are all specialists in Western Canadian history, but the choice of topic is their own. By accident rather than design they relate in almost equal number to the two main divisions of Western History -- pre- and post-1870. Both periods are also represented in Dr. Thomas' own teaching and research.

In addition to the contributors, I am greatly indebted to Mr. Leslie Gutteridge, chairman of the University Press Committee, who has given encouragement and advice, and to Mrs. Norma Gutteridge for her perceptive and expert editorial assistance. Mrs. Lillian Wonders kindly prepared the map and graphs. Mrs. Jonesy Thomas provided helpful information for my introduction. The expert typing of Mrs. Olive Baird of the Department of History was invaluable.

L.H.T.

Contributors

Walter H. Johns. Professor of Classics, University of Alberta (1938-73; Dean of Arts (1952 to 1957), and President of the University (1959 to 1969). Now Professor Emeritus of Classics.

Carl F. Betke, Assistant Historian, Royal Canadian Mounted Police Archives, Ottawa.

David H. Breen, Assistant Professor of History, University of British Columbia.

John E. Foster, Assistant Professor of History, University of Alberta.

Edward J. Hart, Archivist, Archives of the Canadian Rockies, Banff, Alberta.

R. C. Macleod, Associate Professor of History, University of Alberta.

E. A. Mitchener, Head of the Social Studies Department, Ross Sheppard High School, Edmonton.

John Nicks, officer responsible for historic sites administration, Government of Alberta, 1969-74. Currently a graduate student, Department of History, University of Alberta.

Frits Pannekoek, Chief of Historical Research, Prairie Region, National and Historic Parks Branch.

James M. Parker, University Archivist, University of Alberta.

T. D. Regehr, Professor of History, University of Saskatchewan.

Sylvia Van Kirk, Assistant Professor of History, University of Toronto.

Editor:
Lewis H. Thomas, Professor of History, University of Alberta.

Foreword

The production of volumes of essays in honour of retiring scholars has had a long and distinguished tradition in European countries and is beginning to occur with increasing frequency in the United States and Great Britain. The list of such works in Canada is very short indeed and I know of none produced at the University of Alberta prior to the present volume in honour of Professor L.G. Thomas. It is therefore a tribute not only to the recipient but to his friend and colleague (but no relation) Professor L.H. Thomas who has initiated and edited the present studies.

The contribution of a university scholar to the society he serves rests not only on his writings but on the students who have been inspired and whose lives have been enriched by his teaching and his example. The essays in the present volume, all written by former students, provide ample evidence of the influence of Professor Thomas on those who have pursued his special interest in the history of the Canadian West and there are many others who are currently applying the lessons they learned from him in universities, colleges and high schools across the country, in the civil service of Canada, particularly the foreign service, and elsewhere.

Professor Lewis H. Thomas has provided a comprehensive outline of his colleague's career and has pointed out that Lewis G. was the first native-born Albertan to hold the Chairmanship of the Department of History at the University of Alberta. Today that Department includes no fewer than five Alberta graduates on its roster of faculty representing a broad spectrum of interests in historical study.

The essays collected in the present volume cover a wide variety of topics and indicate the rich heritage which we in western Canada enjoy and which justifies the continued research of scholars in the field. It is hoped that they will prove to be of interest to a wide public and an inspiration to other students as well as a tribute to Dr. Thomas in whose honour they have been written and published.

Walter H. Johns

Walter H. Johns
Past President and Professor Emeritus

Lewis Gwynne Thomas
Lewis H. Thomas

When Lewis Gwynne Thomas enrolled at the University of Alberta in 1930, the History Department had a three-man staff -- the head, Professor George Smith, Dr. Ross Collins, and Professor Morden Long. By today's standards this seems very small, but it must be remembered that a similar situation prevailed in the other western Canadian universities. Moreover, student enrolment was small -- 1,824 in 1930-31, of which 718 were in the Faculty of Arts and Science. Yet despite the limited staff, the standard of teaching and scholarship was not lower than today. So far as the History Department was concerned the chief differences were in the library holdings and the less numerous course offerings. The history of western Europe, two or three courses in British history, Canadian history, and occasionally American history were the staple diet, and it was assumed that a professor could teach in two different fields.

Lewis Thomas was the son of a rancher, and his childhood years were spent on the home ranch "Cottonwoods," in the Millarville district, a few miles west of Okotoks and south of Calgary. His father, Harold Edward Thomas (1876-1966), had had a varied and adventurous career before settling down at Millarville. The son of a banker in North Wales he had, like so many young men of his generation, succumbed to the lure of life on the Western range, and, in 1896 came to South Dakota as a ranch pupil, later moving to Montana. The gold rush of 1899 in Nome, Alaska, lured him north, but in the following year he returned home via Victoria. In 1901 he retrieved his baggage and horses in Montana and moved across the boundary into British territory, settling in Okotoks, where he established a livery business and built a house. In 1912 he and a partner acquired a ranch on Sheep Creek, and he was able to indulge his love of good horses.

It was in this district that Harold Thomas met Edith Agnes Louise Lewis, a clever and charming English governess, who had come from Britain in 1904 in the employ of a family who were intent on ranching in the foothills country near Okotoks. Harold Thomas and Edith Lewis were married in 1905.

The beautiful country where "Cottonwoods" and other ranches were located, with the mountains on the western horizon, had appealed strongly to the British immigrants who began to arrive in the ranching district of Alberta in the 1880s, and composed the predominant element in the area. Their ranches surrounded the town of Okotoks and the tiny hamlets of Priddis, Millarville, Kew, Bragg Creek,

De Winton, and others. A general store, blacksmith shop, Anglican church, and
elementary school (if the bachelors could be induced to pay taxes to establish it)
were usually the only buildings. Of the ranchers and their families Lewis Thomas
has written:

> ....they came in such numbers from 1884 to 1914 as to give a definite
> and pervasive flavor to the manners and customs of the region. Their
> pastimes, their ways of building and furnishing their houses, their cul-
> tural interest, and their political and social attitudes were to persist
> beyond the first generation. The foothills region was particularly
> favorable to the small-scale ranching which provided a congenial live-
> lihood to those who liked an outdoor life and had brought with them
> sufficient capital to moderate the rigors of pioneering.[1]

Lewis was the youngest of the three children of the Thomas family. His two
sisters were Dorothy and Gwynydd. In addition to her activities as a rancher's
wife, their governess-mother, with her husband's assistance, taught the girls at
home for a few years. When Lewis was old enough to attend school Mrs. Thomas
and the three children moved to the house in Okotoks, while Harold and his
bachelor-partner, Mr. R.W. Thompson, remained on the ranch, although with
frequent visits back and forth to Okotoks.

Lewis Thomas was enrolled for his high school years at Mount Royal College in
Calgary -- a good boarding school operated by the United Church of Canada. His
summers were spent on the ranch where he and his sisters and their friends learned
to swim in Sheep Creek. Horseback riding was another recreation, for his father was
primarily a horseman. But the son showed marked academic aptitude, and there was
no parental pressure to make him into a rancher; hence it was natural that he should
be given a university education.

In 1934 Lewis graduated with first class honors in history, and the A.L. Burt
Prize for the highest marks in Canadian history. The following year he registered
in the M.A. program, graduating in the spring of 1935. His thesis was entitled "The
Ranching Period in Southern Alberta." It was a congenial theme, and he brought
to it a first-hand knowledge and feeling for the subject. The thesis was the first
comprehensive examination of the cattleman's frontier in Western Canada. The
first half of the study is economic history -- the creation and evolution of the industry, and its characteristics and problems. The second half is social history --
perceptive and in the best tradition of English literary style. Obviously the author
is enjoying his investigation and presentation of the rancher's domestic and community life. Two examples must suffice. The first from a discussion of diet and
cooking:

> Ranch meals were simple: meat, vegetables, and bread, followed by
> puddings or cake. Cooking was very cosmopolitan and recipes were
> constantly exchanged in an effort to secure variety. For great festivals
> Mrs. Beeton's monumental handbook was produced and the glories of

English cookery attempted and, one gathers, achieved. Tea and coffee, with the advantage of the former, were the most popular beverages. Beer, and other slightly alcoholic drinkables were often made at home. The men consumed a good deal of brandy and whisky. Meals in the grand ranch manner were great occasions reminiscent of Dickensian banquets. They were served with the utmost informality but a dim reverence brooded over them as if the ghost of not-quite-forgotten Victorian mahogany sanctified the rougher boards of the last frontier.[2]

The conclusion of the section on sports and pastimes reads as follows:

The ranchers enjoyed themselves. Life was easy enough to allow a plentiful leisure and they used it pleasantly without the conscientious scruples which might have troubled those who had known a harder pioneering. Every occasion was seized for entertainment and the ranchers foregathered upon the slightest excuse. Sometimes work was neglected for a more attractive diversion, but very rarely; haying meant staying at home and gaiety ran highest when work was slack. It would be unfair to call the ranchers a lazy people, equally unfair to stigmatize them as over-industrous. They were not always financially successful; but they did introduce into Alberta a tradition of leisure, a more graceful mode of living, in welcome contrast to the glorification of labor as an end in itself which has been so characteristic of the Canadian and American way of life.[3]

The thesis demonstrates the young author's gift for an apt phrase. In later years he became known as a distinguished stylist. As a conversationalist he possessed the happy gift, when the occasion required it, for an apt or witty phrase.

Like so many of his contemporaries who graduated in the depression years Lewis found it impossible to find work suited to his academic qualifications. But he was adaptable, and found a job as advance agent for an Albertan theatrical company. Theatrical companies, however, were particularly vulnerable in the "Dirty Thirties," and the enterprise expired in Fort Macleod leaving its employees stranded there in the early winter of 1936.

After a fruitless search for alternative employment, Lewis registered as a Ph.D. candidate at Harvard University. One reason for his choice of Harvard was the presence on the staff of Professor Frederick Merk, a distinguished Turnerian who had published a number of important works relating to the Hudson's Bay Company and the Oregon Question. During his two years at Harvard he was unable to return home for Christmas, but the summers were spent on the ranch. Having completed his course work at Harvard and selected a dissertation topic, which Merk was to supervise, he was appointed in the autumn of 1938 as Sessional Instructor in the Department of History at the University of Alberta replacing Professor Long who was on sabbatical leave that year.

Professor George Smith, who had studied at Toronto and Oxford, had succeeded

A.L. Burt as head of the department in 1930. He was an outstanding teacher and administrator, and during his tenure the comprehensive examination for the honors program was introduced and the M.A. requirements revised. The other two professors, Long and Collins, continued to offer their specialties. Smith was most at home in modern history and during his headship (1930-47) taught International Relations Since 1871, and Contemporary Canada. But he also assisted his colleagues by offering courses in post-Medieval European and British constitutional history. Lewis greatly admired George Smith and one can detect his formative influence on his own career. Smith's approach to history was once characterized as follows:

> He was not a narrow specialist, but was familiar with the history of many countries and many periods. Keenly aware of the links between political and social history and the history of music, painting and literature, he missed no opportunity of tying subject to subject and of giving shape and coherence to the work of his students.

In addition to heading the Department of History, Smith accepted the onerous responsibilities of Dean of Arts in 1938, serving seven years in this capacity. His successor paid him this tribute at the time of his death:

> He was not a research man. He often said that three kinds of work were open to a member of a University staff: teaching, administration, research; and that one could scarcely hope to do well in all three. He excelled in two. He made the choice deliberately; and nobody who knew him can doubt that, if he had chosen to avoid administrative duties, he had the ability to do research work of real distinction. One result of the devotion of much of his time to the understanding, enforcement, and improvement of the rules and principles under which a University does its work was that he gave freedom to his colleagues to do research. His students both in Toronto and Alberta, especially his best students, will long remember the teaching of George Smith....

Smith was anxious that Lewis be retained on staff. His appointment was renewed and he taught British History Since 1485. In 1941 he was also assigned the History of the British Commonwealth. Meanwhile he involved himself with the C.O.T.C. in 1939-42. The training program, which included Sarcee Camp in the summers, was more extensive than it had been in pre-war days. In 1942 Lewis was commissioned as a Lieutenant in the Royal Canadian Navy, and left for basic training in the Halifax-Dartmouth area. He then went to Ottawa where he was involved in naval intelligence. Here he married (October, 1943) Muriel Eleanor ("Jonesy") Massie, an Edmontonian who was a 1934 graduate in home economics, then working in the National Research Council. From Ottawa he was transferred to St. John's, Newfoundland in 1944 where, in addition to his regular duties, he and Jonesy extended hospitality to many lonely sailors and their wives, and where Lewis attained the rank of Lieutenant Commander.

President Newton and the University of Alberta administration were anxious to have their promising young staff members return to their duties. Anticipating an upsurge of veteran attendance, Professor Long was particularly concerned that Lewis should return rather than accept a position with the historical section of the armed forces or become Provincial Archivist under anticipated Alberta archives legislation. In the end Lewis chose to return to teaching at the beginning of the 1945 fall term, after receiving his discharge as a Lieutenant Commander. He was appointed Lecturer in History, a promotion for which Smith had argued several years earlier. Smith had been given leave of absence in 1943 for war work in Ottawa but a breakdown in health prevented his return until the autumn of 1947, and he died shortly thereafter. During the four years of his absence from the campus Professor Long was acting head of the department, and succeeded to the headship in 1947.

In the session of 1949-50 Lewis introduced the History of the Canadian West, a subject which was taught either as a lecture or seminar course, or both, and continuously since then. The course description read:

> The social, political and economic history of Canada west of the
> Great Lakes, with emphasis on the period of settlement.

From this time on Lewis must be credited with teaching every year the only course on the Canadian West at any university in Canada. It had been pioneered by A.S. Morton at Saskatchewan, but following Morton's retirement it had not been continued, and later was only offered intermittently. It was not until 1969 following the appointment of Lewis's first Ph.D. student, Professor T.D. Regehr, that it was again taught on a regular basis. Closely related to this course was the support which Lewis gave Smith and later Long in their efforts to secure the creation of a provincial archives for Alberta. His contribution to the department was belatedly recognized by his appointment as Asistant Professor in 1946 and as Associate Professor in 1951.

During these years he carried a heavy teaching load in addition to the course on the Canadian West -- the British Commonwealth, International Affairs Since 1871, and Tudor and Stuart England. He accepted appointment by the Board of Governors as secretary of the Faculty of Arts (1947-52) with an annual honorarium of $300. Following Professor Long's retirement in 1952, he assumed the sole responsibility for offering Canadian history. He usually offered three different courses, very rarely two, and one year (1950-51) four. In 1947 his first publication appeared, "The Liberal Party in Alberta," published in the *Canadian Historical Review.* This was followed in 1948 by *The University of Alberta in the War of 1939-45,* a well organized, thoughtful analysis which is much more than a collection of names, dates, and administrative details. In 1948 he also wrote a pamphlet for the Historical Society of Alberta entitled "History is a Mosaic."

Faculty salaries were still very low in this period, and members of the staff would augment their incomes by teaching evening courses. This has produced an anecdote told by one of his senior colleagues to the effect that on one occasion Lewis was offering a course in Canadian history, and found he would have a large registration. The

University administration was willing to sanction a second course if a sufficient number of students expressed an interest. An uncommonly kind person, Lewis was concerned about a colleague's financial needs, and when he met the class proceeded to argue that Canadian history was a very difficult subject, as compared with, say, the British history course which his colleague down the hall was offering. Carried away by his own eloquence, he was finally interrupted by one of the students who said "You'd better stop now Professor Thomas, half the class have left."

In 1952 Lewis received a sabbatical leave, which he spent on research activities in England. He examined the voluminous records of the Hudson's Bay Company and the archives of the Anglican Missionary bodies active in Western Canada in the nineteenth century -- the Society for the Propagation of the Gospel in Foreign Parts (S.P.G.), the Church Missionary Society (C.M.S.), and the Colonial and Continental Church Society (Col. & Con.), each with its own field of activity and representing its own brand of Anglican churchmanship. The first paper which he read at the annual meeting of the Canadian Historical Association, in Winnipeg in 1954, was a report on these resources,[11] which was followed by a lively discussion of the limitations of Canadian historical scholarship in this neglected field of social history.

In the previous year (1953) he received his Ph.D. degree from Harvard University. His dissertation dealt with the political history of Alberta from 1905 to 1921. In 1959, the year following his appointment as head of the department, a condensed version of his dissertation was published by the University of Toronto Press under the title of *The Liberal Party in Alberta: A History of Politics in the Province of Alberta 1905-1921.* It appeared as one of the noted series of original works of scholarship "Social Credit in Alberta: Its Background and Development" edited by Professor S.D. Clark of the University of Toronto. Clark, in his foreword to the Thomas work, wrote:

> The people of Alberta turned against the old parties in 1921, and, with the conditions of the 1930s breeding even a greater distrust of things connected with Ottawa and the East, they were not likely to reverse their position in 1935. What happened in 1935 can be traced back to events and developments occuring in the years before the First World War which had the effect of seriously weakening the position in Alberta of the old parties....There are too few provincial political histories in Canadian literature. Professor Thomas has set an example, and a standard, which it is to be hoped will be followed by many other scholars.

The reviewer in the *Canadian Journal of Economics and Political Science* echoed Clark's comments when he wrote:

> The book has the merit of being tightly written, packing a great deal of solid information into a concise two hundred pages. Still, for all its solidity this is emphatically not a dull work. Professor Thomas presents a graphic case study of a party machine.

The reviewers in both this journal and the *Canadian Historical Review* pointed out that the real scope of the work was indicated by its sub-title, being a general political history of Alberta during these years. The author devoted considerable attention to the Conservative party and to the organized farm movement.

Lewis was particularly interested in church history. His first publication venture in this field was "Canon William G. Newton" in a 1950 issue of *Edmonton Churchman.* Later (1958) he published "Mission Church in Edmonton: An Anglican Experiment in the Canadian Northwest" in the *Pacific Northwest Quarterly.* In 1956 he read "The Church of England and Higher Education in the Prairie West Before 1914" to the annual meeting of the Canadian Church Historical Society. In 1963 he became a member of the editorial committee of this society's journal, retaining this position to the present. These publications assure him a place among the pioneers of Canadian social history.

A faithful churchman and lay worker, Lewis spent much of his time and energy during these years in the interest of the Anglican church. For a period he was a member of the executive committee of the synod of the Diocese of Edmonton and knew its bishops well, particularly the scholarly and cultivated Rt. Rev. W.F. Barfoot (1941-53). He and Jonesy were active members of St. George's Church, whose liberal tone appealed to students in the university residences as well as numerous laymen living in the Windsor Park and Garneau districts bordering the campus. For several years he was also a vigorous promoter of St. Aidan's House in the Garneau area, which was a small residence for Anglican men, and which some hoped would develop as an Anglican college in the University.

Lewis found escape and relaxation during the intensive academic activity of these years in the garden of his home in the Garneau district and his cottage on Lake Wabamun, for he was an enthusiastic and knowledgable horticulturist. This hobby was a natural activity for "A Little Bit of Old England from Okotoks," as his students sometimes affectionately called him. Whether at home or the lake, colleagues and friends were always warmly welcomed and frequently entertained by Lewis and his wife and their two sons -- Dennis Roland Gwynne and Gregory Edward Gwynne. Another interest was the preservation of Alberta's architectural heritage, and he was an active supporter of every effort to ward off the destruction of Rutherford House. Success was achieved when the provincial government restored it to its original condition -- one of the very few surviving examples of Edwardian elegance in Edmonton.

When Professor Collins retired in 1958, Lewis G. Thomas was the logical choice as his successor as head of the department. The first Alberta-born staff member to occupy this position, he had given devoted service to the department and the University during the preceding twenty years. The Board of Governors had promoted him to a full professorship early in 1958, and subsequently directed that he assume the headship on September 1.

This year the full-time permanent staff numbered five, including Lewis -- F.D. Blackley, W.D. Farnham, R.H. McNeal, and W.J. Eccles -- all vigorous young men, with strong opinions on teaching and scholarship, most of them well advanced on important research projects which were to issue in significant publications. Their ideas can be traced in the deliberations of the department, for Lewis inaugurated a policy (which has continued to the present) of recording the discussions and decisions of department meetings in full.

Lewis was particularly interested in promoting the honors program and in improving the system of honors comprehensive examinations. Early in his term he carried forward the negotiations which enabled the department to offer doctoral work. He encouraged members to bring forward their ideas on course offerings, budget for history, and on University Library acquisitions in history. He established departmental committees on graduate studies, library maps, and the freshman course. He organized an executive committee to advise the head. In general, he followed the practice of consulting his colleagues, but did not relinquish his powers and responsibilities as head in an era which still held him accountable for the conduct of the affairs of the department. Had his term, which ended with his resignation in 1964, extended into the era when faculty opinion favored the concept of limited-term chairmanship, there is little doubt that he would have agreed.

The minutes of the department recorded spirited discussion and sometimes inconclusive debates on such hardy perennials as pre-requisites, sectioning of the freshman class, standards of grading, weighting of term work, the Ph.D. program, and a departmental style guide. But on the proposed revision of the high schools' Social Studies course there was unanimity. The minutes record that Professor Farnham

> gave...a vivid and impassioned description of the present Social Studies course on 'Canada and the Modern World'. The structure of the course was chaotic....Dr. Farnham observed that two questions were involved: the introduction of a new optional history course, and the revision of the social studies course so that it would follow an historical plan. Educators...were not yet aware that historians had long abandoned the idea that history is past politics and nothing more.

One of the responsibilities of the head of the department during these years was the supervision of history instruction at the Calgary branch of the University. Lewis's relations with the Calgary staff were cordial, and he welcomed the academic autonomy which was granted in 1963 under the headship of Professor Frederick Heymann.

By the 1961-62 term the present structure of course offerings at all levels had been established. This was made possible by the appointment of specialists in a variety of fields. It reflected the dramatic growth in university registration, from 8,157 in 1958-59, to 13,570 in 1963-64. From the permanent staff of five when Lewis had assumed the headship, the numbers had grown to thirteen when he retired from this post six years later. He had carried a heavy burden of recruitment with notable success.

During these years the department occupied offices on the second floor of the Arts Building, supplemented later with quarters in the neighboring Powerhouse. When the University authorities decided to relocate the social sciences and history

in the projected Henry Marshall Tory Building, the planning of the space to be occupied by the department became a matter of vital concern. Professor Farnham
served on the planning committee for the building. Lewis and his colleagues
favored an arrangement which would place the faculty, graduate and honors students, and seminar rooms in close proximity on the same floor. Each graduate
student was to be provided with an office adjacent to a faculty office. Lewis
hoped that the sense of community of teachers and students would be enhanced
by this arrangement. In *The University of Alberta in the War of 1939-45* he had
written of the improvisations made to accommodate the veteran enrolment:

> The overcrowding and the exacting timetable had their compensation
> in the quality of the student. The most serious loss was in the close
> personal relationship that used to be possible between teacher and the
> taught. For that, there can in the educative process be no adequate
> compensation. But it is doubtful whether in any academic society
> that essence of the university can be wholly and permanently destroyed.

In the history quarters of the Henry Marshall Tory building, he believed, the essential "essence of the university" could be restored.

Lewis spent a good part of a sabbatical leave in 1972-73 in Ottawa and London
working on a project which was particularly congenial to him personally, and to the
cause of historical scholarship in Canada -- the preparation of a new edition of A.S.
Morton's *History of the Canadian West to 1870-71.* This seminal work, over 900
pages in length, originally published in London in 1939, had long been out-of-print.
He had used it as a text in his courses on the Canadian West, and lamented its un-
availability to students and to the profession, except in a few libraries. The University of Toronto Press decided to reprint it with an introduction and notes by Lewis.

The task would have seemed simple to many, but in reality was a formidable one.
Morton had documented his history in very general terms, but his widow, Mrs.
Vivian Morton, made Morton's proof copy, with its footnotes, available for the new
edition. Morton had provided "Brief Bibliographical Notes" for each chapter of his
text, consisting of important monographs and record groups in the Hudson's Bay
Company's archives. But specific citations (footnotes) were lacking. He had, however, placed citations in his proof copy of the massive manuscript. In preparing his
edition (which appeared in 1973) Lewis G. Thomas listed all important monographs
on the history of the fur trade which had been written since 1939, placing them at
the beginning of each chapter of his notes. These were followed by the footnotes,
based on Morton's citations on the proof copy. He reproduced them wherever they
were exact, supplementing them where necessary with comments based on his own
meticulous examination of the primary sources -- chiefly the Company's archives on
which Morton had relied so heavily. It was a formidable and time-consuming effort.

Lewis provided an editorial introduction dealing with Morton's career, his various
publications, and his methodology, preconceptions, and philosophy of history. He
praised "the detachment that enabled Morton to discern new directions in which
the interpretation of Western History might move." While he was sympathetic to

Morton's approach, he was not uncritical. "There is little evidence," he concluded, "that Morton cared much about the why of history and no one would claim him as a master interpreter of the past; it was not for him to illuminate the whole glade of history. But he opened his chosen preserve to the light of day and occasionally he shed a searching beam down some obscure or even unsuspected by way."

The 10 last years of Lewis's academic career were spent in teaching graduate courses and lecture or seminar courses on Western Canadian history, and in advising M.A. and Ph.D. candidates. A tangible evidence of the interest he took in the careers and personal concerns of former colleagues and students, and their affectionate regard for him, is to be found in his voluminous correspondence. He had too, perceptive and well informed acquaintance with members of the historical profession across the country. It is not surprising that he was elected to the prestigious office of President of the Canadian Historical Association in 1972. His presidential year was marked by conscientious and time-consuming activity during a sabbatical leave in 1972-73.

Freedom from intense departmental administrative activity enabled Lewis to resume scholarly publishing -- articles in *The Newsletter* of the Bibliographical Society of Canada,[20] *The New Trail*[21] ("The Rutherford House and its Place in Alberta Architecture"), the *Alberta Historical Review,* the *Transactions of the Royal Society of Canada,*[23] the *Papers of the 7th Annual Conference of the Western History Association,*[24] two encyclopedia articles, and numerous book reviews in the *Canadian Historical Review, The Beaver,* and other scholarly journals. His presidential address to the Canadian Historical Association, "Associations and Communications,"[25] displayed his capacity to relate the microcosm of the development of the Association to the macrocosm of Canadian inter-regional communications, or, as was the case in his own region, weaknesses in communications which produced the phenomenon of western alienation.

In the articles published since 1958 his first love reasserted itself -- the social history of the West, and in the first year of his retirement (1975) he contributed perceptive analyses to a local history of the ranching district he knew so well as a youth. Earlier in the year he was Visiting Professor in the Department of History at the University of Massachusetts at Amherst. But equally important is the fact that one can anticipate further contributions to Western Canadian historiography, and it remains only to wish him well in these endeavors while he finds relaxation in his garden at Lake Wabamun.

PART I
THE FUR TRADE PERIOD

The Diary of a Young Fur Trader:
The 1789-1790 Journal of Thomas Staynor
John Nicks

This article is based primarily upon a daily journal of occurrences kept by Thomas Staynor during the winter of 1789-1790.* Staynor had been hired by the Hudson's Bay Company in 1787 as a writer and assistant trader at Churchill. Born in London on March 27, 1770 he presumably grew up and was educated in that great metropolitan centre. He appears to have been educated for a career at sea as he was considered by the Company to be "acquainted with marine affairs" and kept his personal journal from noon to noon in accordance with the traditional practice in keeping a ship's log. It is apparent that he also had some training or experience in taking astronomical observations as he was chosen in the summer of 1789 to act as Philip Turnor's assistant in the proposed Northern Expedition which had been organized to lay the groundwork for a concerted push by the Hudson's Bay Company into the Athabasca country.[1]

Due to inadequate logistical support Turnor and his party were unable to proceed beyond Cumberland House in the fall of 1789. As a result Thomas Staynor was sent up the Saskatchewan River with instructions to survey the country beyond that already traversed by Turnor a decade earlier, and "to go on to the Stony Mountain" to winter there with the Piegan Indians as David Thompson had done two years earlier.[2] Presumably it was hoped that with his training in navigational techniques he would be able to obtain accurate observations on the locations of the mountains and other major features of the country he would traverse. Unfortunately this was not to be. Staynor missed his opportunity to take his place as one of the pioneers in the scientific exploration of Canada by a scant four weeks when he arrived at Manchester House too late to join the Piegan Indians on their return to their homeland in the foothills.

Nevertheless, the journal that Thomas Staynor kept that winter offers some interesting insights into the internal economy and operation of a Hudson's Bay Company trading post as recorded by someone who was seeing and experiencing

* The journal of Thomas Staynor is in the Hudson's Bay Company Archives where it is classified as item B.121/a/5. Permission to quote from the journal and other documents in the Company's archives has been granted by the Hudson's Bay Company archivist, Provincial Archives of Manitoba, Winnipeg, and is gratefully acknowledged.

it for the first time. He was not totally new to the fur trade having spent two years already at Churchill and it is likely that he had heard a great deal about inland life. At Churchill he had been assistant to Samuel Hearne, the famous inland traveller and founder of Cumberland House, the first inland post on the Saskatchewan River. Despite this, his viewpoint was fresh and the journal he kept provides a different perspective than that normally seen in the official post journals. Perhaps its greatest interest, however, stems from the fact that it appears to be unique in recording the daily occurrences in the outlying hunting and wintering camps and the horse guards which were essential though shadowy companions to every inland post.

On October 9, 1789 Thomas Staynor left Cumberland House bound up the Saskatchewan River towards the upper settlements of South Branch House and Manchester House. His initial reaction to the life of an inland traveller seems to have been less than enthusiastic. He was indignant at having been compelled "to work the same as a labouring man"[3] on the passage up from York Factory. Due to the shortage of men to man the inland establishments the custom had developed that all inland officers were expected to assume their fair share of the work while on the road. Staynor felt that this was only a custom sanctified by use and no longer a necessary duty. He argued further that "People, who have been brought up to Labour from their Infancy are much fittest for your Honors Inland Service where such duty is required from them. For my part I don't find myself fully capable to carry Weights of burthen 200 lbs or more on my back across Carrying places of a mile to 3 or 4 miles long neither can I conceive it to be required for me to do so..."[4]

Staynor's trip up to South Branch House does not appear to have demanded so much of him. He left Cumberland House with the fall express which consisted of a small brigade of two canoes carrying little payload except for Staynor and his equipment and supplies. This was most unusual as the Company normally chose to send additional trade goods inland with the fall canoes. Clearly Staynor's mission to accompany the Piegan to the Rocky Mountains was considered to be important enough to consider substituting his belongings and instruments for badly needed articles for trade. Staynor himself appears to have received greater deference on this voyage although he voluntarily took one turn on the tracking line. He found it to be very hard work comparable to "Nothing but the Labour of a Horse."[5] Indeed it must have seemed strange to him to see men performing the same function as that assigned to horses along the towpaths of the canals which were then the latest thing in transportation technology. From this experience Staynor gained little but bruised feet and the beginnings of some insight into the hardships experienced by his men who had to pull the canoes most of the way up the river knee-deep in the icy mid-October waters of the Saskatchewan River.

When Staynor arrived at South Branch House he took a series of astronomical observations in order to establish an accurate position for the post. To his dismay the readings were erratic and he concluded that his sextant must have been damaged during the voyage inland. One of the primary reasons for his trip to the upper posts was thus stymied. To cap his frustration he was delayed at South Branch House for three weeks as the winter began to set in and he saw any opportunity to accompany the Piegan on their return to the Rocky Mountains retreat with every passing day.

While he remained at South Branch House Staynor assisted William Walker who had just received his commission to be Inland Master in place of the retiring William Tomison.[6] Walker was a Londoner and although a few years senior to Staynor in years and experience he appears to have got along very well with the young clerk. Walker decided to leave his present quarters and to establish his residence at Manchester House which had served as Tomison's headquarters since 1786. Accordingly Staynor helped Walker wind up his affairs at South Branch House and by November 11, 1789 they were ready to leave.

The weather was cold and the ground was covered with a light skiff of snow when they set off on the morning of Novembr 12 with one man to assist them, William Folster,[7] and two packhorses and two teams of dogs to haul their belongings. The dogs were a last-minute replacement for some of Walker's horses which could not be found. The dogs proved to be quite unmanageable, as Staynor wrote the next day, "having torn our bags & stolen our meat, also rendered incapable of going much further owing to the Bites they had received from each other by fighting."[8] It is not clear whether this was due to the bad temper of the dogs or the inexperience of their handlers.

Be that as it may, the trip was off to a difficult start. Matters were made even worse when only a few miles out Staynor broke the stock of his gun, which was the only gun they had with them. As it was his responsibility, it was incumbent on him to return for another, which he did without any untoward experience. However, in attempting to catch up again with Walker he took a short cut and soon found himself to be lost. He kept his head and returned along the river to the House, arriving there in the evening "exceeding Stiff and tired."[9]

Early in the morning he set off again with one of the men as a guide. They had no more success as they got diverted by the tracks of a Canadian, which led them about six miles out of their way. No doubt they might have persisted for some time in their folly, but men sent out by Walker in search of Staynor caught up with them and guided them in the right direction. Paradoxically, the delay proved to be most beneficial. Besides demonstrating to Staynor how easy it can be to lose one's way, even on the treeless plains, it allowed time for Walker's men to locate his wayward horses which were now available to replace the feckless dogs.

Despite this false start, the remainder of the overland journey to Manchester House went well. The weather turned unseasonably warm, so much so that on November 22 they did not even need to pitch their tent for the night. The trip turned into a pleasant ride through a parkland which teemed with game. Thousands of bison were sighted along the way and they were able to take their pick of prime cuts of meat. In the evenings they were treated with the sublime sight of the *aurora borealis* which on one occasion consisted of a fine red streamer which Staynor remarked "cast a great light below, much superior I think to Moonlight."[10]

On November 26 they arrived at Manchester House and William Walker received charge of the post from the temporary incumbent, James Tate.[11] Manchester House had been established by William Tomison in 1786 and was at the time the furthest inland establishment of the Hudson's Bay Company. It was located on an island in the North Saskatchewan River about 50 miles upstream from the present city of North Battleford, Saskatchewan. The island itself was about a mile in length and had originally been clothed with a fine stand of conifers, from which it got its name, Pine Island. When Walker and Staynor arrived it was denuded of all trees, as were the valley walls adjacent to it, because of the traders' need for timber to build with and wood to feed their numerous hearths. In summer the island locale could render its occupants most uncomfortable because of the mosquitoes and the heat, but in fall and winter its sheltered nature was advantageous.

Within a few hundred yards of Manchester House and on the same island was the post operated by Peter Pangman[12] for the North West Company. The old Yankee trader was entering his last season as a wintering partner and his enmity towards the English company was mellowed by his determination to retire and a consequent willingness to take things a bit easy. Accordingly, although competition remained keen, it does not appear to have been characterized by the rancor which had tainted social relations between him and the officers of the Hudson's Bay Company in previous years.

For the next few weeks Staynor appears to have settled in to his new responsibilities as clerk and assistant to William Walker. As a result of his lengthy stay at South Branch House he had arrived at Pine Island a month too late to accompany the Piegan Indians on their return to their wintering grounds along the eastern flanks of the Rocky Mountains. For the first month Staynor was kept quite busy in the trading room helping Walker to deal with the Indians who were bringing in their fall hunt and obtaining an outfit for the winter on credit. He appears to have found the experience interesting, but his initial reaction to the Indians was not wholly favorable. Indeed he soon found that dealing with them could be quite dangerous. One Tent of Blackfoot Indians arrived early in December with a small quantity of dried meat buffalo tongues and fat which they proceeded to trade for liquor. One of the Indians, "not being fully satisfied with what was offered him...immediately retired to the Tent which was within the Stockhades for his Gun, came in to the Masters Room where I was sitting, and was on the point of loading his Gun when Mr. Walker came in and prevented it by insisting on his delivering the Gun up or departing from the Room. He chose the latter, went into the Tent and Sulked for a length of time without opening his lips to anyone around him."[13] It is interesting to note, however, the high level of trust that predominated, as indicated by the fact that the Indians were allowed to Tent within the Stockade and to move freely about the fort, even to the extent of entering the Master's room.

Significantly it was the excesses of the traditional drinking bout that preceded the trade that impressed Staynor most. His first experience of it came on December 8 with the arrival of a large band of Sarcee Indians.

> before Night there were many amongst them, could scarce stand & as many Voiding what their Voracious Appetites had caused them to force down. About 10 o'clock they were all pretty peacable & retired to Sleep.[14]

In the main he seems to have found nothing reprehensible in the practice, which was universally followed by the traders, and on the contrary seems to have regarded the evening celebrations as welcome diversions from the everyday routine. A few days later he looked on as "the Gun Man was walking along the Ribband of the Stockhades, from that on the Roof of the House and was as Mad I think as ever I see a Mad Man in Bedlam in my days."[15] As viewing the antics of the insane "in Bedlam" was a fashionable *divertissement* of the day in London, the import of his characterization is clear. Staynor's reaction on another occasion was similar. As Christmas drew near the Indian hunter employed by the Company to obtain fresh meat for the post came to the House "desirous of getting Drunk." Staynor observed that he had obtained "a Sufficiency of Liquor" for the purpose and subsequently "favoured us with a Stave or two on his Vocal Instrument in Consort with the rest of his Travellg Mates at their Tent without the Stockhades."[16]

The fact that these rather pathetic events were highlights in Staynor's account of his first few weeks at Manchester House is suggestive of the monotony of the day-to-day routine. There was little work to do when there were no Indians in to trade and there was little cultural or social life to interest a young Londoner imbued with the attitudes if not the means of a gentleman.

Festival occasions, like Christmas Day, only emphasized his isolation from all that was familiar to him.

> this being Christmas Morning, our small stock of Flour, afforded us, a Cake to eat with a little Tea & Chocolate, (which we all apparently enjoyed very much) no one can know what it is to want Bread but those who experience it which we here daily do in this wild country; particular holidays only excepted. Nothing particular intervened thro' the Day, scarce any Merriment going forward.[17]

The lack of "merriment" probably reflected the fact that all of the men were Orkneymen, to whom Christmas was a religious occasion and not a great social event. The different backgrounds of the men tended to heighten the difference between them and their two English officers, Staynor and Walker, adding cultural distance to the distinctions of rank.

On January 3 Staynor set off to see the plains with James Spence,[18] one of the most experienced employees of the Company. The weather was clear and warm, making it "middling pleasant Riding"[19] and the fresh air was a welcome change to the smoke-filled rooms within the House. The purpose of the trip was ostensibly to visit the Hunter's camp and the encampment of the men who were fending for themselves for the winter, but it seems likely that Staynor's main incentive was simply to get away from the post for a few days and, if possible, to participate in a buffalo hunt. That afternoon they arrived at the camp where the Hunter was staying along with four employees[20] who were stationed there to bring meat in to the fort as it was brought in by the Hunter.[21] Not under any pressure to hurry on, they stopped here for the remainder of the day and the night.

The next day they proceeded on to the encampment of those men who were maintaining themselves for the winter. It was situated about two and one-half hour's ride east, and a little north, of the Hunter's camp in the hummocky terrain north-east of Turtleford. It was standard practice at the Saskatchewan River posts for a significant number of the men to be sent out on to the plains to maintain themselves through the winter months. It was a time of year when surplus man-power was a problem as there was nothing for them to do at the posts. Their presence there merely added mouths to feed. Exile to the plains was not con-sidered to be a punishment. On the contrary it appears to have been thought a privilege sought by many of the more experienced men, who appreciated the freedom it afforded and the opportunity it opened for them to augment their income by hunting or trapping fur-bearing animals. They could also trade their own belongings or necessaries to the Indians in return for furs on which a hand-some profit could be made. An additional attraction was the opportunity it afforded to contract a liaison of a more lasting nature with an Indian woman and to beget and raise a family. Regulations of the Company did not allow the men to keep their wives and families inside any of the forts, but these rules did not extend outside the palisades.

The encampment consisted of two tents containing 10 men. At least some of the men had wives and children, but there is no clear indication of the total size or composition of the small community. The tent that Staynor stayed in housed James Spence, his wife and children, and three other men, William Flett, James Batt, and John Grott. Although there is no positive evidence it seems likely that the other men also had wives. William Flett had served inland since 1785 and was near the beginning of a lengthy career in the Company which lasted until he retired with his family to the Red River Colony in 1822. James Batt was a brother to Isaac Batt, James Spence's father-in-law, and had come up to Manchester House in the fall from Cumberland House in an Indian canoe "with his old wife."[22] John Grott or Grout was an American who had deserted from the North West Company the previous fall.[22] Considered an experienced steers-man it seems likely that he would have acquired an Indian helpmate during his time with the Canadian traders.

Although Staynor clearly hoped to have an opportunity to participate in a buffalo hunt this was denied him as the weather proved to be unsuitable. Indeed it turned so cold that their stock of brandy "froze equal to a thick paste."[23] His visit was cut short, and after a stay of less than two days he set off once again for the fort in company with several of the men who were in charge of a long string of pack horses laden with dried meat and other produce of their hunting activities. With cold so intense that they could not ride for any length of time without dismounting to restore circulation by taking to their own legs they made as good time as possible arriving back at the fort in time for supper.

This brief taste of life on the plains had fired the imagination of the young fur trader and he dreaded spending the rest of the winter confined within the four walls of Manchester House with little to keep him occupied and in a house so ill-constructed that "there was no living in it."[24] The chimney was so bad that smoke poured out of it forcing everyone to take to their beds as soon as evening came, presumably so that they could dispense with using the fireplaces any more than necessary.[25] Accordingly, Staynor "begged permission of Mr. Walker to continue in the Meadows"[26] for a month and with approval granted, Staynor returned to stay with James Spence on January 9, 1790.

For the next month, Staynor's principal interest and occupation was the buffalo hunt. At last he had found an activity he could share fully with the men, an activity which fitted the code of a gentleman and fired the imagination of a youth. He soon found, however, that the skill of being a hunter is neither inborn nor easy and he did not achieve an instant success.

The standard method of hunting used during the winter was that of stalking the game, making use of broken terrain or tree cover when available. Special camouflaged clothing was worn and care was taken to keep downwind from the intended quarry. Unlike the Indians, who frequently used the pelt of a wolf as a disguise, the white hunters adopted a costume entirely made of white duffel or blanket cloth with which they could melt into the snow-covered landscape. This technique of hunting was made more difficult by the habits of the buffalo which would bunch up when threatened, with the bulls covering the retreat of the cows. As the cows alone were desired it was often difficult to approach them without arousing the bulls and starting the whole herd. Skilled hunters were able to avoid detection and frequently were able to get off several shots from close range before the confused animals were fully aware of their danger.[27] Staynor's first hunt came on January 18.

> I found it exceeding hard work crawling for some Hours, I was going sometimes on my hands & knees, at other times on my belly, the snow being very deep made it both fatigueing & cold. in short my fingers paid the Debt all of them having got touched with the frost... it was near sunset when I returned to the Tent having broke the fore Leg of a young Bull that was in my way crawling to a large herd of Cows, my hands were so entirely benumbed with Cold, I could not fire a second Shot.[28]

Staynor's hunting prowess only slowly improved. On January 23 the wind was so variable that they were not able to get close enough to the animals for a shot. The third time he went hunting he was a little luckier, but his trophy left something to be desired. As he remarked later in the day,

> The cows keeped continually Walking & feeding and prevented us from getting near them. I killed a 6 year old Bull, that I really believe had not two ounces of hair on his whole carcass (head & top of the Neck excepted).[29]

Although the times spent hunting appear to have been highlights of his stay, they constituted only a small proportion of his time. Staynor appears to have fitted in, taking his turn helping to bring in the meat of animals brought down by the more successful hunters and doing chores around the encampment. In order to hunt more efficiently the community had split up in the middle of January with James Tate and five of the men moving east while Staynor and his companions moved west to a new site about two miles away close to a high hill which commanded "a great Prospect of several miles...[with] the pleasing sight of several herds of Buffalo at one look."[30] In the latter part of January there was a lengthy thaw accompanied by rain which removed all of the snow on the hilltops and made travel temporarily more difficult. At the same time outdoor activities were more pleasant and Staynor took the opportunity to follow the example of the men in setting out traps for wolves. The normal practice, and the one followed by Staynor, was to set a gun or guns using a bait to attract the wolves and trip wires to set off the firearms when the wolves took the bait. Staynor did not indicate whether his set was successful, but in general the method appears to have been uncertain and risky. Two years later two of the men at Manchester House suffered serious injury by accidentally triggering setting guns.[31]

On February 3 Staynor set off to return to the House, his month being almost up. The journey back was "very irksome Travelling"[32] due to the deep snow covered with a thin but hard icy crust which he broke through at every step, and must have been made more so by the thought of returning to the monotony of life at the post. For a week he stuck with it and then, finding the House "exceeding dull & lonesome,"[33] he sought permission to return to the tents for the remainder of the winter. Permission granted he left the next day. He did not reach the tents that night, losing his way as it started to become dark, and he spent the night on the trail, "a Star light Night with squalls of Wind at times."[34] He survived but found it by no means a pleasant experience.

> My lodging was by no means good having only a few Scrubs or small dried Sticks to the wind'd of me, & most of them blown down - tho' I made a good fire & had plenty of bedding, etc., still my feet were excessive Cold the whole Night.[35]

With the return of daylight and with the aid of his compass, he soon found the right track and by noon had reached his intended designation.

For the next month Staynor indulged in frequent hunting excursions but his skill, or luck, did not improve. His first excursion netted him another old bull, worthless except as a source of marrow fat.[36] For the remainder of the month he was unable to improve on his luck despite the fact that buffalo were very numerous and hunting conditions generally favorable. Other men at the tent, especially James Batt, James Spence, and William Flett, were more accomplished and the small community was well supplied with fresh meat.

Wolves were very numerous and, perhaps because of the deep, encrusted snow, they were becoming much bolder. As a result the men were encountering difficulty in keeping them away from freshly killed carcasses of buffalo. The usual precaution was that of "hanging up something that has a human smell such as a Handkerchief, Cap, etc., which if not left too long in the plain will sufficiently shy them from coming near."[37] As the wolves grew bolder it became necessary to bring the meat in as soon as possible. On one occasion the wolves got so brave as to attack the dogs

of a small party consisting of two women and a young boy who had gone out to
bring in a cow.

> During the time of their being engaged in cutting up the Beast, a large
> Grey Wolf appeared before them, within the Distance of about 3 Yards.
> Fear immediately possessed them. the wolf began his attack on the Dogs,
> one of them being easy prey, having the Sled fast to him, prevented his
> Escaping, the other ran off, the eldest of the Females was the Mother
> of 3 children, the other, a Young Girl of 14 years. The former con-
> stantly kept betwixt the Wolf and the Children, she hove her Hatchet,
> knife & some Flesh at him, he only jumped on one side while he was
> tearing at the dog, they made use of the Opportunity to get off, took
> to their heels for the Tent, leaving their Blankets & everything of
> burthen behind them...[38]

Subsequently William Flett killed the wolf not 20 yards from the tent to which he
had trailed the dog and the woman.

On March 12 Staynor and his companions received orders from William Walker
to return to Manchester House. With spring approaching the pace of work at the
fort was quickening and soon every man would be required to assist in the spring
trade and preparations for the voyage down to York Factory. Within two days
the men had struck camp and started on their return. Spring snow conditions made
travel difficult and in places they left the beaten track, which was now soft and dangerous, and kept to the bare ridges.

They arrived at the House at noon on March 15 to find that the Piegan with their
Blood and Blackfoot allies had already completed their spring trade. Thus Staynor
was not even to see the Indians that he had intended to winter with. The trade
with these Indians had been disappointing to Walker as a significant number of
them had gone over to trade their furs with Peter Pangman of the North West
Company, despite the fact that the wily old Yankee trader had not gone to the
trouble and expense of sending any men to winter with them. Staynor, in a passage virtually parroting a concurrent entry in Walker's journal, argued that this was
probably due primarily to the fact that the Governor and Committee of the Company
had changed the Comparative Standard of Trade by reducing the official value of
wolves from 2MB to 1MB. As wolves made up the majority of the skins brought by
the Plains Indians, Walker was not in a position to give them "encouragement" on
the same scale as his predecessor, William Tomison. Thus many of the Indian
leaders were attracted to the Canadian post where they received lavish presents
of liquor, tobacco, paints, rings, hawk's bells, gun worms, needles, awls, fire steels,
and even knives. In consequence, the near monopoly the Hudson's Bay Company
had previously enjoyed with these Indians was broken and Walker received a bare
majority of 770 out of the 1,400 skins that they brought with them.[39]

This incident provides insight into the dynamics of the trade relationship which
existed between the European traders and most of the trading Indians. It is generally acknowledged that commercial intercourse was governed mainly by political

alliances established and periodically reconfirmed through the exchange of gifts and other demonstrations of friendship. It appears highly probable that the political alliances were contracted on a personal level and often embodied the contracting of kinship obligations through the institution of the *mariage à la façon du pays*. Analysis of trading patterns at the Pine Island posts yields information that suggests that the trading alliances were remarkably stable and normally resisted such competitive techniques as the offering of better prices or more lavish gifts.[40] William Walker was unable to hold the allegiance of some of Tomison's former customers because Peter Pangman, with a much larger supply of goods, was frequently able to outbid him in the scramble to establish and firm up new personal alliances to replace those broken by Tomison's departure.

This was especially so with the Piegan and their allies. For many years the Hudson's Bay Company had operated with a double Comparative Standard of Trade under which their traders had actually traded wolves at the rate of 1MB.[41] At many of the inland posts this had provided the majority of the factor's Overplus, the difference between the value of furs needed to offset the official valuation of goods traded for them and the value of furs actually received. With the revaluation of wolf pelts in the official Standard, a major source for the factor's Overplus was wiped out. As the Overplus served as the source of unofficial profit which could be drawn upon in order to make presents to establish and confirm trading alliances, such a drastic reduction in the Overplus proved a severe blow to the Company's competitive position.

The men now returned to the House were soon busy with their fellows on the usual round of springtime activities. The preparation of provisions for the trip down required them to beat or pound the dried meat until it reached the consistency of a fine powder which was then mixed with fat to make pemmican. At the same time the men's women were kept busy "splitting" fresh meat and drying it.[42] The pemmican was made and stored in leather bags each containing 66 pounds of the concentrated food.[43] During the same period the fur press was refurbished and new wedges and mallets made so that the furs could be put up into tight bundles or packs.

While most of the men were so employed, a few of the more experienced men who had acquired the necessary skills started to work on the construction of new canoes and the repair of the old ones. The work started on March 31 with two men shaping and planing pieces of birch to serve as part of the framework while the women were busy preparing the pitch which would later be used to seal the seams of the canoe in order to make it watertight. Throughout the month of April Magnus Twatt[44] and one or two assistants concentrated all of their energies on their task as canoe builders; locating, cutting, and hauling in the raw materials and shaping and bending the timbers. The following month was spent in actually assembling the new canoes and mending or repairing the old ones.

Canoe building was a skill which the Hudson's Bay Company deliberately tried to encourage through the payment of a bounty or bonus of 20 shillings per canoe to the men responsible for its construction. As Staynor remarked on the practice,

> I think if I may presume to speak, that your honour's generosity is not
> badly bestowed on those men who build canoes. From first of the
> Spring these people toil morn[g], noon and night until the canoes go
> down, which other people have little or nothing to do but attend to
> their wolves traps which brings in'a great many skins to your Honours.[45]

More importantly the system worked. Given the number of men available to man
them, a sufficient number of canoes were being built. On the other hand, the bounty
system tended to make it more difficult to convince the ordinary laborers to assist
the canoe builders. Some at least argued that they were not paid for it and should
therefore not have to do such work.[46]

Staynor's journal contains little information about his own activities between
March 15 and April 18. Presumably he spent much of the time assisting Walker
with clerical duties. He took over some of the trading responsibilities at the end
of March, obtaining experience in dealing with small groups or families of Assiniboine
and Cree Indians who were bringing in meat and leather to trade for liquor.[47] The
trade brought in was felt to be most disappointing, as many of these Indians had once
been good suppliers of furs. Worst of all, they continued to expect the same kind of
treatment they had previously received. Walker lost all patience when a band of
Assiniboine, which had only a small quantity of meat to trade,

> had the impudence to send for Tobacco, Ammunition etc., also the
> cullers [sic] to be hoisted & guns to be fired for them...What makes
> these Indians so bad his [sic] the Canadians gives such encouragement
> for Provisions on the Account They have their Partners to Supply that
> comes from the Northward which for every pound weight they receive
> 3 livres when made into pimmeecon, which is deducted from the others
> furs.[48]

This incident provides a glimpse into one of the factors which was encouraging
large numbers of Cree and Assiniboine to opt for a way of life more completely
dependent upon the hunting of bison out on the plains. It is likely that many of
them were the trading Indians who had held a middleman position so long as the
Hudson's Bay Company had remained at their forts along the coast of the Bay.
Over the course of decades they had built up a special relationship with the
Company.[49] This had always been reflected in the elaborate ceremonial and
lavish gift exchange which preceded each trading encounter. The shift to a
new role as buffalo hunters and provisioners was encouraged by the Canadians
and discouraged by the English traders who did not have the same need for
dried meat and pemmican. This appears to have been a significant factor in
enhancing the competitive position of the North West Company. By refusing
to provide the traditional ceremonial welcome Walker ran the risk of alienating
customers who might in future have furs as well as meat to sell.

For the first two weeks of April Staynor was employed pressing furs with the
men. Presumably his task was to tally the pelts as they were packed, making

accurate shipping bills and maintaining a proper account for the year's trade.

About the middle of April several Canadians arrived with a large quantity of furs to sell. They were Freemen, in the sense that they were no longer under contract with the North West Company, and they wished to enter the service of the Hudson's Bay Company. It seems likely that they had been among those who were released by the North West Company when it cut back on its manpower after absorbing the McLeod-Gregory concern in 1787. This particular party had apparently spoken with William Tomison the previous spring and had reached a tentative agreement with him. At the time it was Company policy to encourage the recruitment of experienced Canadian voyageurs whenever possible. Despite this, William Walker did not welcome them with open arms. Presumably he was happy to receive their furs but he was not anxious to acquire them as employees. Staynor made no comment about them but Walker was explicit in referring to them as "a parcel of Shifting Fellows."[50] Prejudice against the Canadian voyageurs was clearly present, both among the Orkney servants who viewed any outsiders with suspicion and among the English officers who held little respect for the "frenchmen."

Once the furs had been packed there was a lull during which there was little for Staynor to do at the House. Accordingly he asked and received permission to go out for a week to stay at the Horse Tent. Horse raiding was already an endemic problem on the plains. Indeed it was so pervasive as to be almost a national sport among the Plains Indians. The traders, with the large numbers of horses they had acquired, were considered to be a worthwhile opponent; but they were not anxious to play the game. They were not in a position to stage retaliatory raids in order to recoup their losses. On occasion they were able to negotiate the return of stolen horses or payment for them,[51] but more usually stolen horses constituted a serious permanent loss to both the Company which depended on them for many essential services and the men who owned them. Consequently it was usual to pasture the horses at some place away from the posts where they would be less visible and to assign a small party of men to stand watch over them.

On April 17 Staynor set off on horseback with Robert Garson and Hugh Beakie,[52] arriving safely at the horse tent late in the afternoon. As the ground was too hilly and broken-up where they were it was decided to move to a more open location where it would be easier to keep the horses together. Once this had been accomplished the men found time for their favorite summer sport, running the buffalo on horseback. Staynor's success with this new way of hunting was no better than with the old. Nevertheless his first run made a deep impression on him.

> I only wounded one [cow] which had liked to have cost me dear only
> just escaping my horse being ripped by the horns of that wild Animal.
> The Badger holes are very numerous here which gives many a brave
> fellow a fall by the Horse treading in them, it brakes the bones of some
> & terminates the Life of others. The Horses are possessed of much
> Sagacity hav^g a quick Eye, they avoid the holes as much as possible.[53]

Two days later another small herd of cows was spotted and some of the men ran them but Staynor had to stay behind when he could not catch his horse. On his last run he "wounded a Cow as usual" and remarked in disgust in his journal, "I can't say but I have very bad luck."[54]

All too soon his week was up and he returned once again to the fort. Spring was well advanced and it was now time to bring in the horses and load them up with furs for the overland journey to South Branch House, then the main canoe-making centre owing to its proximity to the Birch Hills. After a delay caused by a spring storm which deposited 10 inches of wet snow on the ground, Staynor set off in company with 11 men and a string of horses carrying 64 bundles of furs. Two of the men were French Canadians from the North West Company post who accompanied them for protection and company on the road.

For the first few days they were slowed down by the snow but for Staynor the entire journey provided one last extended opportunity to prove his prowess as a hunter. Game was plentiful and, through the efforts of Staynor's companions, they were well supplied with fresh meat. On May 8 they killed two cows and three calves, "2 of the Calves [having] follow'd the Horses for 6 or 7 mile untill their Strength was entirely exhausted, after the same manner as they would to their Mothers."[55] Staynor went hunting virtually every day and on May 13 perseverence paid off. At last he was successful in bringing down "for the first time a very good Cow & calf."[56]

The route followed by the brigade skirted the river keeping to the north side and cutting across country from the vicinity of Jack Lake to the Crossing Place near the later Fort Carlton in order to avoid a lengthy detour around the elbow on the North Saskatchewan. When they arrived at their destination they found they were ahead of the canoes and with the river now open they had no means of crossing in order to continue on to the South Branch House with the furs. Accordingly they set up camp and settled in to wait. The French Canadians took the initiative of making a skin or hide boat which they used to cross the river and they continued on to their post on the South Saskatchewan River. Two days later, probably in response to the arrival of the two Canadians, a pair of men from South Branch House arrived in a small canoe bringing a supply of fresh beaver meat, as there were no bison in the area. The first of the canoes from Manchester arrived on May 19 and after considerable effort loading and unloading canoes and horses they had ferried all the furs to South Branch House in little more than a day.

While at South Branch House Staynor had one last opportunity to observe trade with the Indians. Large numbers of them were congregated there and they spent most of their time going from one company to the other bartering for liquor and other luxuries. On May 24 Staynor wrote:

> I cannot but take Notice of the hardship I think an Inland Master is
> under when he is compelled to sit up Night after Night to attend to
> this [sic] Drunken Sots & serve out Liquor to them which it is true
> is all to the Company's Interest, for without that many a skin would
> go to our Neighbours that now comes to us.[57]

It is not clear whether he was writing from observation of another's travails or from his own bitter experience. In any event the tone is significantly different from that which characterized his description of similar scenes the previous fall.

As soon as the new canoes were off the stocks they were put in the water and loaded up for the trip down to York Factory. Walker arrived on May 28 and while most of the canoes were sent on ahead Staynor remained behind with Walker to take stock and check over the accounts. While doing this they received letters from Cumberland House containing very discouraging news about the prospects of the Northern Expedition. George Hudson, who had been appointed to head up the trading aspect of the expedition, had died suddenly a few weeks earlier, but not before consuming all of the brandy set aside for the expedition. To make matters still worse they were completely out of dried provisions and were now totally dependent on the daily catch of ducks, geese, and presumably fish, the staple of all northern posts at the time.[58] At the end of the month they set off for Cumberland House arriving there four days later. Here they found that conditions had not been exaggerated.

It was apparent that the Northern Expedition would not be able to make a start until after the return of the canoes bearing a fresh supply of goods from York Factory. Staynor does not appear to have been unduly disappointed. Indeed he had made up his mind that he preferred the life of an inland trader to that of an explorer. The physical exertions of travelling had no appeal, especially when compared with the attractions of the hunt. One might speculate that he may also have acquired some other attraction while wintering on the plains. In any event Turnor chose Peter Fidler to take his place and Staynor a second time lost his opportunity to make a major mark on history.[59]

The return trip to York Factory was generally uneventful and Staynor's Journal comes to a close with his arrival at the Bay on July 7, 1790. Staynor's request to return inland was accepted by the York Fort Council and he was appointed to be Master at South Branch House. On his return up the river some of his equipment proved to be faulty and he returned to York Factory to await the arrival of the ship. The return of William Tomison led to the rescinding of his appointment and he was sent back to Churchill to take up again his former position there, still hoping that he would be able to return and take up an inland posting the following year. This was not to be. He remained at Churchill for the rest of his career until recalled to London in 1801. It was during his later career as chief officer at Churchill that his interest in the inland trade found expression in an aggressive program to develop an inland trading system out of Churchill parallel to the one at York Factory. His inland experience in the winter of 1789-1790 may have been a major factor in motivating this new strategy and in defining the approach he took. In any event his hope to return to the prairie that had captivated him as a young man was never fulfilled.

The Struggle for the Athabasca
James M. Parker

During the last two decades of the eighteenth century, the fur trade reached the Athabasca country. Inspired by the visions of Peter Pond,[1] Alexander Mackenzie persuaded his cousin, Roderick McKenzie, to remain inland and establish a northern rendezvous which would enable him to carry out his ambitious plans for exploration of the Canadian northwest. Founded in 1788, Fort Chipewyan* on Lake Athabasca still functions as a fur trade post and, indeed, is the oldest continuing settlement in Alberta, 400 air miles northeast of Edmonton. Roderick McKenzie established the fort's reputation as the "Emporium of the North." In 1791, while surveying Lake Athabasca for the Hudson's Bay Company, Philip Turnor described it as "the compleatest Inland House I have seen in the country...the Grand Magazine of the Athapiscow country."[2] With a two years' supply of trade goods in store, the fort held a commanding position in the expansion of the Canadian northwest.

Today, however, Fort Chipewyan has fallen victim to the ravages of time. Although two of the old log buildings lie in disrepair elsewhere in the settlement, crumbling cellars are the most visible remains on the old fort site.[3] The main path leads from the chief factor's house across the outline of the east stockade to the high rocky point where the look-out tower and the powder magazine once stood. Here stands the base of the fort sundial which faithfully recorded time until the 1940s. Southeast across the lake, where willows mark the line of the encroaching delta, can be seen the outline of Goose Island, a former fishing station, now embedded in silt from the Athabasca River. Beyond Goose Island, old Fort Point, the first site of Fort Chipewyan, can be distinguished on clear days. A mirage frequently forms and magnifies the proportions of both the island and the point. To the southwest are the entrances to the Riviere des Rochers and the Quatre Fourches. Between them lies English Island where Peter Fidler failed in his attempt to establish a post for the Hudson's Bay Company. Directly west of the settlement, Dog Head, a massive hill of granite, juts into the lake. Nothing remains of the XY Company's post about a mile away on Little Island, a piece of rock separated only by a few feet of water from Mission Point. One mile south of the settlement, across the channel of water leading from the lake, sits Potato (formerly Coal) Island, whose sombre spruce-

---

* This site was situated on the south shore. Fort Chipewyan was relocated on the northwest shore in the 1790s.

covered hills scarcely reveal that they once harbored Fort Wedderburn, witness to the final struggle between the Hudson's Bay Company and the North West Company.

With the advent of the European trader into the Athabasca came conflict. Rival traders fought over the spoils and struggled to establish an ascendancy over the original people, the Tinné, who had survived by extracting what meagre resources they could find. And it is the interplay between the white traders, the Indians, and the natural elements of air, water, and rocky soil which make up the struggle for the Athabasca. The traders encountered an immense challenge in their encounter with the rugged landscape, but even more critical to their success was the attitude and culture of a shrewd Indian people who provided the knowledge and the techniques so necessary for success and survival. These three protagonists, the trader, the Indian, and the land occupy the stage in the struggle for "the fur trade Eldorado of the North-west"----the Athabasca.

The Athabasca is part of the Mackenzie River basin which stretches north from the 53rd to the 69th parallel and lies between the 104th and 140th meridians of longitude.[4] This general area became the North West Company's Athabasca district in 1802.[5] Of direct significance to the expansion of the fur trade into the area are the rivers which served as natural highways. The west end of Lake Athabasca is situated at the hub of the Mackenzie drainage system. Rising in the Rocky Mountains, the Athabasca River flows northeasterly for 765 miles (most of it navigable) to discharge into the lake of the same name. An important tributary, the Clearwater River, joins the Athabasca two hundred miles south of the lake. The course of the Clearwater brings it at one point 13 miles of the Churchill River system.

Forming at the junction of the Findlay and Parsnip river, the Peace River winds 1,065 miles through northern prairies to join the Slave River, 10 air miles north of Lake Athabasca. Two channels connect the Peace River to Lake Athabasca, the Quatre Fourches and the Riviere des Rochers. These rivers carry the overflow of the Peace River into the lake during spring break-up. During this period the normal flow of the current out of the lake is reversed until the later break-up of the Athabasca River raises the waters to discharge into the Peace and Slave rivers.

At the east end of the lake the Fond du Lac River brings its waters from Wollaston Lake which connects with Reindeer Lake and eventually with the Churchill River system. Therefore, Fort Chipewyan was connected by water to the barren grounds to the east, the prairies to the south, the Rocky Mountains to the west, and the Arctic Ocean to the north. These natural highways aided the fur trade in expanding its activities into the northwest. What, then, did the trader find in his immediate surroundings?----a large lake, a vast delta, rock, and muskeg.

Lake Athabasca is about 200 miles in length, 35 miles at its greatest width and covers an area over 3,000 square miles with a shoreline measuring over 750 miles. Its cold deep waters harbored lake trout and whitefish, the voyageurs' gourmet. The north shore is part of the great Laurentian Shield, a composition of precambrian gneiss and granite, stunted spruce, birch clump, pine, and muskeg dotted with innumerable lakes. South of the lake the sandy soil grows forests of balsam poplar, white spruce, and jackpine. To the southwest sweeps the expanding delta, the deposition from the silt-laden waters of the Athabasca and Peace rivers. Encompassing an area of 2,300 square miles, the Athabasca delta was a haven for muskrat, beaver, and water fowl. A rich fur bearing region was the prize to be won.

Reaching this eldorado required an organization of finance, transportation techniques, and men with a knowledge of water routes and ability to deal with the Indians. It was the Frobisher brothers, Joseph and Thomas, who were instrumental in developing a line of supplies and transport up the Saskatchewan to Cedar Lake, and over the height of land into the Churchill River. Isle-a-là-Crosse was established by Thomas Frobisher in 1775-76.[6] The successful interception of the trade from the Hudson's Bay Company and the resultant disorganization of the Indian middleman trade was a stimulus to other traders in the Northwest.[7]

Peter Pond, an American trader from Connecticut, had been on the Saskatchewan since 1775 and he formed a 'concern' with six other pedlars at Sturgeon Fort in 1778. He "believed...that he could realize a large profit if he and the men employed by him could reach the Chipewyan Country at or near Lake Athabasca."[8] With five canoes Pond made his approach through the Churchill River system, past Isle-a-là-Crosse, through Buffalo Narrows, across Buffalo Lake, and up the shallow Methye River into the Methye Lake where at the north end he encountered his first real obstacle, the Portage la Loche, a formidable 13-mile height of land separating the waters flowing east to Hudson Bay from those flowing north to the Arctic Ocean. Portage La Loche proved to be a major obstacle until steam transportation, both rail and boat, made other routes possible.

One of the few accounts of crossing the portage is given by John Richardson. He states that the average load of the Canadian on a long portage was two "pieces," each weighing 90 pounds, "and in shorter ones, often a greater load."[9] Each man was given an equal number of packs in addition to the boats and their equipment. The ordinary, i.e., expected, carry was two miles a day which, if each man carried five pieces, meant walking approximately 20 miles, 10 of these with a load. There were nine resting places along the portage. A discomfort which added to the miserable work on the portage is mentioned by Back,

> For about six or seven miles on this portage, the voyageurs are exposed to temporary but acute suffering, from the total absence of good water to quench the thirst, aggravated, in our case, by carrying loads of 200 lbs in an atmosphere of 68° Fahrenheit.[10]

Horse-flies, or "bull-dogs," and mosquitoes also added to the misery of portaging.

Once over the portage, Pond led his canoes down 60 miles of the Clearwater River which involved six more portages. Coming to the confluence of the Clearwater with the Athabasca River, he turned northward, followed the steep sandy oily banks, and finally reached the head of the Athabasca delta. Here he stopped and selected a trading site, about 40 miles above the lake and approximately 2,500 miles inland from Montreal or 1,500 miles from the mouth of the Saskatchewan River on Lake Winnipeg.

Selecting a site for a post depended upon several factors. With little knowledge

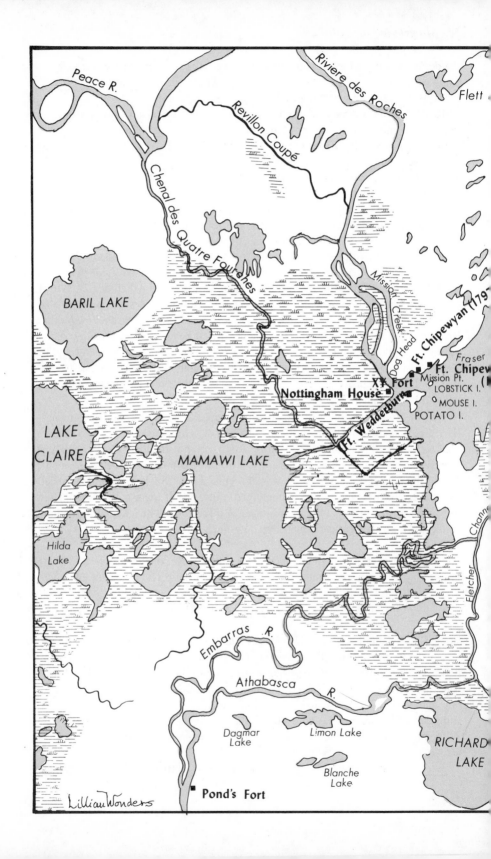

Peace R.

Riviere des Roches

Flett

Revillon Coupé

Chenal des Quatre Fourches

BARIL LAKE

Mission Creek

Ft. Chipewyan (179

Dog Head

Fraser

Ft. Chipew

Mission Pt.

XY Fort

LOBSTICK I.

Nottingham House

Ft. Wedderburn

MOUSE I.

POTATO I.

LAKE CLAIRE

MAMAWI LAKE

Channe

Hilda Lake

Fletcher

Embarras R.

Athabasca R.

Dagmar Lake

Limon Lake

RICHARD LAKE

Lillian Wonders

Blanche Lake

Pond's Fort

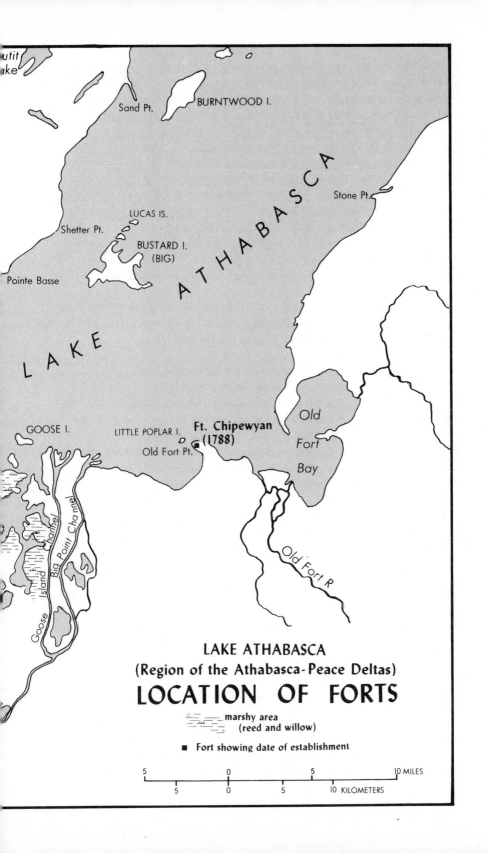

LAKE ATHABASCA
(Region of the Athabasca-Peace Deltas)
LOCATION OF FORTS

marshy area
(reed and willow)

■ Fort showing date of establishment

of where the Indians lived and with no knowledge of possible sources of provisions,[11] traders like Peter Pond depended upon native advice and experience. In the Athabasca country the posts were shifted north from Pond's first site to a final location on the northwest shore of the lake. Naturally, the proximity to furs was a prime factor in any site selection but there were other important factors involved. The location of the Indians had to be considered. It was important to have a fur post situated in a place where trade with the Indians could be intercepted, especially during times of competition. Transportation to and from the immediate vicinity of the fort was also important. Another consideration was the nearness of a food supply, both for the fort inhabitants and the men of the brigades. Finally, the entry of rival traders could make the relocation of a fort necessary.

The site which Pond selected was on the east bank of the Athabasca River, about half a mile past the point where the Embarras River branched away. The site was noted in 1791 by the Hudson's Bay Company surveyor, Philip Turnor:

> ...the river at this place parts into two branches followed the Eastern one, the river passed this day much as before, went in the East branch N-1/2 and came to Peter Ponds old House...[12]

The Historic Sites Branch of Alberta place the location of Pond's post in NE 14-108-10-W4th, but aerial photographs show this location to be on the west shore of the river and part of an island. Guy Blanchet said that the fort was located near the cut bank where the Embarras River branches from the main channel although he found nothing of the original site in the 1920s.[13] The erosion is quite heavy along the banks and it is probable that the original site has been washed away. Old-timers from Fort Chipewyan recall that they were told that "Old Fort" was the first high sandbank on the east side of river, coming upstream.[14]

In the choice of a site, Pond was undoubtedly influenced by three considerations, the availability of a food supply, the proximity of a water route, and the prospects of trade. Provisions were necessary for survival through the long winter months. The banks of the Athabasca were a haven for moose and deer while big game would be scarce on the delta. Pond also had to appreciate the fact that spring break-up meant a long upstream journey to Portage La Loche and the ice on the river would go out before that on the lake. Furthermore, it is extremely doubtful whether Pond's Indian guides knew the delta, which presents a bewildering maze of creeks and channels to all but the most experienced traveller.

Because of the differences in languages and customs between the Crees and Chipewyans, Pond probably encountered further difficulties. He and his men would be more familiar with the Algonkian language of the Crees and it is significant that his post was located near the northernmost edge of the Cree country. If he wintered in Chipewyan or Beaver country he might experience difficulty in collecting provisions, because the Chipewyans were never noted for their generosity when it came to trading provisions.[15] More significant was the fact that the Crees and the northern Athabascan tribes were on unfriendly terms.[16] A letter from

Alexander Henry the Elder to Joseph Banks in 1781 on the possibility of a route to the Pacific through the Athabasca country certainly implied problems:

> ...when everything is ready and provisions procured for the summer, as no dependance can be put, on what you are to receive in an unknown part...A new sett of interpretors and guides must be procured....[17]

Since Henry never travelled beyond Isle-a-là-Crosse Lake, his information about the Athabasca probably came from Peter Pond.[18]

Finally Pond chose a location where the Indians could be intercepted when they travelled out with their furs to Isle-a-là-Crosse, Cumberland House, and Hudson Bay. The trade route followed the Churchill River, accessible by the Athabasca and Clearwater rivers and Portage La Loche. The best point of interception would be where the Athabasca River splits into two main channels; the Embarras River meanders in a northerly direction while the main channel makes an easterly swing before flowing into the lake.

Pond's choice of a site soon proved inadequate when the fur trade expanded into the northwest. The distance between Lac la Pluie and Lake Athabasca made it impossible to trade furs on an annual basis. Alexander Mackenzie, who served as Pond's lieutenant between 1786 and 1787, was,

> ...certain, if the Chipeweans could be drawn away from there, the other nations would draw near, and if a *rendezvous* could be established, an advantageous trade would be carried on...[19]

The possibility of the existence of a river which would lead to the Pacific Ocean was foremost in Mackenzie's thoughts. The exploration which he determined upon was only practicable if there could be a base of operations in the Athabasca. Any exploratory venture would be facilitated by having a base of supplies and provisions in the far northwest. The "rendezvous" would also become a centre for the Chipewyan trade. After being informed of Alexander's plans, cousin Roderick McKenzie established Fort Chipewyan on the south shore of Lake Athabasca in the autumn of 1788.[20] The first Fort Chipewyan was situated on the west side of a point of land known as Old Fort Point. One of its chief advantages was that it lay near to a never-failing supply of whitefish and trout, the food required to sustain the fort's inhabitants. The fisheries around Old Fort Point still provide an abundance of whitefish and pike to the people of Fort Chipewyan. In 1820-21 the fort caught approximately 57,000 fish and in 1831-32, over 48,000 were taken.[21] Although the number of fish taken seems prodigious, the daily allowance probably averaged eight pounds per man, which meant 100 men would consume 800 pounds each day. Assuming the average weight of a whitefish to be from three to four pounds, 100 men would require nearly 200 fish.[22] In the early years of the fort's history, it became a practice to send the wintering voyageurs out to the fisheries to fend for themselves. On December 4, 1799 three men ate 23 whitefish and a dish of pounded meat and grease.[23] Fish, then, was the mainstay of the fort's food supply. When available, buffalo and moose meat were added to the rations; and gardens, when not destroyed by beast or frost, produced a welcome variety for the table. In 1834 a cow and calf were shipped by boat from Peace River and supplied "luxuries till then untasted at Fort Chipewyan."[24] However, times of starvation stalked the fort during prolonged periods of freezing and thawing conditions when fishing nets could not be set and other food supplies were low.

While the fisheries provided for the inhabitants of Fort Chipewyan, a problem in the logistics of the trade was to gather an adequate supply of provisions for the brigades. Fresh rations of fish and meat could not sustain the men of the brigades which made the long annual voyage to and from the Athabasca. In the short season of open water, these brigades had not the time to collect provisions by fishing and hunting as they travelled; great quantities of pemmican were required to assure the success of the brigades in reaching their destination. These dried provisions were gathered at Fort Chipewyan from the Athabasca and Peace River regions in preparation for the outward journey.

Evidently Peter Pond, or possibly Alexander Mackenzie, discovered that the Peace River country was a prairie teeming with wood buffalo. Dried buffalo meat provided the main ingredient for pemmican which Pond and the Northwesters employed to advantage in extending the travel of brigades to and from the Athabasca Country. The advantage of pemmican lies in its concentrated food value and light weight. Stefannson stated that dried meat is one-sixth of its original weight and that one pound of dried meat is equal to six pounds of lean meat in food value.[25] Whereas a man required eight pounds of fish or fresh meat per day, pemmican supplied the equivalent nutrition in one-and-a-half pounds.[26] Pemmican was packed in leather bags, 30 inches long, 20 inches wide, and only four inches thick, thereby making them suitable for canoe transport.[27]

In 1791 Philip Turnor observed that,

> ...the Canadians send a single large Canoe up it [Peace River] with only three men and fetch down two tons of dried Provisions at a time and this Canoe keeps working most of the Summer on purpose to supply the Athapescow Settlement which is the grand Magazine of those parts from which the Slave Lake, Peace River and Athapescow River Canoes are supplied in the fall of the year and reserve a stock of provisions for the Spring....[28]

In August, just before the arrival of the fall brigade, a load of provisions would usually arrive from Peace River so as to ensure a plentiful supply of food for the brigades travelling on to the Great Slave Lake and Mackenzie River. Provision posts were also established on Lac Claire, and at Pierre au Calumet, about one hundred miles upstream on the Athabasca River. This was the system which the North West Company developed for its trading operations in the far northwest.[29] This system of collecting dried provisions was one reason which necessitated a relocation of Fort Chipewyan.

When the trade expanded into the Peace River and Great Slave Lake regions, the Fort on the south shore proved inadequate, except for the fisheries, as a northern entrepot. The northwest shore proved to be more accessible and central than Old Fort Point. Although the main channels of the Athabasca River enter the lake near Old Fort Point, the Embarras River and smaller delta streams flow in a more northerly direction to the west end of the lake. These streams are usually the first free of ice in the delta.

All of the northwest shore forts[30] were situated adjacent to the channel of water which leads from Lake Athabasca. Around Dog Head the Riviere des Rochers runs north for some 30 miles to join the Peace River. South of the entrance to the Riviere des Rochers the Chenal des Quatre Fourches flows four miles west to a junction with streams from the south and west. The west channel connects with Mamawi and Claire lakes while the Quatre Fourches channel winds north for about 40 miles to join the Peace River. Both the Rivière des Rochers and the Quatre Fourches normally drain Lake Athabasca except when the Peace River flooded in the spring and early summer.[31] During flood time the current of the two channels was reversed until the water level of the lake was brought up by the spring floods of the Athabasca River.

The time of the ice break-up was undoubtedly a factor in relocation. At Old Fort Point the ice does not break up as soon as the ice on the northwest shore channel. The ice of this channel is broken up by the reversal of the current. The real problem of ice at Old Fort Chipewyan was noted by Philip Turnor in 1791:

> ...began to haul the Furrs &c to within about 1-1/2 miles of the mouth of the Athapescow River to be in readiness to proceed up the river so soon as it is clear of ice...if we had remained at the House in expectation of going out of the Lake at water we might have been detained many days by the wind setting the Ice from the Westward in upon this shore....[32]

Furthermore, the ice was not only pushed against Old Fort Point by a west wind, but also by the other main prevailing wind from the east which coming down the lake, tends to lock the drift ice against the south shore.

The other considerations were the Peace River provisions supply, which could be delivered earlier to the northwest shore, and the proximity to the Slave River leading down north. From the northwest shore, the earliest open water route to the south was up the Embarras River and its tributaries.

Finally, the convenience of the Indians was a factor in relocation of the trading post. Roderick McKenzie probably found that the south shore site, although situated near abundant fisheries, was not a convenient place for meeting the Chipewyans. Their lands lay north and east of Lake Athabasca. Because they were not adept in handling canoes, considerable difficulty was experienced in crossing the lake. Wind conditions also made the lake crossing difficult and the first Fort Chipewyan was closer to Cree territory than Chipewyan territory, an undesirable situation from the Chipewyan point of view.

Consequently, Fort Chipewyan was relocated on the northwest shore before 1799. The exact date is unknown, but it is obvious from an early account that the fort was on its new site and that it had been there for possibly two or three years.[33]

Although the North West Company succeeded in finding the best sites, fisheries, and provisions, one development which the Hudson's Bay Company introduced to the Athabasca was the use of the York boats. Until their demise in 1821, the Northwesters relied upon the birchbark canoe,[34] a marvellous craft introduced by the Indians and to which the Canadian voyageurs readily adapted. The Athabasca country was not the best source for canoe construction materials; there was birch toward the Birch Mountains, and pine instead of cedar could be used for frames, but the material was more suitable for repair than construction.

Despite their speed canoes had certain disadvantages. The gummed seams cracked in colder weather and the seams had to be repaired several times *en route;* these delays often caused the brigades to fail to reach their destination.[35] The Great Slave Lake region lacked canoe materials and this probably caused the closure of this district in 1814.

In 1823 a boat builder was employed at Fort Chipewyan by the united companies. All of the required materials were located around the fort and on May 21, 1823, four York boats departed for Portage La Loche. These boats carried approximately 200 "pieces" with 25 to 30 men while it took 10 canoes with 50 to 60 men to transport approximately 250 "pieces."[36] Boats held an economic advantage over canoes.

With the introduction of boats the Hudson's Bay Company had incoming and outgoing brigades meet at Portage La Loche so that only the "pieces," not the boats, were carried over the Portage. This, too, was an improvement over the old system. By the 1820s the fur traders had developed an organization which, by and large, coped with the natural challenges of the Athabasca, but the most important factor in the trade was the Indians and their culture.

The struggle between the companies for the Athabasca fur trade alternated between periods of competition and monopoly. During times of competition the cost of supplying the Indians with gifts, their indolence in times of plenty, and the resulting decrease in fur returns, combined to reduce fur trade profits. The Athabasca fur country was far inland and it was only during monopoly conditions that the above hazards could be minimized. Control of the trade permitted the traders to set prices without any threat of competition. During competition,

> the end of the line [of transportation] lay in the hands of the Indians who rapidly seized the chances which competition gave them, to enhance their prices and to demand more liquor and more debt.[37]

Professor Rich has shown, in his excellent article on Indian trade habits, that the Indians had concepts of property and commercial value which did not correspond to European ones.[38] Their trading was not only motivated by economic necessity, but also by concepts of social behavior. The immediate needs of food, clothing, and shelter were paramount in the Indian approach to trade and the basis of fur trading was to persuade them to trade their furs for European articles. Indian trade habits involved an exchange of pleasantries before the serious business of bargaining was begun. Therefore the social exchanges became very critical during competitive periods. When one Company controlled the outlet of trade goods, the Indians were more susceptible to trading furs:

> It was the Indians lack of sense of property (as the word was used by the Europeans) which made the fur trade the only branch of commerce which needed some other branch of control and some other incentive than the European controls and incentives which arose from a sense of property. This was the reality which explained the perpetuation of monopoly....[39]

Monopoly, then, was the solution which both the North West Company and the Hudson's Bay Company relied upon to ensure a successful return in furs. Both companies realized that competition readily answered the Indians' desire to supply their needs without effort. Offering higher prices for their furs only made them that much more satisfied with the quantity of furs they were already bringing to the fort. In place of European concepts of prices and supply, the fur traders devised other methods of making successful returns. These methods developed from an understanding of Indian culture.

The Chipewyan Indians, or Tinné, as they called themselves, differed to a certain extent in their cultural traits from the southern Cree Indians. Samuel Hearne, whose account is still one of the best, called them "the greatest philosophers, as they never give themselves the trouble to acquire what they can do well enough without."[40] This attitude, termed deceitful and fraudulent by Alexander Mackenzie, belies the fact that the Chipewyans occupied a harsh environment and a large territory. Their original lands were around Hudson Bay[41] but the intervention of the fur trader caused their migration to the country north of the Churchill River in the eighteenth century.[42] The extent of their lands meant that they held an advantage which other tribes did not have,

> ...they can never be rendered dependant, much less become stationary... as many of the other Indian tribes, from the obvious circumstance of having their lands to resort to when caprice or necessity prompt them retiring thither.[43]

Since the Chipewyans followed the caribou migrations they were able to maintain an independence from the amenities European trade goods offered. As a result of the trade the Chipewyans tended to separate into those who followed the fur trader, and those Indians who preferred to remain as "caribou eaters." The effects of the trade were noted by George Simpson in 1821:

> ...they shook off their indolent habits, became expert Beaver hunters.... The greater proportion of them however remain on their own barren

lands, where they procure sustenance with little exertion as the country abounds with Rein Deer, and some years nearly the whole of them resort thither...having laid up...an abundant stock of European articles (being very provident)...[44]

This was a constant factor in the fur trade and the Chipewyan Indians.

Fortunately for the fur traders the Chipewyan Indians had other traits which assisted them in making good returns. The most important of these was their timid, peaceable nature:

> ...let their affronts or losses be ever so great, they will never seek any other revenge than that of wrestling...murder...is seldom heard of in them...[45]

Because they had little regard for private property, they did not hesitate to plunder their neighbors of goods and wives. The common method of plunder was wrestling and this cultural trait provides an insight into the Indian acceptance of what appears to be excessive brutality by the fur traders. Samuel Hearne told of a woman found by his group, and before the evening was over, "the poor girl was won and lost at wrestling by near half a score different men...."[46] Mackenzie observed that women were used as "objects of traffic" in the sense that a father could sell a daughter "as companions to those who are supposed to live more comfortably than themselves."[47] Consequently, there was traffic in women at Fort Chipewyan by the Northwesters.[48]

Marriages *en facon du nord* allowed the fur traders to establish contacts with the Indians. As George Simpson explained, the alternative was a greater dependence on the Indians.

> ...who have no other feelings than those which interest and mercenary views create towards us; it is never matured to attachment and a price is only required to make those on whom our existence depends our inveterate enemies.[49]

In an effort to entice those Indians to hunt and trade furs, the traders placed a great emphasis on the manner of making chiefs of the more productive hunters. There were no actual chiefs in Chipewyan culture, but when it was time to trade furs the more influential leaders formed large bands to give them more authority at the trading post[50] and required "the stamp and impression of the Sovereign to indicate their value and rend them current."[51] These chiefs never became influential in Indian society except for skill in bartering furs.[52] Normally a chief was entitled to tobacco and liquor for his band, a salute of firearms and hoisted flags followed by a suit of clothing.[53]

The hunt for furs, however, was not assisted by the indifference of the Chipewyans to liquor. They usually came to the trading hall with "...a regular and uninterrupted use of their understanding, which is always directed to the advance-

ment of their own interest...."[54] Although liquor was used to induce the
Chipewyans to part with their furs, few of them became habitual users. Philip
Turnor said, "...the Chipewyan tribe will not trade liquor consistently are not
fond of parting with their provision, but powder and shot will draw it from
them."[55] John Porter also complained in 1800 that "any person who trades Rum
with the Chipiwians requires a Great deal of Patience they...would almost as soon
part with their Blood as Part with a Piece of meat or anything else for Liquor..."[56]
Hence liquor was not regarded as a trade article but a gratuity in the Chipewyan
trade. The Chipewyans, however, were unlike their southern neighbors, the Crees,
whose taste for liquor was so pronounced that a separate post, Pierre au Calumet,
was maintained for them on the Athabasca River. The objective was,

> ...to keep the Northern Indians apart otherwise when they are drinking
> the Southern Indians are sure to insult the Northern Indians...[57]

At Lake Claire, John Porter was able to trade the Crees rum for their provisions and
then gave them more liquor on credit.[58]
  As a result of the Chipewyan attitude toward liquor, the Hudson's Bay Company
was able to withdraw it from the Athabasca trade in 1826.[59] Although the Indians
were upset at the new regulation and threatened to withdraw to their own lands, the
reports and journals after this date show the rule had little effect upon the returns
of the post. John Richardson reported in 1848 that "the present race of Chipewyans
are ignorant of the use of spirituous liquors."[60]
  When competition entered the Athabasca country, the attitudes and trading
habits of the Indians changed. Competition meant that their furs were sought by
rival traders and the Indians soon realized the advantageous position they held. It
meant that they could get out from under the yoke of monopoly exercised by the
Northwesters. Samuel Hearne analyzed their shrewdness when he noted,

> ...if the least respect be shown them, it makes them intolerably in-
> solent...by giving him [the Indian] the least indulgence...he will
> grow indolent, inactive, and troblesome, and only contrive methods
> to tax the generosity of an European.[61]

It is not surprising that they welcomed opposition traders. Philip Turnor reported
that the Chipewyans became insolent to the Northwesters because they expected
the Hudson's Bay Company to establish a rival post. The opposition, however, did
not arrive until 1799 when the XY Company set up a trading house and the Hudson's
Bay Company arrived in 1802. During this time of competition the Indians were
wooed, cajoled, and intimidated by the competing companies, but they tended to
remain loyal to the North West Company because it had the most men and goods.
They were afraid to change to the new companies for fear they would not return
another year. The Indians had expected the English to return after Philip Turnor's
visit in 1792, but it took 10 years. They became dubious about the men from the
Bay.[62] With the amalgamation of the two Canadian Companies in 1804 the

strengthened North West Company turned its superior force against the English, who were no match for the Canadians. The Hudson's Bay Company withdrew in 1806.

During the next nine years the Hudson's Bay Company reorganized and decided that it would actively oppose the North West Company. An Athabasca enterprise was recognized to be a conclusive part of the struggle.

> ...as the discussions of 1814 and 1815 emerged...it became more and more clear that an Athabasca venture was accepted as the decisive issue....63

Two ex-Northwesters, Colin Robertson and John Clarke, were engaged by the Hudson's Bay Company to lead the Athabasca campaign. Their first move was to establish Fort Wedderburn across the channel from Fort Chipewyan. For the next five years these men played the same tactics as the Northwesters. With an ostentatious display of men and goods the Hudson's Bay Company succeeded in winning the loyalty of the Indians away from the North West Company.64 The Indians took advantage of the situation by settling,

> ...among themselves who are to join the French and who the English... individuals frequently take credit at each Fort and divide their hunts....65

The chaotic state of the trade was indicated in Simpson's decision to reduce Indian debts by one-half in 182066 and they were again reduced by 40 percent in 1822,67 obvious signs that the Indians were the only beneficiaries in the final struggle for the Athabasca trade. Their brief moment of superiority soon ended with the surrender of the North West Company in 1821. Colin Robertson's determination to return each year with a force of men and a plentiful supply of trade goods convinced the Indians that the Hudson's Bay Company was there to stay. -- and so it was. The struggle for the Athabasca was over, the time of high prices, gratuities, and free trade goods was finished; the necessity of adapting to a new monopoly was the order of the day.

"The Custom of the Country": An Examination of Fur Trade Marriage Practices

Sylvia Van Kirk

Although extensive work has been done on the economic and political aspects of the fur trade in Western Canada, historians in the past have neglected the important social side of this far-flung enterprise. From the interaction between two very different cultures--European and Indian--grew an early Western society which was a blend of Indian, British, and French attitudes and traditions. Little appreciated has been the extent to which this society developed its own mores and customs in response to the particular needs of the environment which gave it birth. This paper will attempt to trace the evolution of a fundamental institution in fur trade society-- marriage *à la façon du pays*.[1] It was according to this rite that hundreds of fur traders formed unions with Indian and, later, mixed-blood women.

If the concept of marriage *à la façon du pays* is not actually articulated in the early annals of the Hudson's Bay Company, it is because of the official policy formulated by the remote London Committee which prohibited any social contact between its servants and the Indians. Almost as soon as posts were established on the Bay, the men showed a tendency to form relationships with Indian women, but to the Committee this seemed a reprehensible practice which could only result in the debauching of its servants, the wasting of provisions, and illicit trade. The London Committee admonished its governor on the Bay in 1683:

> We are very sensibly [sic] that the Indian Women resorting to our Factories are very prejudiciall to the Companies affaires...It is therefore our possitive order that you lay your strict Commands on every Chiefe of each Factory upon forfiture of Wages not to Suffer any woman to come within any of our Factories...[2]

Although similar remonstrances were to be sent out many times in future, the Committee's regulation remained only loosely or, at best, sporadically enforced. However sensible the official policy may appear in theory, in practice it proved largely unworkable because it failed to make allowances for the realities of fur trade life.

---

*This chapter was read by Ms. Van Kirk at the annual meeting of the Canadian Historical Association, University of Toronto, 1974.

Sex was, of course, a motivating factor in the development of intimate ties between white men and Indian women. No white women were permitted to accompany their men to Hudson Bay, a situation which precluded the possibility of connubial comforts in the conventional European sense.[3] It is apparent, however, that many Englishmen found Indian females not unattractive representatives of their sex. According to James Isham, Cree maidens were most enticing:

> ...very frisky when Young &...well shap'd...their Eyes Large and Grey yet Lively and Sparkling very Bewitchen...

It was certainly within the context of their own moral code for the Indians to sanction liaisons between their women and the Company's men. As Richard White, a witness at the parliamentary enquiry of 1749, put it: "The Indians were a sensible people, and agreed their Women should be made use of..."[5] Both the Cree and the Chipewyan practised the custom, common among primitive people, of offering their wives or daughters to strangers as a token of friendship and hospitality.[6] To an Englishman, it appeared that an Indian took a wife with scant ceremony and a rather shocking disregard for the precepts of chastity and fidelity.[7] However, the Indian was not without his own standards. When found guilty of a clandestine amour, a wife could expect violent punishment or even death, but a husband deemed it perfectly proper to lend his wife to another man for anywhere from a night to several years, after which she was welcomed back together with any children born in the interim.[8]

If the sexual mores of the Indians encouraged the growth of intimate relations, the development of a body of "Home" Indians around each post meant that frequent contact was unavoidable. Traders on the Bay, who soon appreciated the essential role to be played by the women in making mocassins and netting snowshoes, defended the necessity of admitting women to the factories:

> ...we cannot do without Snowshoes & other Necessarys for our Men who are always abroad & requires a Constant Supply of Shoes for the winter otherwise we can Kill no partridges nor, be able to provide our Selves with fireing.[9]

In spite of the Committee's ruling, the governors or chief factors themselves took the lead in forming unions with Indian women. Such alliances, they realized, helped to cement trade ties. Among the Cree, a daughter was esteemed because, once married, her husband was obliged to contribute to the maintenance of her parent's household.[10] To have a fur trader for a son-in-law would thus be seen to promise unlimited security and prestige. Although the specific identity of most of the Indian women kept by the early H.B.C. factors remains unknown, it appears that they were usually the daughters or wives of leading "Home" Indians. During his governorship of Albany in the 1760s, Humphrey Marten formed a union with Pawpitch, a daughter of the "Captain of the Goose Hunters."[11] Several decades earlier, another factor, Joseph Adams, had had a child by a Cree woman described as being of "ye blood Royal."[12]

Among the Cree, as in most Indian tribes, polygamy was an economic necessity, and a man's prestige was enhanced by the number of wives he could support. Significantly, a number of H.B.C. factors appear to have adopted the practice which, however contrary to European morality, would have found favor in Indian eyes. James Isham, described as the "Idol of the Indians" during his rule at York Factory in the 1740s and 50s, maintained more than one Indian lady.[13] Similarly, Robert Pilgrim kept two Indian women with their children in his apartments at Fort Prince of Wales in the 1740s.[14] One of his successors, Moses Norton, who assumed command of Churchill in 1762, was reputedly a most notorious polygamist. If the very unsavory character-sketch written by his arch-enemy Samuel Hearne is to be believed, Norton kept a selection of five or six of the finest Indian girls to satisfy his passions, being quite ready to poison anyone who dared refuse him their wives or daughters.[15]

By the mid-eighteenth century, it had become an established practice for a Company governor to take an Indian "wife." Andrew Graham, who himself fathered at least two children during his time on the Bay, affirmed that "the Factor keeps a bedfellow within the Fort at all times."[16] The term "wife" is not inappropriate when one considers that from the Indian point of view these unions would have been seen as marriages. Furthermore, the appearance of such phrases as "father-in-law" and "son-in-law" in the post journals indicates that the English themselves were beginning to acknowledge a marital relationship.[17] Children were a strong factor in cementing ties between mother and father, and the resulting domesticity must have done much to alleviate the loneliness of life on the barren shores of Hudson Bay. Humphrey Marten's intense concern for the Indian girl Pawpitch, for example, was revealed when she fell ill of a fever. He must have been watching over when she died for he records her death, an unusual step in itself, as occuring at precisely ten minutes to three on the morning of January 24, 1771. The father worried about the fate of his "poor Child" now motherless. He feared to entrust the little boy to his in-laws, as would have been customary, because Pawpitch's father was now old and already burdened with a large family.[18]

The extent to which the Committee's policy was applied to the lower ranks of the service varied with the capability and inclination of each individual governor, most of whom had exempted themselves from the ruling. The situation at York Factory in the mid-eighteenth century is illustrative. James Isham, one of the Company's most successful governors during the early period, readily permitted his men to have the company of Indian women outside the fort at the goose hunters' tents or on short journeys where they were especially useful. Some women were allowed to reside with servants inside the factory as well since Isham undoubtedly observed that such liaisons had a conciliating effect upon the men. His successor Ferdinand Jacobs, however, roundly denounced such license when he took over in 1761, declaring that "the worst Brothel House in London is Not So Common a Stew as the men's House in this Factory." He refused to admit Indian women to men they regarded as husbands, a move so unpopular that several servants feigned sickness and refused to work.[19] This vacillation in enforcing the rules led to a good deal of resentment on the part of both the men and the Indians.[20]

Although its prohibition regarding Indian women was frequently ignored, the official policy of the Hudson's Bay Company during its first century did work to prevent the widespread development of marriage relationships between its servants and Indian women. As a general rule, only a chief factor was permitted to keep a woman permanently within the factory. "At proper times," a factor might allow an officer to entertain an Indian lady in his apartment provided she did not stay there overnight, but ordinary servants were usually limited to chance encounters and took to sneaking over the walls at night.[21] Even these restrictions were to break down when the Company began to move inland to confront a powerful Canadian rival which actively encouraged the formation of intimate ties with the Indians.

The men of the Montreal-based North West Company, inheritors of the framework and traditions of the French colonial fur trade after the conquest of 1763, readily adopted the attitudes of their predecessors with regard to Indian women. The coureur de bois had realized that his adaptation to and understanding of Indian society on which his success depended could be greatly facilitated by an Indian mate. Besides helping to secure trade ties and familiarizing the trader with the customs and language of her tribe, the Indian woman performed a myriad of domestic tasks essential to wilderness survival.

The North West Company, therefore, gave its sanction to unions between its employees and Indian women, and it was among the Nor'Westers that marriage *à la façon du pays* first developed into a recognized and widespread custom. All ranks, bourgeois, clerk and engagé, were allowed to take a woman, and the Company accepted the responsibility for the maintenance of Indian wives and families.[22] It irked more than one H.B.C. officer to observe the high style in which his Canadian counterpart travelled. The bourgeois always had "his girl" who was carried in and out of his canoe and shared the luxury of his tent and feather bed; furthermore, if a clerk "chuses to keep a girl which most of them does the Master finds her in Apparel so that they need not spend one farthing of their Wages."[23] The only restriction placed on an engagé taking an Indian wife was that he had to obtain the consent of his bourgeois to his proposed match.[24]

It is important to emphasize the extent to which "the custom of the country" derived from Indian marriage rites. The active involvement of the Indians in securing unions between their women and the Nor'Westers is much in evidence. According to one observer, many among the Cree kept one or more of their daughters specifically to offer as wives "for the white People."[25] Simple as the Indian notions of matrimony appeared to the Nor'Westers,[26] a trader could not take a wife without giving credence to the customs of her people. Of fundamental importance was the consent of the girl's parents. In the words of an old voyageur:

> On ne se joue pas d'une femme sauvage comme on veut....Il y aurait du danger d'avoir la tête cassée, si l'on prend la fille dans ce pays, sans le consentement des parents. C'est le père et la mère qui donnent les femmes, et s'ils sont morts, ce sont les plus proches parents.[27]

To obtain the consent of the parents, the Nor'Wester was required to make a suitable present. This bride price could vary considerably, but it usually took more than a few trifles to gain the hand of an Indian maiden. At Fort Alexandria in 1801, Payet, one of Daniel Harmon's interpreters, gave the parents of his Cree bride rum and dry goods to the value of two hundred dollars.[28] According to the younger Henry, the common medium of exchange was a horse for a wife.[29] On the Pacific coast, the marriages of several Nor'Westers to the daughters of the powerful Chinook chief Concomely involved more elaborate ceremony with a mutual exchange of gifts. In July 1813, for instance, a rich dowery of pelts accompanied the bride of proprietor Duncan McDougall, but it took McDougall until the following April to discharge his part of the bargain:

> Mr. D. McDougall this afternoon completed the payment for his wife... he gave 5 new guns, and 5 blankets, 2½ feet wide, which makes 15 guns and 15 blankets, besides a great deal of other property, as the total cost of this precious lady.[30]

Before being consigned to her new husband, it became common for an Indian woman to go through a "ritual," performed by the other women of the fort, designed to render her more acceptable to a white man. She was scoured of grease and paint and exchanged her leather garments for those of a more civilized style. At the Nor'Wester posts, wives were clothed, usually at the expense of the Company, in "Canadian fashion" which consisted of a shirt, short gown, petticoat, and leggings.[31] The trader then conducted his bride to his quarters and, without further ado, the couple was considered man and wife. The women assumed their husbands' last names, and the engagés respectfully addressed the wives of the bourgeois as "Madame."[32]

Initially marriage *à la façon du pays,* in accordance with Indian custom, was not viewed as a binding contract.[33] Should the relationship prove unhappy, both parties were free to separate and seek a more congenial union. Even a moralist such as Daniel Harmon, as he became more familiar with the ways of the fur trade, conceded that this attitude had merit:

> for I cannot conceive it to be right for a Man & Woman to cohabit when they cannot agree, but to live in discontent, if not downright hatered [sic] to each other, as many do.[34]

In contrast to Indian practice, however, the Nor'Westers appear to have taken a definite stand against polygamy both for moral and economic reasons. The Indian was understandably slow to comprehend white man's morality since in his view "all great men should have a plurality of wives." Such was the argument used by Alexander Henry the younger's father-in-law, himself the husband of three sisters, when he pressed the trader to take his second daughter.[35] The reluctance evinced by Henry in taking his first Indian wife and his adamant refusal of a second typifies the attitude of many bourgeois, and polygamy was never part of "the custom of the country" as practised by the Nor'Westers.[36] While H.B.C. officers, in their isolation on the Bay, appear to have been susceptible to polygamy, the economic implications of such a practice when moving into the interior served to reaffirm the desirability of monogamy. By 1780, according to Philip Turnor, English officers stationed inland from York Factory found themselves besieged with offers of wives:

> the Masters of most of your Honors Inland settlements...would Labour under many difficulties was they not to keep a Woman as above half the Indians that came to the House would offer the master their Wife the refusal of which would give great offense to both the man and his Wife; though he was to make the Indian a present for his offer the Woman would think her self slighted and if the Master was to accept the offer he would be expected to Cloath her and by keeping a Woman it makes one short ready answer (that he has a Woman of his own and she would be offended) and very few Indians make that offer when they know the Master keeps a Woman....[37]

Thus marriage *à la façon du pays* was essentially an adaptation and not an adoption of Indian marriage rites. In particular, the Indian attitude that marriage did not constitute a union for life was corrupted to suit the needs of the transient fur trader. The men of both companies never intended to remain permanently in the Indian Country, but the growth of family ties during their sojourn placed many traders in an agonizing dilemma when it came time to retire. After the unhappy experience of one of its officers, the Hudson's Bay Company actively discouraged any attempt on the part of its servants to remove their families from Rupert's Land. In 1750 Robert Pilgrim had taken his Indian wife Thu a Higon and their infant son to England. Unfortunately, Pilgrim died within a few months of his arrival, having stipulated in his will that, while the child was to remain in England with his brother, Thu a Higon was to be properly looked after until she could be sent back to Churchill.[38] An irritated London Committee, fearing that dependents brought to Britain might easily become a burden on the Company, sent Thu a Higon back to Hudson Bay accompanied by a strict order forbidding all ship's captains to allow any native man, woman, or child to be brought to Great Britain without its express written consent.[39]

Whether Thu a Higon could have overcome the almost insuperable problems of adjustment she would have had to face in England is doubtful. This consideration helps to explain the action of most early bourgeois. Many of the Nor'Westers were men of education who, having won sizeable fortunes, intended to retire to enjoy the fruits of civilization in Eastern Canada or Britain. An Indian family had little place in such a design; the wife especially would have to cope with an alien way of life where too often she might meet with "impertinent insult" and "unmerited obloquy."[40] While many of the early wintering partners sent their children east to be educated, most forsook the Indian mothers of these children and felt at liberty to marry white women upon retirement.[41]

Yet until the founding of the Red River settlement in the early 1800s, even the most devoted father could not have remained in Rupert's Land with his family after his contract had expired.[42] It distressed more than one H.B.C. officer to witness the suffering caused by the breakup of families owing to "the want of an Asylum in this part of the Country to which a Parent might retire with a prospect of supporting his Family and which would prevent the Miseries of a Separation and check the Increase of a Burden on the Factories."[43] Before the creation of the colony, it had of necessity become customary to leave one's Indian family behind. Although the unions between H.B.C. men and Indian women had shown an increasing tendency to last for the duration of the husband's stay on the Bay, the usual and accepted course had always been for an Indian wife and her offspring to return to her own relations in the event of his death or departure. An Indian husband, whether old or new, readily adopted "the Englishman's children," an act which reflected the strong kinship ties and great love of children characteristic of Indian society.[44]

While the London Committee had tacitly had to accept that it could do little to prevent its men from having native families, it refused to assume any official responsibility for their maintenance. This accounts for the fact that the Indian families of H.B.C. men were absorbed back into the "Home Guard" bands, but it was also a spur to conscientious fathers to make some provision for their families. Many of the officers' and servants' wills which have survived from the late eighteenth and early nineteenth centuries clearly reveal the growth of definite family ties and a marked concern for the welfare of native dependents. The action of John Favell, an early inland officer in the Albany district, is typical. Upon his death in 1784, Favell left an annuity for his Indian wife Tittimeg and their four children, earnestly requesting "the Honorable Company" to implement this part of his will so that his family would receive an annual supply of goods from the Company's warehouse.[45]

Similarly, an Indian woman who had formed a union with a Nor'Wester could expect to be taken back into her tribe. According to the elder Henry, Cree women who had been kept by the men received a ready welcome along with their progeny:

> One of the chiefs assured me, that the children borne by their women to Europeans were bolder warriors, and better hunters, than themselves... The women, so selected, consider themselves as honoured.[46]

However, there was less impetus for a family of a Nor'Wester to return to live with the Indians. The Company itself accepted the responsibility for at least feeding the families of its servants who had died or left the country, and some traders did provide their wives with a small annuity to purchase cloth and other goods from the company stores.[47] Furthermore, the Nor'Westers were not insensible to the problems which could arise from divorcing an Indian wife and her children from the life of a fur trade post to which they were accustomed. A concomitant of marriage *à la façon du pays,* therefore, was the growth of another custom, known as "turning off," whereby a trader leaving the country endeavored to place his spouse under the protection of another. Ross Cox declared that many a voyageur for "a handsome sum" would be happy to take over *"la Dame d'un Bourgeois."*[48] On his wedding day in 1806, Daniel Harmon was obviously expressing a contemporary attitude when he confided to his journal that he intended to keep his wife, as long as I remain in this uncivilized part of the world, but when I return to my native land shall endeavour to place her into the hands of some good honest Man, with whom she can pass the remainder of her days in this Country much more agreeably, than it would be possible for her to do, were she to be taken down into the civilized world, where she would be a stranger to the People, their manners, customs & Language.[49]

Although Harmon, like others, may be accused of wanting to enjoy the best of both worlds, there was a good deal of truth in the generally-held view that this was the kinder course of action.

Since the late eighteenth century, the men of both companies had, in fact, been espousing the daughters of their predecessors, an action which emphasizes the extent to which micegenation had taken place. Owing to the restriction of marital unions in the Hudson's Bay Company, most of the marriageable mixed-blood girls were initially daughters of former officers.[50] Of Matthew Cocking's daughters, for example, the eldest, Ke-the-cow-e-com-e-coof, became the country wife of Thomas Staynor, governor at Churchill in the 1790s, while another, Agathas, married William Hemmings Cook who took charge of York Factory in the early 1800s.[51] As the British moved inland, the pattern of intermarriage spread among the servants. Although Neskisho, the wife of Orkney servant James Spence, is referred to as "Indian" like many other daughters of H.B.C. men, she was actually a daughter of the early inlander Isaac Batt.[52]

The daughters of the French-Canadian engagés, on the other hand, constituted the largest group of eligible females for the Nor'Westers. Many of the bourgeois wed the daughters of voyageurs or freemen in unions which cut across both class and racial lines. Ross Cox tells the story of one doughty old voyageur Louis La Liberté who felt he could address himself with familiarity to one of the Company's proprietors because he was father-in-law to three wintering partners.[53] Like Indian girls, the daughters of the men of both companies were given in marriage when very young. To cite a famous instance, Daniel Harmon took his metis bride Elizabeth Duval when she was only fourteen years old.[54]

By the early 1800s, the replacement of the Indian wife by one of mixed-blood had become a widespread phenomenon in fur trade society. As the mixed-blood population grew, it naturally evolved that wives should be drawn increasingly from its ranks. In the first place, a fur trader's daughter possessed the ideal qualifications to become a fur trader's wife. A very child of the fur trade, she knew no other way of life. From her Indian mother, the mixed-blood girl learned those native skills so valuable to the trade such as making mocassins, netting snowshoes, and preparing pemmican. Her familiarity with Indian language and customs enabled her to act as an interpreter,[55] and on more than one occasion, her timely intervention reputedly saved the life of a white husband.[56] The mixed-blood wife was thus in a position to adequately perform the functions which had made the Indian woman such a useful helpmate but, unlike the Indian woman, there was little danger of her becoming a source of friction between Indian and white. In fact, by the turn of the century, partly because of the violence and drunkeness occasioned by the trade war, Indian-white relations had seriously deteriorated. In well-established areas, marriage alliances were no longer so important, and many Indians deeply resented the flagrant way in which the Nor'Westers in particular now abused their women.[57]

Secondly, the white man generally evinced a decided personal preference for a mixed-blood wife whose lighter skin and sharper feature more closely approximated his concept of beauty. Many, according to Alexander Ross, were captivating with "their delicacy of form," "their nimble movements," and "the penetrating expression" of their bright black eyes. The officers especially considered the greater potential of a mixed-blood girl for adapting to "civilized ways" as increasingly desirable. "With their natural acuteness and singular talent for imitation," Ross declared, they could acquire considerable grace and polish.[58]

Furthermore, the fur traders had a collective responsibility for the fate of their daughters. They were not Indian; even those raised among the "Home Guard" were taught that their paternity gave them a definite superiority.[59] But they were not white; fathers were actively discouraged from sending their daughters to the civilized world to be educated.[60] Being women, however, the only way in which mixed-blood girls could remain an integral part of fur trade society was through marriage, either to new men coming in or at least to fur traders' sons. This consideration can be seen in the ruling introduced by the North West Company in 1806 which prohibited men of all ranks from taking any more pure-blooded Indian women as wives. Although primarily instigated to reduce the enormous cost of maintaining the growing families of its servants, the resolution can also be seen as encouraging Nor'Westers to marry "the Daughter of a white man" in an effort to ensure them husbands.[61]

Significantly, as mixed-blood wives became the rule, the "custom of the country" increasingly evolved towards white concepts of marriage. There is much evidence to suggest that the men of both companies came to view a union contracted *à la façon du pays* as a union for life. A respected H.B.C. officer, J.E. Harriott, explained that "the custom of the country" involved a solemn agreement between the father of the girl and the man who was taking her to wife. When Harriott espoused Elizabeth, a daughter of Chief Trader J.P. Pruden, he "made a solemn promise to her father to live with her and treat her as my wife as long as we both lived. I kept this promise until her death." He further declared that he considered his union as binding as if celebrated by an archbishop:

> It was not customary for an European to take one wife and discard her, and then take another. The marriage according to the custom [of the country] was considered a marriage for life...I know of hundreds of people living and dying with the woman they took in that way without any other formalities.[62]

Although it was more difficult for the lower ranks to maintain permanent unions, the engagés, in general, recognized the permanency of the marriage bond. According to one old voyageur Pierre Marois, whose marriage *à la façon du pays* lasted over 20 years, "nous regardons cette union comme union de mari et femme ...et union aussi sacrée."[63]

Within fur trade society, "the custom of the country" was undoubtedly regarded as a bona fide marriage rite. As one clerk declared, "I never knew or heard of a man and woman living together in the North-West without being married."[64] Although the actual ceremony remained simple, the union was accorded public recognition through festivities similar to those found at European weddings. It became customary to celebrate a fur trade marriage with a dram to all hands and a dance which might see the fun-loving engagés jigging till norning.[65] When the young clerk Robert Miles took Betsey Sinclair as "a Femme du Pays" at York Factory in the fall of 1822, a friend recorded, "we had a Dance & supper on the occasion, when no one but the happy Swain was allowed to go sober to bed."[66] Whereas initially a trader had been required to make a substantial present to his Indian in-laws for his bride, it was now not unusual for a fur trader to provide his own daughter with a handsome dowery.[67]

Numerous examples of the development of lasting and devoted relationships between white men and their mixed-blood wives could be cited. H.B.C. officer George Gladman, for instance, emphasized that he considered Mary Moore to be his "lawful wife."[68] Like many of his contemporaries, he made generous provision for her in his will, specifically entreating his sons to see that their mother was well cared for in her old age.[69] Significantly, growing numbers, especially among the Nor'Westers, now took their wives and families with them when they retired to the East. A most famous example is that of Daniel Harmon who took his wife back to his home in New England in 1819. Although the deeply-religious Harmon could never deny the sanctity of a church marriage, he, like others before him, had come to realize that something much deeper than mere ceremony bound him to his wife:

> Having lived with this woman as my wife, though we were never formally contracted to each other, during life, and having children by her, I consider that I am under a moral obligation not to dissolve the connexion, if she is willing to continue it. The union which has been formed between us, in the providence of God, has...been cemented by a long and mutual performance of kind offices....How could I spend my days in the civilized world, and leave my beloved children in the wilderness? The thought has in it the bitterness of death. How could I tear them from a mother's love, and leave her to mourn over their absence, to the day of her death?....On the whole, I consider the course which I design to pursue, as the only one which religion and humanity would justify.[70]

Once outside fur trade society, though some maintained it was unnecessary,[71] most submitted to a church ceremony if only to conform to "civilized" convention. Such action was seen, however, as merely "un bénédiction" and not an admission that no marriage had existed before. J.E. Harriott maintained that he would have gone through "the civilized form of solemnizing marriage...to please people and to conform to the custom of society. I would not consider myself more strongly bound to that woman than before."[72]

Within fur trade society, however, one was expected to conform to its own social norm with regard to marriage, that of "the custom of the country." While no laws existed to enforce morality in the Indian Country, it is evident that the society itself exerted considerable pressure on a newcomer to adopt a code of behavior which had gained its own legitimacy through long usage. One can observe this social conditioning working on Nor'Westers such as Daniel Harmon, Alexander Henry the younger, and George Nelson. Arriving fresh from a society which recognized only the legitimacy of church marriage, these young men were initially shocked by "the custom of the country" which seemed only a form of concubinage. They therefore began by refusing all the offers of wives made to them, but eventually an increased understanding of the ways of the fur trade, coupled with the loneliness and the attractiveness of the girls themselves, led them to follow in the footsteps of their predecessors and take a wife *à la façon du pays*.[73] As James Douglas very perceptively observed, only through such adaptation could one become reconciled to fur trade life:

> There is indeed no living with comfort in this country until a person has forgot the great world and has his tastes and character formed on the current standard of the stage....To any other being...the vapid monotony of an inland trading post would be perfectly unsufferable, while habit makes it familiar to us, softened as it is by the many tender ties, which find a way to the heart.[74]

Even though the desirability of a lasting union had become widely acknowledged, the security of a native wife ultimately depended upon individual conscience. Because "the custom of the country" had evolved from two very different sets of attitudes towards marriage, it was inevitable that irregularities should persist. "Turning off" remained a problem, it being not uncommon for a mixed-blood woman to have two or three husbands in her lifetime.[75] After the amalgamation of the two companies in 1821, the Hudson's Bay Company took definite steps to regulate country marriages by introducing marriage contracts which were signed by both parties in the presence of witnesses. In 1824 the Council of the Northern Department further resolved:

> That no Officer or Servant in the company's service be hereafter allowed to take a woman without binding himself down to such reasonable provision for the maintenance of the woman and children as on a fair and equitable principle may be considered necessary not only during their residence in the country but after their departure hence....[76]

Since marriage *à la façon du pays* contained all the elements of "civilized" marriage except the blessing of the church, it might be supposed that the arrival of missionaries in Rupert's Land would have been welcomed. In fact, the intolerant and unsympathetic attitude of particularly the Protestant missionaries toward "the custom of the country" provoked a good deal of hostility. The Reverend John West, the first Anglican chaplain of the Hudson's Bay Company who arrived at Red River in 1820, refused to acknowledge that marital relationships already existed. In his view, all couples were merely "living in sin" and too often a man might "turn off" his woman after having enjoyed the morning of her days.[77] While abuses undeniably existed, West in seizing upon the exception rather than the rule encountered much resentment. To many an old trader, the pronouncement of a clergyman could add no more legality or sanctity to a country union which had existed for decades. Although West, who firmly believed that "the institution of marriage and the security of property were the fundamental laws of society," performed a total of 65 marriages before his departure in 1823, it is clear that he had had to force his view in many cases.[78] Resistance seems to have come from some of the most prominent settlers in Red River such as James Bird and Thomas Thomas, retired H.B.C. chief factors, who continued to live with their Indian wives *à la façon du pays.* West, being especially concerned that such men set an example to the rest of the community, was much gratified when both couples agreed to take the vows of the Church of England on March 30, 1821.[79]

West's successors, David Jones and William Cockran, continued to rail against the immoral habits of the fur traders. Jones's dogmatic stance was hardly conciliating. It had been West's custom to baptise traders' wives immediately before the marriage ceremony, but Jones was adamant that it would be a sacrilege to pronounce "our excellent Liturgy" over persons entirely ignorant of its meaning. When several traders maintained that there would be little point in having a church marriage since their wives would still be regarded as "heathens" unless baptised, Jones declared they were merely looking for an excuse to continue "living in sin."[80]

By the end of the 1820s, however, Cockran, the assistant chaplain, was optimistic about the changing attitude in Red River:

> It is encouraging to view the growing attention of the people to divine ordinance. Many that could not be prevailed upon formerly to marry their women have now seen the sin of despising the ordinance, and have felt truly sorry for the contempt and neglect of it.[81]

Equally gratifying to the missionaries was the spread of the church rite along the route between the colony and York Factory. On his way out to England in 1828, Jones was rejoiced "to unite two officers of high standing to their partners" at Oxford House. These proved to be Chief Factor Colin Robertson and his half-breed wife Theresa Chalifoux, and Clerk James Robertson and Margaret, a daughter of Chief Factor Alexander Stewart and his half-breed wife Susan Spence.[82]

In the post-1821 period, the Red River colony became the hub of fur trade society since increasing numbers retired there with their families, and schools were established for the children of the men in the field. Thus, the doctrines of the missionaries gained widespread acceptance. In 1835 Parson Jones jubilantly observed that it had become customary for traders passing through Red River to seek religious sanction for their unions: "This laudable practice is now becoming General, in fact

the revolution in these respects during the past 10 years had been immense."[83]
Indeed, the mid-1830s mark a definite change in attitude toward "the custom of
the country" in the environs of the settlement. Chief Trader Archibald McDonald
emphasized that the acceptance of the church rite was now the only proper course
for an honorable gentleman:

> All my colleagues are now about following the example, & it is my
> full conviction few of them can do no better--the great mistake is in
> flattering themselves with a different notion too long--nothing is
> gained by procrastination, but much is lost by it.[84]

After attending the annual meeting of Council, McDonald himself had had his
union with his half-breed wife Jane Klyne blessed by the church in a well-attended
ceremony at the parsonage in Red River on June 9, 1835. Yet he could not resist
pointing out the humor in the solemn pronouncements of the clergy as he and his
beloved Jane had lived in a most exemplary fashion since he had wed her *à la façon
du pays* 10 years before:

> [we] were joined in Holy wedlock & of course declared at full liberty
> to live together as man & wife & to increase & multiply as to them
> might seem fit--And I hope the validity of *this* ceremony is not to be
> questioned though it has not the further advantage of a Newspaper
> Confirmation.[85]

Even old die-hards eventually gave in. Although William Hemmings Cook had
retired to Red River with his wife Mary [Agathas] and family in 1815, it took till
1838 before he could be persuaded to tie the solemn knot. As one of the guests at
his wedding feast sarcastically observed, old Cook had "stood manfully forth...
bringing his 35 years courtship to an early close."[86]
Just at the time when Red River was becoming firmly reconciled to the European
form of marriage, a bitter feud over this issue erupted at Fort Vancouver, the headquarters of the Columbia district. The desirability of a mission to the Columbia
had been suggested as early as 1824, but Governor Simpson, in enumerating the
qualities such a missionary should possess, issued a prophetic warning:

> ...he ought to understand in the outset that nearly all the Gentlemen &
> Servants have Families altho' Marriage ceremonies are unknown in the
> Country and that it would be all in vain to attempt breaking through
> this uncivilized custom.[87]

Simpson appears to have forgotten his own advice, however, when selecting the
Company's first Pacific coast chaplain because, in spite of his name, the Reverend
Herbert Beaver could not have been a more unfortunate choice. According to
Beaver Fort Vancouver, upon his arrival in the fall of 1836 with his English wife
Jane, presented a "deplorable scene of vice and ignorance."[88] He refused to give

any credence to "the custom of the country," styling the traders' wives as concubines and chastizing the men for indulging in fornication.[89] This most insulting and inappropriate assessment of the well-regulated domestic situation at the fort provoked much hostility.

No one resented Beaver's slanders on his wife's character more than the fiery-tempered ruler of Fort Vancouver, Chief Factor John McLoughlin. Around 1811, while a young Nor'Wester in the Rainy Lake area, McLoughlin had wed Margeurite Wadin McKay *à la façon du pays.* Four children were born to the couple, and when McLoughlin assumed charge of the Columbia district in 1824, Margeurite and the youngest children made the long journey overland with him.[90] McLoughlin treated his wife with respect and devotion, and the remarks of contemporaries indicate that she played her role as first lady of Fort Vancouver well. According to Chief Trader James Douglas, Madame McLoughlin was respected by all for "her numerous charities and many excellent qualities of heart."[91] Narcissa Whitman, the wife of one of the first American missionaries to reach the post, is unlikely to have been guilty of bias in describing Margeurite as "one of the kindest women in the world."[92]

But to Beaver, good Mrs. McLoughlin was only a "kept Mistress" who could not be allowed to associate with respectable married females such as Mrs. Beaver.[93] He demanded that McLoughlin set an example by entering into a legal union with Margeurite. This, McLoughlin, who had Catholic predilections, absolutely refused to do. However, in order to silence once and for all any charge of illegality against his union, he had James Douglas, acting in his capacity of Justice of the Peace, perform a civil ceremony.[94] When Beaver and his wife, therefore, continued to heap invective upon Mrs. McLoughlin, her husband's anger reached such a pitch that on one occasion he could not refrain from giving the parson a sound drubbing with his own cane.[95]

Beaver also encountered stiff opposition when he attempted to prevent the "country marriage" of the clerk A.C. Anderson to a daughter of Chief Trader James Birnie. Anderson, at this time stationed in New Caledonia, had commissioned Chief Factor Peter Skene Ogden to conduct the girl north with the annual brigade. Beaver refused to baptise the girl prior to her departure and wrote a scathing letter to Anderson denouncing the contemplated union as "immoral and disgraceful"; he threatened to deny Anderson the church's blessing forever if he persisted in wilfully denying God's ordinance.[96] Ogden paid no heed to Beaver's rantings, declared that he would have the girl baptised by the American missionaries en route or do it himself and, as a Justice of the Peace, ultimately presided over Anderson's marriage.[97] Anderson himself wrote a spirited letter to Beaver giving a sophisticated defence of his action. In the first place, he claimed, legal authorities acknowledged that marriage was essentially a civil contract, the religious ceremony being merely a social convention. Scottish law, he pointed out, did not require church rites for marriages to be considered legal.[98] Furthermore, laudable as Beaver's presence at Fort Vancouver might be, he was of little use to Anderson hundreds of miles away. Even Church authorities had previously recognized that, marriages contracted in these wild and secluded regions in positions where the intervention of a person duly ordained may not be immediately available are valid and irreproachable.[99]

While few officers actually denied the desirability of a church marriage when a clergyman was present, Beaver's insufferable attitude alienated even the most devout. Such was the case of James Douglas who had wed Amelia, a daughter of Chief Factor William Connolly and his Cree wife, according to "the custom of the country" at Fort St. James in 1828. Douglas was anxious to have his marriage recognized by the church, however, and on February 28, 1837 Beaver performed the Church of England rite for the first, and almost last, time.[100] Even though she was now regularly married, Beaver still regarded the kind and gracious Mrs. Douglas as "little calculated to improve the manners of society."[101] Douglas, who was extremely sensitive to such unjust slanders, stoutly defended the honor of the ladies of the country when he assumed temporary command of Fort Vancouver in 1838. To Beaver's accusation that the Factor's house was "a common receptacle for every mistress of an officer in the service, who may take a fancy to visit the Fort," Douglas retorted that only the *wives* of officers visited the fort when their husbands were on brigade business:

> I neither have nor would suffer any person, of whatever rank, to introduce loose women into this Fort, an attempt which, to the honor of every gentlemen here, was never made.[102]

Beaver and his wife created such friction that all were gratified when he was relieved of his post and the haughty pair departed in the fall of 1838.

The dismal failure of Beaver was in sharp contrast to the success of the Pacific Mission established by the Catholic missionaries F.N. Blanchet and Modeste Demers who travelled overland to the Columbia in 1838. Although the majority of the populace at Fort Vancouver were Catholic, the priests' conciliatory attitude toward "the custom of the country" also contributed to their welcome. The Protestant missionaries in Red River had denounced their Catholic counterparts for refusing to marry persons of different religious persuasions "as though it were better for them to live in fornication, than that they should violate the rigid statutes of the Papal see."[103] Blanchet and Demers, however, had received special dispensation, and the records show that a considerable number of the marriages they performed in their progress across the country were between Protestant and Catholic. Although the Catholic Church did not recognize the sanctity of a "country marriage," the priests did acknowledge the existence of a marital bond by considering that every cohabiting couple were living in a state of "natural marriage." The only children stigmatized with illegitimacy were those whose parents could not be identified. Furthermore, the general tenor of the Catholic rite was that the parties were "renewing and ratifying their mutual consent of marriage" and formally recognizing the legitimacy of their children.[104] On November 19, 1842, to the priests' unboubted satisfaction, McLoughlin, who had just turned Catholic, had his union with Margeurite "his legitimate wife," blessed by the church:

...wishing to renew their consent of marriage in order to discharge the grave bonds on receiving the sacrement of marriage, we priests...have received the renewal of their consent of marriage and have given them the nuptial benediction...[105]

The coming of the missionaries to Rupert's Land with their insistence on the prerogative of the church in the sphere of marriage made it inevitable that "the custom of the country" would become a thing of the past. Even the "civil" contracts enacted by the Hudson's Bay Company contained the proviso that the marriage would receive the sanction of the church at the first possible opportunity.[106] The slow spread of missionary activity to more remote areas, however, meant that for many this opportunity never actually arose. As a result, official civil powers were granted to the chief officers of the Company; in 1845 the Council of the Northern Department resolved that, in the absence of a clergyman, chief factors only could solemnize marriages, but no person could take a wife at any establishment without the sanction of the gentleman in charge of the district.[107]

If the missionaries introduced "civilized" conventions into Rupert's Land, it was not without painful repercussions for fur trade society. "The custom of the country" had been regarded as a bona fide marriage rite, entailing all the obligations toward wife and children that marriage implies. Around the time of the union of the two companies, however, a significant change in the behavior of newly-arrived men toward native women can be observed. The stand of the church, it can be argued, worked to block the traditional conditioning process by which a newcomer had adapted to fur trade custom. The native woman was now often reduced to the status of mistress or even prostitute--someone with whom to gratify one's passions but never actually marry.

Unfortunately, the classic practitioner of this new attitude was the Governor himself, George Simpson, a man who had only wintered one year in Rupert's Land before assuming control of the Northern Department. Simpson showed little sympathy for the marital concerns of his associates partly because he did not recognize "the custom of the country." His lack of understanding is shown in his initial liaison with Betsey Sinclair, a daughter of the late Chief Factor William Sinclair and his native wife Nahovway. While Betsey was acknowledged as "Mrs. Simpson" by his contemporaries, the Governor treated her as a casual mistress and felt little compunction in getting rid of her when he tired of her charms.[108] Simpson, in fact, gained a notorious reputation for his womanizing,[109] and his behavior is not typical of officers who had had long experience in the fur trade.

He further shattered the norms of fur trade society by bringing a British wife out to Red River in 1830, even before he had severed his connection with Margaret Taylor whom all had come to regard as his "country wife."[110] Although none dared openly criticize the Governor for this action, widespread shock was expressed when a former Nor'Wester John George McTavish followed suit and renounced Nancy McKenzie, his "country wife" of long-standing. His unfeeling violation of fur trade custom provoked one old comrade John Stuart to declare their friendship at an end:

...what could be your aim in discarding her whom you clasped to your bosom in virgin purity and had for 17 Years with you, She was the Wife of your choice and has born you seven Children, now Stigmatized with ognominy...if with a view to domestick happiness you have thus acted, I fear the Aim has been Missed and that remorse will be your portion for life....[111]

That white women might become the wives of fur traders had been a possibility ever since the founding of the Red River settlement. But, because her numbers were so few, the white woman tended to be put on a pedestal, to be regarded as a "lovely tender exotic."[112] The presence of white women helped to reinforce the attitudes and customs of the society their men had previously left behind, which made native women appear less desirable as marriage partners. As the clerk James Hargrave observed in 1830, "this influx of white faces has cast a still deeper shade over the faces of our Brunettes in the eyes of many."[113] Hargrave himself, however, was not immune to "the fascinations of dark-eyed beauty,"[114] but studiously avoided any permanent attachment, ultimately bringing a Scottish bride Letitia Mactavish out to York Factory in 1840.

Significantly, the church gave support to this trend. William Cockran, who actively discouraged young officers from marrying mixed-blood girls, upheld Chief Factor Duncan Finlayson as worthy of emulation since he, though almost alone, had managed to evade "the snare which has ruined many of our countrymen."[115] So great was the Rev. Beaver's concern to prevent his wife from being tainted by association with "loose females" that he actually proposed that all who had not been married by a clergyman should be barred from Fort Vancouver. They might, however, be maintained outside the walls where the men could visit them on the sly to at least conform with the "outward decorum" which men in civilized societies observed in relation to their mistresses,[116] Such a plan which would have completely subverted the existing state of morality provoked an angry rebuttal from Chief Trader Douglas. A *wife* according to "the custom of the country" bore no resemblance to a prostitute in European society:

> The woman who is not sensible of violating [any] law, who lives chastely with her husband of her choice, in a state approved by friends and sanctioned by immemorial custom, which she believes strictly honorable, forms a perfect contrast to the degraded creature who has sacrificed the great principle which from infancy she is taught to revere as the ground work of female virtue; who lives a disgrace to friends and an outcast from society.[117]

Native women were particularly victimized by the introduction of the Victorian double-standard. While men might indulge their pleasure without obligation, women were now expected to abide by rigid European standards of propriety. It was grossly unfair to blame native women for perpetuating immorality, even though they were influenced by Indian sexual mores which were much more lenient compared to those

of white society.[118] Beaver, for example, proposed to punish the women directly
for the sinful state of affairs at Fort Vancouver by denying them rations and medical
attention to bring them to a sense of their shame.[119] A major concern of the boarding school established in Red River in the 1820s for the daughters of officers was to
estrange them from their Indian heritage and inculcate proper notions of feminine
virtue, particularly chastity.[120] After the stern disciplinarian John MacCallum took
over the school, the children were even forbidden any contact with their mothers
if they had not had a church marriage. One tragic victim of this situation was the
poor Indian wife of a trader Kenneth McKenzie who had gone off to join the
American Fur Company. She never saw her two daughters who had been placed in
the school, except when they, at risk of severe punishment, would sneak out to
visit their mother. Wives who could claim "benefit of clergy" were taught to look
upon those who could not as most debased creatures. But Letitia Hargrave, though
not always charitable in her remarks about native women, protested against such
hypocrisy:

> This may be all very right, but it is fearfully cruel for the poor un-
> fortunate mothers who did not know that there was any distinction
> & it is only within the last few years that anyone was so married. Of
> course had all the fathers refused, every one woman in the country
> wd have been no better than those that are represented to their own
> children as discreditable.[121]

Although "the custom of the country" had fallen into disrepute in fur trade
society by the mid-nineteenth century, the purpose of this paper has been to show
that it was in itself an honorable and recognized marriage rite. In spite of increasing
pressure to conform to the norms of white society, there were a few notable traders
who insisted upon living with their wives *à la façon du pays* as they had always done.
The romantic story of how the young Nor'Wester John Rowand was rescued
after a serious fall from his horse by the native girl who became his wife has become
legend.[122] Rowand took Lisette Umphreville for his country wife sometime around
1811, and their relationship through the years as Rowand rose to become the most
prominent officer on the Saskatchewan appears to have been a devoted one. Significantly, while the Catholic priests baptised four of his daughters and solemnized the
marriage of one on their visit to Fort Edmonton in 1838,[123] Rowand did not feel
that his "natural marriage" needed further benediction. Perhaps there is no greater
testimony to the bond that existed between them than Rowand's simple lament
when he learned that Lisette had died while he was returning to Fort Edmonton with
the brigades in the summer of 1849: "my old friend the Mother of all my children
was no more."[124] According to tradition, Chief Factor Peter Skene Ogden continually refused the church's sanction for his union with his remarkable Indian wife,
known as "Princess Julia." "If many years of public recognition of the relation and
of his children did not constitute sufficient proof," he declared, "no formal words
of priest or magistrate could help the matter."[125]
This argument was to be used to uphold the validity of marriage *à la façon du pays*

in the famous Connolly case of the late 1860s in which the judges of Lower Canada displayed a degree of tolerance and humanity in sharp contrast to the pious denunciations of the clergy.[126] In 1803 William Connolly, a newly-appointed clerk in the North West Company, had contracted an alliance with Suzanne Pas-de-Nom, the 15-year-old daughter of a Cree chief, partly to secure his influence with this band in the Athabasca country. For the next 28 years, the couple had lived together as man and wife and at least six children were born to them. According to one H.B.C. officer:

> I often saw Suzanne at his house at different posts and he introduced her to me as Mrs. Connolly. She passed and was universally acknowledged as his wife at the different posts where I met her...her children by William Connolly were always acknowledged in public as the lawful issue of their marriage.[127]

Connolly had, in fact, earned a reputation as one who stoutly maintained that it would be "a most unnatural proceeding" to desert the mother of one's children,[128] and he took Suzanne and his family east with him in 1831. The family was first settled in Saint Eustache where two of Connolly's daughters were baptised and Suzanne was introduced to the community as Mrs. Connolly. Shortly after the Connollys moved to Montreal, however, Connolly inexplicably repudiated his Indian wife and married his cousin Julia Woolrich in a Catholic ceremony on May 16, 1832. Nevertheless, Connolly, now stationed at Tadousac, continued to support Suzanne in Montreal until 1840 when he arranged for her to return to a convent in Red River where she remained until her death in 1862. Connolly himself had died in 1849, but his second wife, who had always known of the existence of Suzanne and even cared for some of the children, continued to make annual payments for the Indian woman's support. Then in 1867, Connolly's eldest son by Suzanne instituted a suit against Julia Woolrich as Connolly's executrix, claiming that the marriage of his mother and father had been legal and that, therefore, by law Suzanne had been entitled to one-half of his father's estate. Upon her death, this inheritance would have passed to her children, and John Connolly maintained that, as a legitimate heir, he was entitled to one-sixth of the estate.

The question as to whether a valid marriage had existed between Connolly and his Indian wife was thus the central issue of the case. On the basis of the testimony of numerous witnesses who had lived in Rupert's Land and an extensive examination of the development of marriage law, Chief Justice Monk ruled that their union constituted a valid marriage: firstly, because Suzanne had been married according to the custom and usages of her own people and secondly, because the consent of both parties which was the essential element of civilized marriage had been proved by 28 years of repute, public acknowledgement and co-habitation as man and wife.[129] Connolly had further given his name to Suzanne and shown considerable concern for the care and education of his offspring.

In a moving vindication of "the custom of the country," the Chief Justice summed up:

It is beyond all question, all controversy, that in the North West among the Crees, among the other Indian tribes or nations, among the Europeans at all stations, posts, and settlements of the Hudson's Bay, this union, contracted under such circumstances, persisted in for such a long period of years, characterized by inviolable fidelity and devotion on both sides, and made more sacred by the birth and education of a numerous family, would have been regarded as a valid marriage in the North West, was legal there; and can this Court, after he brought his wife and family to Canada, after having recognized her here as such, presented her as such to the persons he and she associated with, declare the marriage illegal, null and void? Can I pronounce this connection, formed and continued under such circumstances, concubinage, and brand his offspring as bastard....I think not. There would be no law, no justice, no sense, no morality in such a judgment.[130]

The Origins of the Mixed Bloods in the Canadian West

John E. Foster

For many historians of Western Canada prior to 1870, the question of the origins of the Mixed Bloods seems to be answered with casual reference to the parentage of the progenitors. An Indian mother and a European father, never the reverse, seems to provide the biological base from which historians can extrapolate assumptions concerning the nature of the culture of the Mixed Bloods. The recurring theme of the blend of savagery and civilization indicates possibly an inordinate concern with the questions as to what aspects of mixed blood behavior constitute "Indianness" and what aspects constitute "whiteness."[1] In such a perspective unacceptable value judgments are avoided only with difficulty. While "Indianness" in the Mixed Blood heritage may encourage "brave" and "loyal" behavior, historians seem to sense an absence of "steadfastness" leading to success in "civilized" pursuits.[2] When the "Indianness" of the Mixed Bloods is combined with the *"joie de vivre"* of the Canadien the results may be romantically dashing but never "progressive" and "stable."[3] An infusion of Celtic or Anglo-Saxon genes seems to serve as a substantial cultural corrective.[4] But in terms of civilization the problems of the Mixed Bloods' Indian heritage remain considerable.[5] It would appear to be self-evident that such unacceptable assessments of the cultural ways of the Mixed Bloods spring from equally unacceptable historical understandings of the nature of the origins of the Mixed Blood peoples in the Canadian West.

Before examining the factors responsible for the origins of the Mixed Blood peoples, it is well worthwhile to perceive them in the context of North America north of the Rio Grande in the century preceding Confederation. Throughout what is today Canada and the United States the process of *metissage* accompanied the fur trade. The presence of adult European males isolated from their women-folk, as well as the concepts of "good manners" and "hospitality" of many Indian bands, ensured as much.[6] In most instances, however, the biological Mixed Blood grew to maturity as an Indian.[7] In a few instances, a very few, Mixed Bloods were enculturated as whites.[8] In only one region, the northeastern fringe of the Great Plains, did the Mixed Blood emerge as a distinct socio-cultural entity. Thus, in the valleys of the Saskatchewan and the Red and Assiniboine Rivers, not one but two culturally distinct Mixed Blood peoples emerged in the century preceding Confederation.

At this point it is necessary to clarify the meaning of frequently encountered terms. "Métis" and its anglicized equivalent "Meetis" are used extensively to refer to the Mixed Bloods in western Canada today. For the pre-Confederation period historians have drawn a more precise cultural profile. With due notation of the fact that exceptions exist to any system of labelling or classifying peoples, Métis, in historical parlance, has come to refer to the French and Cree or Saulteaux-speaking, Roman Catholic buffalo hunters. Through the institution of the buffalo hunt they became the "New Nation" whose increasing prominence marked the closing decades of the pre-1870 West. Their Cree or Saulteaux heritage was evident in such patronyms as Desjarlais, Parenteau, Nolin, and Lagimodière and, of course, the ubiquitous Cardinal. But what of such Métis names as Jean-Baptiste Wilkie, Bastonnais Pangman, and Cuthbert Grant; what of surnames such as Dease, Fisher, and McGillis? Such names reflect the ebb and flow of European peoples involved in the fur trade system based upon the St. Lawrence River and the Great Lakes. Following the fall of New France, Yankees, Englishmen, and Highland Scots aspired to control this vast fur trade system. They left their names in the parish registers of the Métis communities of the West. More important, they left the legacy of their participation in the St. Lawrence fur trading system in the socio-cultural ways of the Métis.[9]

In the documents and the literature of the pre-Confederation West an additional set of Mixed Blood surnames appear which seem to cause scholars some difficulty. Historians have given significant scholarly attention to individuals in this group, but as a collectivity historians have virtually ignored them.[10] Who were the Birds, Bunns, and Cooks, the Favels, Fletts, and Gaddys? Who were the Prudens, Sinclairs, and Sutherlands? It is readily apparent in the documents that they were not Métis. English-speaking and Anglican, a few of them hunted the buffalo on the plains. Most of them, however, were farmers in the Red River Settlement. Some served as officers and tripmen in the Hudson's Bay Company's service. A few were merchants. And one, Dr. John Bunn, was a medical doctor. Who were these "non-Métis Mixed Bloods?"[11]

Some historians of the pre-1870 West have used the term "halfbreed" or "English-speaking halfbreeds" to identify the non-Métis Mixed Bloods as a collectivity.[12] The term "halfbreed" would appear to be unacceptable on two grounds. In the first place it seems to continue the biological perspective that has evoked questionable cultural assumptions. At the same time, after a few generations, the term is scarcely accurate. Perhaps a more important reason for questioning the use of the term is the pejorative sense that can be associated with it, both in the past and today. A solution to the problem in terminology should appear in the term used by the non-Métis Mixed Bloods to describe themselves. In this respect the documents are not as helpful as one might assume. The term "halfbreed" was used but it was clearly a synonym for "Mixed Blood" as it included the two Mixed Blood peoples within its meaning.[13] In the documents it is apparent that the Mixed Bloods, who historians have designated "halfbreeds," were conscious of their "British" and "Protestant" ways, particularly those ways that set them apart from the "French" and "Catholic" Métis.[14] Yet when they wished to distinguish themselves from the Métis and from the British-born segment of the population they used the rather vague phrase "my Countrymen."[15] This phrase, however, lends support for an infrequently used term found in documents originating with British-born Anglican missionaries.[16] The term "Country-born," no doubt a polite affectation, was used to designate those Mixed Bloods whose cultural ways were not those of the Métis. While the Country-born did not use the term themselves they would have recognized that it referred to them. At the same time "Country-born" avoids the errors in perspective that seem to arise from the use of "halfbreed." Lastly the term does not have a pejorative sense associated with its use. "Country-born" is the most feasible term to apply to the second Mixed Blood community to emerge in the pre-1870 West.

As the surnames of the Métis suggest cultural antecedents in the St. Lawrence trading system, the surnames of the Country-born suggest that their cultural antecedents lay in the trading system based on the coastal factories of Hudson Bay and the line of related posts stretching westward along the major rivers in the eighteenth century. While an examination of the literature would suggest that the Métis are more familiar to historians than the Country-born, it would appear that, for the moment at least, the historical factors accounting for the origins of the Country-born are more easily identified than those determing the origins of the Métis. For this reason scholarly efforts in this area will tend to emphasize the historical and cultural odessey that gave rise to the Country-born. In turn, an historical understanding of this odessey may prove most helpful in understanding the possibly similar experience of the Métis. To the reader the appearance of the two Mixed Blood peoples as cultural collectivities, in different regions but at the same time, must appear to be something more than an historical coincidence. Thus the question of the origins of the Country-born has scholarly interest beyond that associated directly with the community itself.

The simple fact that European women were virtually absent from the Hudson Bay trading system prior to the nineteenth century dictated Indian bands for the origins of the Country-born.[17] No other community could produce children and raise them to maturity. The trading post in the Hudson Bay trading system consisted solely of adult males. The women and children that could be found within the bastions of the post from time to time were members of surrounding Home Guard Cree bands. The official policy of the Hudson's Bay Company's Governor and Committee in London dictated non-fraternization particularly between Indian women and British-born officers and servants.[18] Distance and the realities of life in Rupert's Land led to a more practical though unofficial policy.[19] In time the results were ties of kinship and occasionally friendship between the members of the Home Guard Cree bands and the British-born officers and servants of the trading posts. Furthermore the unofficial policy recognized that the adult males of an Indian band would permit British-born males to consort with Indian women only in the context of a marriage relationship. The officers and servants were expected to behave in a manner that demonstrated their acceptance of this relationship.[20] A failure to do so could and did lead to tragic incidents.[21]

The marriage relationship between officers and servants on one hand and Home Guard Cree women on the other differed significantly from the European ideal. If

practices in later years reflect ways in an earlier period, many marriages would be
of relatively short duration.[22] In addition, some evidence would suggest that many
of the marriages were polyandrous in nature. While the officer-in-charge of a post
was permitted a "bed-fellow," other officers were limited to occasional visits.[23]
While the record is virtually silent with respect to servants it seems probable that
older servants of some seniority enjoyed relationships similar to those of the officers.[24] The portrait of marriage that emerges from the documents focuses upon
a Home Guard Indian woman with an Indian husband and his children. In addition
she would have a British-born husband with whom she might live for varying periods
of time.[25] In many instances it would appear that the relationship was conducted
through relatively brief visits.[26] From the perspective of the Home Guard Cree
husband the British-born husband was a "brother." And as such he was a most
valuable asset to the family and to the band. No doubt with careful maneuvering
a candidate for "brother" and "husband" could be selected who would prove to be
a valuable pipeline from the warehouse and storehouse of the trading post to the
Home Guard Cree family and their band. In addition it was not unknown for some
officers and servants to make provisions in their wills for their Indian wives and
children.[27] It may well be these historical facts radiating around the Home Guard
Cree women that explain the anthropological findings showing coastal Cree bands
to be matrilocal while those further inland tended to be patrilocal.[28]

It is readily apparent that after a few generations questions as to the biological
make-up of a Home Guard Cree band were largely meaningless. Within a relatively
short period of time various color shadings of eyes, hair, and complexion would
mark the individual members of a Home Guard Cree band. Everyone in the band,
however, would see himself in terms of the socio-cultural ways of the Home Guard
Cree. This way of life came into being in the century preceding the Hudson's Bay
Company's penetration of the interior. It was the cultural fount from which the
Country-born originated.

While much research remains to be done in terms of understanding the ways of
the Home Guard Cree sufficient material exists to provide a sketch with some detail.
Through the fur trade European goods and ways significantly influenced the lives of
the coastal Cree. As suppliers of provisions, "small furs," and goods such as tobog-
gans and snowshoes as well as services such as guide and courier, the Home Guard
Cree were the recipients of many material benefits originating in Britain.[29] In
comparison with the trapping and trading Indians of the interior they acquired
guns, shot and powder, cloth and blankets, as well as beads and brandy out of
proportion to their numbers.[30] Yet the Home Guard Cree utilized such goods in
an Indian context. In their eyes European goods enriched rather than debased the
quality of their way of life.[31] In other areas of their lives the British-born officers
and servants made an impact. But again it would appear to be in terms of enrich-
ment. Before the coming of the Hudson's Bay Company the coastal Cree had not
required names for the days of the week. After sustained contact such names
became necessary. Reflecting their observations on life in the trading post, Sunday
became, in Home Guard Cree, "Talking Day."[32] Saturday, mirroring the practice
of disbursing weekly provisions to the servants, became "Sharing Day."[33] In addi-

tion the various holidays of the British calendar became "Feast Days."[34] Another British accomplishment that became a part of the world of the coastal Cree was the game of checkers. In a short period of time they were virtually unbeatable.[35] Their use of the English language, however, did not give rise to the same accolades on the part of observers.[36] Yet in spite of the numerous and various acculturative forces that influenced the Home Guard Cree their ways remained firmly tied to an Indian tradition. Even the familial context that governed their relationship with the British-born males of the trading post emphasized, from a Home Guard perspective, Indian ways.[37]

For the most part children of marriages involving Home Guard Cree women and British-born officers and servants were enculturated in the ways of the band. The girls learned the ways of their mothers while boys learned skills taught by their Indian fathers or other Indian male relatives. The careers of such Mixed Blood officers as Moses Norton and Charles Price Isham in the service of the Hudson's Bay Company, demonstrated that the paternal interest of the British-born fathers could play a significant role in shaping the lives of individual children.[38] Nevertheless the vast majority of children, no matter what their parentage was, saw life from the perspective of a Home Guard Cree of the appropriate age and sex.

Today the historical descendants of the Home Guard Cree are the coastal Cree of Hudson Bay and James Bay and to a lesser extent the Muscaigo Cree of northeastern Manitoba and the Monsoni Cree of northern Ontario. If the Country-born of the pre-1870 West were to derive their cultural origins from the Home Guard Cree it becomes necessary to postulate a mechanism or a sequence of events directing some Home Guard Cree along a diverging historical route. Their route was one of cultural change leading to the English-speaking Anglican Mixed Blood farmers in the Red River Settlement and elsewhere in Rupert's Land. Such a sequence of events began with the Hudson's Bay Company's penetration of the interior in strength a century after the voyage of the *Nonsuch*.

During the last quarter of the eighteenth century the Hudson's Bay Company faced what seemed to be insurmountable problems.[39] At a critical juncture in their competion with the traders of the St. Lawrence, fur trading system wars in Europe further exacerbated their difficulties. The shortage of skilled labor proved to be a particularly damaging problem.[40] In desperation the Company turned to the Home Guard Cree, particularly those young men whose kinship ties drew them close to the trading post and made them at least partially amenable to the ways of command in the Company's service.[41] Beginning in the last decade of the eighteenth century the names of young men whose parish of origin was "Hudson Bay" occurred with increasing frequency on the Company's "Lists of Servants."[42] With this step the young Home Guard Cree males became fully fledged members of the trading posts' complement. No doubt following practices similar to when they served the Company as hunters and couriers, their families were brought into the post to live during the period of their service.[43] In such circumstances it would be difficult, if not impossible, not to offer the same fringe benefits to the British-born. By the end of the eighteenth century Mixed Bloods were a feature of the society of the Company's trading posts.[44] With this step a number of Home Guard Cree began the historical process that would culminate in their emergence as the Country-born.

The first two decades of the nineteenth century witnessed the increasing tempo of the competition in the fur trade that led to violence and death. Amidst this chaos the Mixed Blood children of the Company's trading posts acquired some interesting skills. Although Cree would continue to be spoken, a knowledge of basic English became common.[45] A few could read and write the language of their British-born progenitors.[46] But perhaps the most crucial skill acquired by these children was a knowledge of the social structure, not of one post, but of all the posts that constituted the Hudson Bay trading system. An examination of this society, without reference to the metropolis from which it sprang would suggest an Alice-in-Wonderland world. A relatively small number of adult males structured themselves socially in a pyramidal hierarchy from the unskilled youthful newcomers at the bottom to the experienced Chief Factor (the Trader or the "Uckimow" of the Home Guard Cree) at the top.[47] Life in this authoritarian social system seemed to emphasize an individual's concern for the material goods and social behavior that served to demark his particular status position.[48] Most frequently this concern was expressed in terms of maximizing the privileges associated with a rank.[49] Whether it was a question of the inadequate quantity and quality of rations or the absence of deference by an inferior or respect from a superior, officers and servants seemed to expend much energy in looking to their supposed interests.[50] In learning the intricacies of this social system as their own, the Mixed Blood children of the trading post also familiarized themselves with the other social systems that were intertwined with the formal social structure and influenced its operation. The camaraderie of the various adult male groupings was a significant feature of trading post society.[51] Another important social system of the post was the network of kinship linking various Mixed Blood families with British-born officers and servants and with the members of surrounding Indian bands.[52] The complex interplay of the various social systems into a cohesive whole created a unique social world in the posts of the Hudson Bay trading system at the close of the eighteenth century. To the outsider it was bewilderingly complex and often unpredictable. To the participants, particularly the children born and raised within its limits, the social world of the trading post was the "normal" manner in which human beings interacted.

The children of the Home Guard Cree and the British-born officers and servants, the first generation raised in the trading posts, evolved values appropriate to their social circumstances. It was apparent in the early years of the nineteenth century that there were distinct differences in some values and some attitudes between the British-born and the Mixed Bloods. For those who enlisted in the Company's service in Great Britain the remunerative aspects of work were of cardinal importance.[53] For the Mixed Blood the social aspects of work were of greater importance.[54] Thus the fine was an effective tool for dealing with the refractory British-born servant. With the Mixed Blood servant the fine was ineffective; rather, physical coercion seemed to be the effective means of discipline.[55] Similarly the British-born servants tended to become argumentive over what might be termed the monetary aspects of their work.[56] On the other hand Mixed Blood servants became troublesome when work appeared to disrupt their social interests.[57] Such differences would suggest that a value system distinct from that of many of the British-born influenced the behavior of the Mixed Blood residents of the Company's posts.

The Mixed Bloods, in the early years of the nineteenth century, developed an ethos peculiar to the fur trade society of the Hudson's Bay Company's posts. To them the epitome of the good life was the life-style of the "Indian Trader," the officer-in-charge of the trading post.[58] To the inhabitants his responsibilities must have seemed most noteworthy. In addition to seeing to the profitable conduct of the fur trade in his district he was responsible for the welfare of the inhabitants of the post as well as the members of surrounding Indian bands.[59] In seeing to his responsibilities the Indian trader utilized the authority contained in numerous directives, rules, and regulations emanating from London.[60] Greater authority, however, sprang from his position atop the hierarchical social structure.[61] No doubt significant influence devolved from the kinship connections that linked him to many inhabitants in the post as well as to individuals in surrounding Indian bands. In recognition of the numerous and onerous responsibilities that fell on his shoulders the system bestowed significant privileges on the Indian trader. Living quarters, food, and drink were the best that circumstances could provide.[62] Deference marked the conversation and behavior of those who came within his presence.[63] As a result the aspirations of many in the trading post, particularly the Mixed Bloods, emphasized a style of life imitating that of the Indian trader.

The final step in the historical and cultural process that moved from Home Guard Cree to Country-born witnessed the migration of hundreds of Mixed Bloods from the posts of the Hudson Bay trading system to the Red River Settlement. The migration began when the signing of the Deed Poll in 1821 ended the competition in the fur trade between the North West Company and the Hudson's Bay Company. The revitalized Hudson's Bay Company encouraged the movement of supernumerary officers and servants into retirement in the agricultural settlement founded by Lord Selkirk.[64] At Red River the Mixed Bloods would come under the influence of the institutions of a British and Protestant civilization. Churches, schools, and civil government would create a British agrarian community in the heart of North America.[65] Numbers and circumstances dictated the simple fact that the Mixed Blood migrants from the Company's posts, the Country-born, would be the social foundation on which a British agrarian community in harmony with the fur trade rested. Such was the plan for Red River that prevailed in the board rooms of the Hudson's Bay Company and the Church Missionary Society in London.[66] It remained to be seen whether future practices mirrored present plans.

In Red River the Country-born continued their pursuit of the good life as their years in the trading post had defined it. Although most of them became farmers they did not share the attachment to the land of their Kildonan Scots neighbors whom Lord Selkirk had brought to Red River.[67] Several tried merchandizing but few enjoyed success as businessmen in the social network of kith and kin that was Red River.[68] In terms of their aspirations to emulate the life style of the Indian trader the institutions of Church and State, particularly the schools, appeared to democratize opportunity. A cardinal qualification of the Indian trader was his ability to read and to write fluently in English. For this reason many in the trading posts, who may have felt that they possessed the other necessary attributes, had to admit their deficiencies and set their sights lower. Extensive kin connections were a most helpful asset of an effective Indian trader but such connections did not compensate for an absence of competence with the pen. To many in Red River the Sunday and Day schools of the Anglican Mission seemed to offer a remedy for this deficiency.[69] In so doing the schools held out the promise of increased opportunity for those who would dream. The Anglican missionaries were enthralled with the pursuit of salvation that seemed to galvanize their Country-born parishioners in the 1820s and 1830s.[70] The Country-born found salvation to be no hindrance and, in time, a distinct asset in the pursuit of their goal.

While circumstances in Red River prior to 1850 tended to widen opportunities that the Country-born had defined in the trading posts a generation earlier, the number of Country-born youths who pursued the goal of the life-style of the Indian trader were relatively few. For a variety of reasons, including education and family connections, most young Country-born males would have to be satisfied with a style of life, not in the image of an Indian trader, but in the image of a master of a small outpost.[71] A few could and did aspire to become Indian traders. Frustrated in achieving their ambitions they generated the "Free Trade Movement" in the 1840s.[72] They were joined by the Métis, most of whom participated for very different motives.[73]

By the 1850s the Country-born had completed the historical journey that began a century earlier in the Home Guard Cree bands living nigh to the coastal factories on Hudson Bay. The vehicle that impelled them upon their journey and defined cardinal aspects of their world was the fur trade. The ways of the small family bands associated with the role of the Home Guard Indians in the fur trade was the point of cultural origin for the Country-born. Living in association with the personnel of the trading post the Home Guards were exposed to aspects of British ways. Those ways that were deemed to be of value were incorporated into Home Guard patterns of life and became part of an Indian tradition. The employment of young adult males in the Company's service and year round residence in the posts for their families marked a significant environmental change. In such circumstances British ways took on added importance. As Home Guard hunters the coastal Cree required a knowledge of British social ways sufficient to enable them to identify those individuals who could be of the greatest help to the band. As members of the trading posts' complement a far more sophisticated knowledge of the social system was necessary. Yet in acquiring this knowledge the Mixed Bloods of the trading post did not necessarily acquire the British values that supposedly underlay the social system. If anything the "Uckimow" of the Home Guard Cree took on greater importance and a more precise definition. As the Indian trader the gap between the world of the coastal Cree and the Uckimow of the trading post diminished. A few Mixed Bloods, a very few in fact, could aspire to such a position of material well-being and leadership.

The end of the competition in the fur trade and the migration of many Mixed

Bloods to Red River heralded the final step in the emergence of the Country-born. Under the influence of the institutions of a British and Protestant community the Country-born completed the cultural transformation that began generations earlier on the shores of Hudson Bay. Speaking English and professing evangelical Anglicanism, they pursued in greater numbers than previously the goal of the good life epitomized in the life style of the Indian trader. This aspect of their lives was uniquely their own in Red River. More than anything else it set them apart from the other communities, including the Métis. It would be pointless to pursue the question as to whether the Country-born concept of the Indian trader owed more to the British concept of a gentleman and the head of a patriarchal household[74] or to the coastal Cree concept of Uckimow. What is significant is that the fur trade of the Hudson Bay system gave rise to a concept that embodied the ways of a culturally distinct people. Obviously related to both British and Cree traditions but equally obviously more than a simple mixture of these traditions, the Country-born were a sociocultural creation of the fur trade in the Hudson Bay trading system.

At the moment the historical record does not furnish a clear picture delineating the origins of the Métis. Perhaps that of the Country-born may furnish, if not a "model" at least some helpful suggestions as to possible lines of inquiry.

From the era of New France, Mixed Blood families were familiar features of the posts of the St. Lawrence trading system.[75] Of particular interest were the posts between Lake Superior and the Red River valley among the Saulteaux in the last quarter of the eighteenth century. It would be worthwhile to determine whether "Home Guard" bands were a part of the fur trade in the region. In addition, a comparison of Home Guard bands in both fur trade traditions could be most illuminating. Should later practices reflect those of an earlier date, however, the Mixed Blood women in the posts of the St. Lawrence fur trading system enjoyed a relatively secure position. The various skills she acquired from her mother gave her a valuable role in the conduct of the trade at the post.[76] Her Mixed Blood brother, however, would face difficulties establishing a place for himself in the trading post. Even should he be willing to accept the authoritarian discipline associated with a voyageur's work he would find that servants enlisted in Montreal not in the interior.[77] To survive he needed the skills of the Indian hunter. This was particularly true in an era when an expanding population and decreasing game resources were darkening the future for the Saulteaux.[78] To acquire the necessary skills of survival the young Mixed Blood would probably have lived with the males of his mother's band, her father, her brothers, or her uncles. But still his future would not be secure. With the evolution of family hunting territories whose succession was probably determined by patrilineality, the Mixed Blood male whose claim would have devolved from his mother would have to move on.[79] If he wished to live a life other than that of a "hanger-on" about some trading post or Home Guard band he would have to push westward with others in similar circumstances. As the forest gave way to the Parkland and at the Red River the Plains, animal resources increased significantly.[80] At the same time the Dakota rendered life more hazardous. Armed with the Plains gun and mounted on the horse, another recent arrival to the area, the Dakota could wreck havoc on the pedestrian Saulteaux.[81]

If the Saulteaux were to exploit successfully the resources of the Parkland and the Plain they would require assistance in making an adjustment. Their traditional ally, the trader, could provide such assistance. He would provide assistance because the Saulteaux in their need were more dependable suppliers of provisions and furs.[82] The ranks of such Saulteaux bands were increased in 1804 when the XY Company discharged numerous Canadien servants upon its amalgamation with the North West Company.[83]

The remaining steps in the adaptation of many Mixed Blood Saulteaux bands to circumstances in the Red River are well known to historians. The struggle involving the North West Company and the Selkirk settlers in the second decade of the nineteenth century was particularly important as it evolved the concept of the "New Nation."[84] Another development of significance was the presence of French-speaking Roman Catholic priests from Lower Canada after 1818. From the time of their arrival these men exerted much influence amongst their parishioners.[85] Lastly the emergence of the institution of the buffalo hunt in 1820 signified the successful adaptation of Mixed Blood bands of Saulteaux to circumstances in the Red River valley.[86] In the process, however, they became the Métis. It is possible that a similar scenario could be sketched in the same time period for the Métis who emerged on the Saskatchewan. While their language was Cree and not Saulteaux, limited evidence to date would suggest an historical experience for Cree bands intimately involved with trading posts of the St. Lawrence trading system on the Saskatchewan that was similar to the experience of some Saulteaux bands in the Red River valley.[87]

Detailed and complete studies on the origins of the Métis as well as the Country-born remain to be done. In such studies the process of cultural change over time should he highlighted and perhaps clarified. In the past thirty years historians have virtually ignored the question of the origins of the Mixed Bloods in what was to become the Canadian West. Marcel Giraud's monumental work *Le Métis Canadien* remains the last occasion when a scholar gave serious consideration to the question. It would appear that J.M.S. Careless's landmark article in 1954, "Frontierism, Metropolitanism and Canadian History"[88] rendered unfashionable of inquiry anything that could be considered "frontierist." Past attempts to find an "individualistic and democratic" people in the pre-1870 West have failed.[89] The "free land" frontier and its cultural concomitants simply did not exist. But studies of the origins of the Mixed Bloods will suggest that in addition to being a vehicle reflecting metropolis-hinterland relationships, the fur trade systems were "frontiers" whose particular features created new socio-cultural entities out of the various participants. In studies of the pre-1870 West Frederick Jackson Turner's hypothesis has little validity; but perhaps his perspective has.

A Probe Into the Demographic Structure of Nineteenth Century Red River

Frits Pannekoek

To the casual observer in 1830 Red River appeared a picturesque rural backwater dotted with church steeples and numerous windmills.[1] The impression would not have been inaccurate. By 1830 the settlement had recovered from the violent struggle between the British and Canadian fur companies and the accompanying desolation, barbarity, and destitution. But the golden decade of the half sedentary, half nomadic life (built around the extended family and the neighborhood) that had become Red River by 1830 lasted only a few years. By 1840 the settlement was faced with a crisis of the land that caused the breakdown and disintegration of the extended family and consequently Red River. Until the rush of Ontarians in the later nineteenth century killed the Red River dream forever, the settlement writhed in a confused agony seeking to perpetuate its myth of that impossible half nomadic, half sedentary existence. The 1849 free trade crisis, the unrest of the 1850s, and the Riel affair were all products of this breakdown. This is not to deny that they were a result as well of the Company's attempt to fossilize its monopoly, and Ontario's effort to extend its empire westward.

The first people to struggle for survival in this isolated, flat, and damnable wilderness were a motley and dispirited crew. The only creditable inhabitants were the Scottish remnants of the Earl of Selkirk's endeavors to create a land speculator's dream in North America and the retired officers of the Northwest and Hudson's Bay Company. The vast majority of the population, the English-speaking half-breeds and the French-speaking half-breeds (the Métis) drifted into Red River between 1822 and 1830 upon the encouragement of the Hudson's Bay Company, which had seriously reduced its need for personnel after union with its rival the North West Company. There were other groups but they were of minor significance and tended to identify with one of the above. The handful of Canadian farmers who came at the invitation of Bishop Provencher in 1818 settled around St. Boniface and identified with the Métis who dominated that area. A few Scandinavians and Irish were also sprinkled throughout Red River -- but they formed no distinct community nor identified themselves as belonging to one and could and did serve as a bridge between the various communities comprising Red River.

Early in the 1830s life arranged itself into a pattern regulated by the seasons, the church, the Company, and the family.[2] Families settled on varying sized river lots (retired Chief Factors could claim as much as 1,000 acres while the poorer sorts often squatted on a few acres) with their children and friends about them. These bonds of family and neighborhood became very tight indeed, and tended to re-inforce religious and ethnic divisions. The lower settlement between the two Fort Garrys was, for example, Protestant and English, with the English-speaking mixed-bloods tending to live in the proximity of the Lower Fort and Lord Selkirk's Scots closer to the Upper Fort. The French-speaking Catholic mixed-bloods settled at the forks on the Red and Assiniboine and along the south bank of the Assiniboine.

Each of these Red River families was headed by a patriarch whose position in the settlement and in the family was for the most part derived from his previous status with the Company. The average age of the head of a mixed-blood household was 33 in 1832 and 39 in 1843. Among the Scottish families, residing for the most part in Kildonan parish, it was 42 in 1832 and 45 in 1843.[3] These figures indicate not only that fewer and fewer new families were being established in the settlement, but that married children were remaining with and under the influence of their fathers. That this was true is indicated by an examination of some of the more prominent families.

Among the principal patriarchs of Red River were William Hemmings Cook, James Bird, and Peter Corrigal. Chief Factor William Hemmings Cook was 53 years of age when he arrived in the settlement in 1820. Short, husky, dark-haired and swarthy-looking, Cook had spent 33 years in the service of the Company before petitioning the London Committee of the Hudson's Bay Company in 1815 to let his family settle somewhere in Rupert's Land. Within a few years of 1820 Cook was settled with Mary Cocking, his third wife whom he had married in the custom of the country, and his children: Samuel, 21; Mary, 20; Jeremiah, 19; Charles, 16; and Lydia, Jenny, Catherine, and Joseph all of indeterminate age. Cook first established his household on a narrow piece of land between the Red and Seine Rivers, but in 1824 moved with his family to Image Plain where he had two five-hundred-acre lots. This was a considerably more congenial area already settled by an increasing number of Cook's fur trade friends.[4]

Chief Factor James Bird also entered the settlement in 1820. He was 46 years old and was accompanied by his second Indian wife, Elizabeth, and his children: a married son, five unmarried adult sons, an unmarried adult daughter, and a son under 15 years of age. At first this entire family lived in his house, one of the largest and most pretentious of the settlement.[5] Another, Chief Trader Peter Corrigal, a gaunt, tall, and formidable 42-year-old Orkneyman who had served in posts along the Saskatchewan and at Norway House, arrived at Red River in 1822 accompanied by Christy, his Indian wife, and James, their 20-year-old unmarried son.[6] He established his family on two 125-acre lots above Image Plain near the 1846 site of St. Andrew's church.[7]

The patriarchical pattern was typical of the bulk of the settlers such as Henry Hallet, Humphrey Favel, William Garrioch, and William Flett. Humphrey Favel had been a clerk and retired in the 1820s with his two sons Humphrey Jr. and Thomas. While Humphrey Sr. and Thomas established their household on Image Plain, Humphrey Jr. settled closer to Upper Fort Garry.[8] Henry Hallet, stationed for a number of years at York as a trader, retired in 1824 with Catherine Dansee, his half-Indian wife, and their five mixed-blood children: James, 24; Henry Jr., 23; William, 22; Anne, 16; and Elizabeth, 12, on two lots well over 300 acres.[9] William Garrioch, a trader and second clerk in the Swan River district, arrived in 1825 with six children and settled adjacent to his father-in-law William H. Cook.[10] William Flett, a nondescript servant, settled in 1822 at age 59 with Saskatchewan, his second Indian wife, and with his four children: William, Ann, and Elizabeth (all in their late 20s), and Peter, 10 years old. Flett's eldest children did not live with him, but were married and established their own households.[11] This appears to have been the exception rather than the rule.

The great majority of adult men who married in the late 1820s and early 1830s stayed with their fathers. Samuel, son of William Hemmings Cook, lived with his wife in his father's home, as did both the sons of James Bird after their marriages in 1824. The Bird women reinforced the Red River pattern when they accompanied their husbands to the homes of their fathers-in-law.[12] This dependency of adult children upon their fathers must have reinforced and have been reinforced by the hierarchical traditions of the fur trade, and by the clan structure common to many of the Orkney and Scottish born fathers. The increasing prevalency of the extended family is very apparent from the substantial increase in the number of sons over 16 living at home. The extended family was most common amongst the Scottish families. They had .82 sons over 16 at home in 1843, compared to the mixed-bloods who had only .35. In both cases it must be emphasized that this was double the number of 1838.[13]

The late 1830s must have been years of confidence if not always prosperity for the settlement. The farms must have seemed to have hopeful futures. This is apparent by the significant increase in the birth rate from 1832 to 1843. The increase in Kildonan was especially phenomenal and indicated the confidence the Kildonan Scots must have had in their agricultural endeavors. By 1843 the average number of children in a Scottish household was 5.7, significantly up from the 3.4 of 1832. For the mixed-bloods the increase was less, but nevertheless pronounced, from 3.7 to 4.1.[14]

That this was so is further indicated in the baptismal records of these years. The James Hallet who married Sally Fidler in 1828 fathered three children between 1828 and 1832.[15] The Henry Hallet who married Catherine Parenteau in 1824 fathered two sons soon afterwards,[16] while the John Inkster who married Mary Sinclair on January 20, 1826 fathered four children from 1829 to 1834.[17] Thomas Favel and his wife added one more to an already large family of nine,[18] and William Flett, a son of James Flett, married in 1830 and had a son two years later.[19]

The baptism records indicate that the European and mixed-bloods had virtually similar birth rates. If mixed-blood families were smaller it was because of their staggering rate of infant mortality. Joseph Bird, the eldest son of James Bird, and Betsy his wife, had three children between 1831 and 1836, Emma, born in 1831, died in the spring of 1833; James, born in 1833, died that same year; and Laetitia, born in 1836, died in 1849.[20] James Hallet, the son of Henry Hallet Sr., lost two children between 1834 and 1838, while Henry Hallet Jr. lost a child in 1834.[21] The story of woe is never-ending and examples exist in every family. The tragic loss of children, very often in the spring with the onslaught of fevers, must have made life endlessly sad.

Had the children of mixed-blood parents died in one year or along with the children of Kildonan-Scot parents, then one could have assumed that the cause had been either famine or epidemic. But this was not the case; deaths did not occur frequently among the Kildonans, the most European of the settlers. For example, Alexander Bannerman and his wife had five children between 1833 and 1844, all of whom lived.[22] The high mortality rate amongst the mixed-blood couples suggests that they were not as able to provide a suitable environment for child growth. The food supply for many of the mixed-bloods was uncertain. This cycle of feast to famine must have caused malnutrition.[23] The standard of hygiene was also appallingly low if Alexander Ross, Red River's first historian is to be believed. The mixed-bloods were least likely to have wells and probably drew water from the Red River, into which they had dumped the manure from their barns.[24]

By 1843 it was apparent that a serious demographic and economic crisis was afflicting the Red River settlement. The result was the collapse of the extended family. This is indicated by the decline in the average age of the head of the mixed-blood households from 39 to 36 years from 1843 to 1849.[25] While this may have been due to disease and death from old age, it was in fact probably due to adult children of both the first and second generation finally leaving to establish their own homes. It is interesting to note, however, that the tendency amongst the Scots was the exact opposite. The mean age of the head of the Scots households continued to increase, from 45 in 1843 to 52 in 1849. The Kildonan settlers, in the period of uncertainty that was the late 1830s and early 1840s, seem to have turned even more inward to themselves and to the protection afforded by the security of their families.[26]

The reasons for the break-up of the mixed-blood extended family are not obscure. Pressures on the second Red River generation increased steadily throughout the late 1830s and early 1840s. Unable to gain a certain livelihood from their father's land and with no opportunity for suitable employment in the Company, they turned instead to the plains to trade in furs, to hunt, or to freight goods to St. Paul. Chief Factor James Sutherland knew the problem well.

> I could get him (Sutherland's second son) in the Cos service, but half-breeds as they are called has (sic) no chance there nor are they respected whatever their abilities may be, by a parcel of upstart Scotchmen, who now hold the power and Control in the concern...[27]

The results were predictable. Some like Joseph Cook, Chief Factor William Hemmings Cook's son, served as a laborer.[28] Others were not so patient. Peter Garrioch left the settlement in 1843 to trade furs with the Missouri Fur Company,[29] while William Hallet and his brother James[30] as well as James Bird's two sons joined the Métis on the plains.[31]

When a second generation son joined the illicit fur trade, he usually severed his relations with his father, who more often than not supported the Company's monopoly. When Peter Garrioch became a free trader, for example, his father refused to have anything more to do with him.[32] James Bird was beset by similar anxieties, as his letter to Alexander Christie, in charge of the Upper Fort, indicates:

> I have just received your note and beg to say that I have lately heard with sorrow that the members of my family you name are somehow or other employed in an improper and illegal pursuit of furs...my son Phillip behaved so ill to me formerly that I was obliged to turn him out of doors and resolve to have nothing more to do with him - my son Henry has occasionally behaved nearly as ill, and never allowed me to control him longer than I supported him and Frederick is wholly independent of me though I lent him Smith's tools with a view of inducing him to settle down and work his trade.[34]

But the problem was not entirely with the fur trade's inability to absorb the second generation. By 1835 the choicest land in Red River had been settled. The problem was quite apparent to Chief Peguis of the Netley Creek Indian Settlement near Lake Winnipeg. He emphasized that

> There is nowhere else for them to settle upon, this part of the river is thickly inhabited, there is only a little vacant land in the neighbourhood of the Fort; when this is occupied, a new settlement must either be formed behind or upon land called the Indian reserve.[35]

Certainly the family lots were oversettled. William Cook's land supported five separate families: Samuel Cook's family, Widow Garrioch's family, Joseph Cook's family, Mary Cook's family, and Sarah Cook's family.[36] Even though Henry Hallet had only eight chains of land, it supported about 15 people after 1835.[37] Under such conditions the Image Plain children of the first and second generation had to turn their attention to the land on the fringes of the settlement or to vocations other than agriculture. William Cook for his part attempted to introduce his son Samuel to carpentry and blacksmithing with some success.[38] But whatever livelihood they chose, there was inevitably a disruption in the extended family. While some sons could still live on their father's land or in the same houses as their fathers, the majority of the second generation were finding this an increasing impossibility.

Among the second generation of mixed-blood men who left the family lots in the 1830s to locate elsewhere were men from the Hallet, Bird, Garrioch, Cook, Flett, and Favel families. They moved from the patriarchal lots either to hunt the plains, to work for the Company, to trade, or to farm in the newer districts along the Red River. While his two brothers remained on the family plot of land, William Hallet, a son of Henry Hallet Sr., settled on lot 1388 that his father had received from the Company in the 1820s. Near to the Pembina Plain, it was a great distance from lots 226 and 227 where the majority of the Hallets lived.[39] The Garrioch children also moved from the family lots as did three of the Favel children.[40]

With the disintegration of the extended family the number of children per household also declined, although the total number of children in the settlement did not, and merely levelled off. The number of children in Scottish families declined from 5.7 in 1843 to 4.9 in 1847, while those in Rupert's Land born families declined from 4.1 to about 3.8 children.[41] This decline was in all likelihood not due to disease but rather to a probable decrease in the marriage and birth rates. Four of James Bird's nine sons, Peter Favel, and George Flett, to mention but a few, remained bachelors.[42] More important, of the men who did marry, few had children. Thomas Favel and his wife remained childless.[43] Samuel Favel's first wife died in 1845 without giving birth to any children and the woman he married in 1846 similarly died in 1849 also without offspring.[44] The John Garrioch who married in 1843 did not father any children until the 1850s[45] and the Jeremiah Cook who married in 1833 did not have any children until after 1838.[46] Only Richard Favel and his wife seem the exception with eight children all born during the 1840s.[47]

The 1840s were becoming, then, years of crisis, of disorientation, and disintegration for Red River. Those who knew the relatively more generous and prolific years of the early 1830s, must have despaired at the increasing unpleasantness of their world. For Red River the scapegoats were obvious: the Company and the Church. Red River did not realize that it was in the clutches of an inexorable dilemma which had no solution and for which no scapegoat could be found.

The Company, because of its economic, political, and social dominance, was an obvious target for dissatisfaction.[48] It was the only employer, the only route by which sons of the first and second generation could acquire the position of respect and wealth held by their fathers. The Company seemed to hold the keys to the door that had shut forever on the golden decade of the 1830s. There seemed no alternative to smashing the Company, for by 1840 the only other legitimate and popular source of prosperity, the land, was closed by overcrowding.[49] But a wholesale destruction of the Company's monopoly would not have brought back the closeness and the security offered by the extended family and close neighborhoods in the 1830s -- it would offer only anarchy. In fact during the 1850s and 1860s the settlement edged closer and closer to total social and political disintegration.

The church was equally responsible for exacerbating the crisis. Both the Catholic and Protestant churches had taught the value of subservience, of hierarchy, and of family; and the Protestants the value of an agricultural existence.[50] Throughout the 1830s the teachings of the clergy had struck a responsive chord, reinforcing as they did patterns taught by the fur trade and the European traditions of Red River. The church had, in fact, in a few years won an astounding following. By 1840, however, the goals of farm and family set by the church were no longer possible. The failure to achieve these goals must have served again and again to underline the desperateness of the situation. As important were the social pretentions of the clergy, and more important their support of the Company, which meant, too, that they were unable to empathize with the dilemma of the mixed-bloods.

By 1845, then, the second generation of mixed bloods of the settlement were in a state of confusion. The major points of reference for nineteenth century society, the farm, the state (the Hudson's Bay Company), and the church were in disrepute. Red River would have to seek new reference points, a new identity. In the end they found it not in Red River or the fur trade, but rather in Canada.

Appendix I

Mean age of head of household

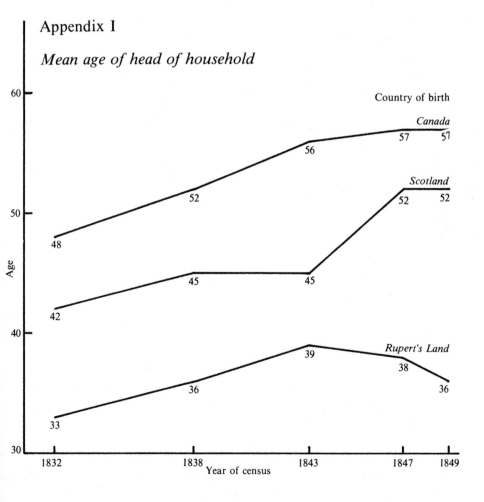

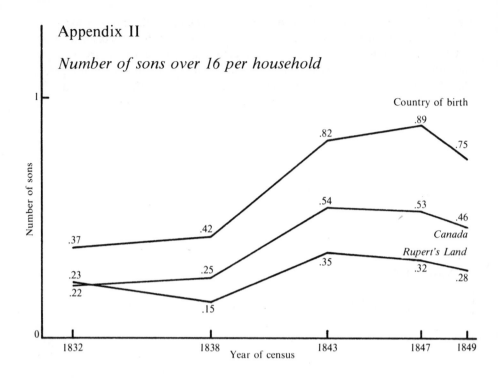

Appendix II

Number of sons over 16 per household

Country of birth

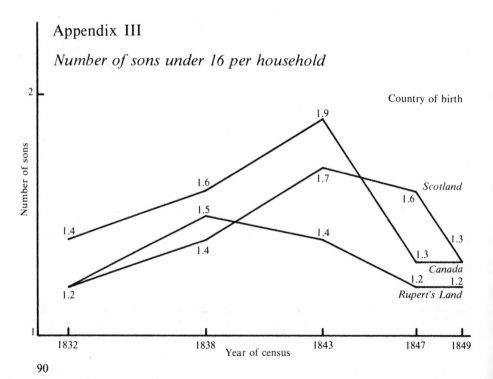

Appendix III

Number of sons under 16 per household

Country of birth

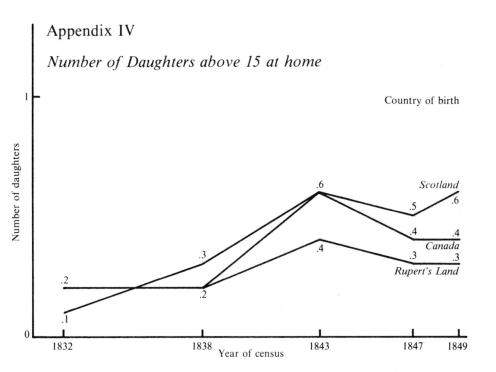

Appendix IV

Number of Daughters above 15 at home

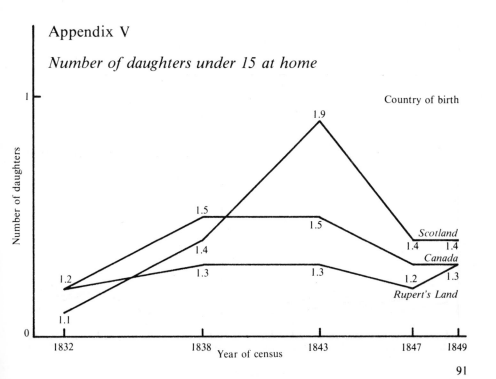

Appendix V

Number of daughters under 15 at home

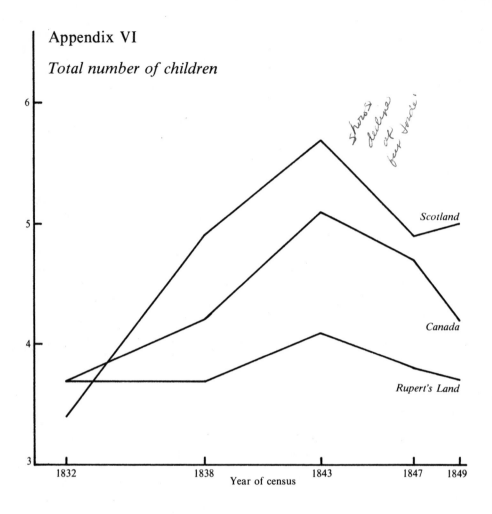

Appendix VI

Total number of children

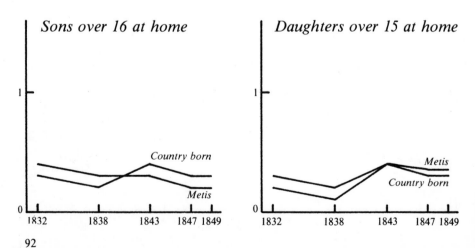

Sons over 16 at home

Daughters over 15 at home

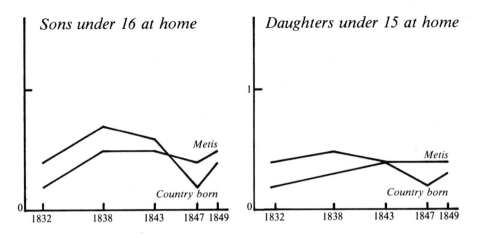

Sons under 16 at home

Metis

Country born

0

1832   1838   1843   1847 1849

Daughters under 15 at home

1

Metis

Country born

0

1832   1838   1843   1847 1849

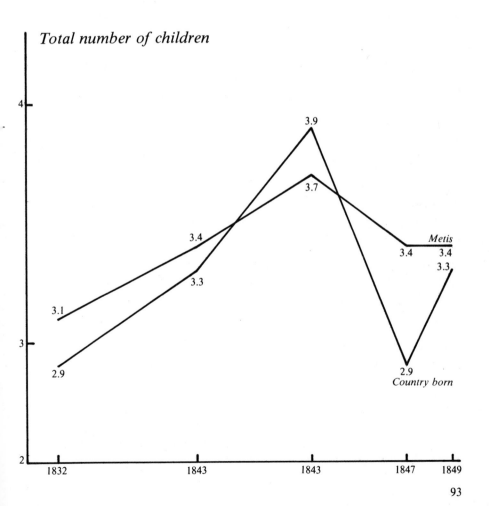

Total number of children

4

3.9

3.7

3.4

3.4   3.4

Metis

3.3

3.3

3.1

3.4

3.3

3

2.9

2.9

Country born

2

1832   1843   1843   1847   1849

Appendix VII

The information for the graphs was calculated from 1832, 1838, 1847 censuses in the Manitoba archives using the Statistical Package for the Social Sciences (SPSS). While the censuses are for the most part reliable, they do have shortcomings. For example, many of the ages of the head of household are missing. Originally this meant a significant prejudice towards an older mean age since it was apparent when first coding the material that the first settlers, and the older members of the family tended to record their ages while the younger members did not. It was possible fortunately to fill many of the gaps from the Red River baptismal and marriage registers.

Geographic designation also changed from census to census. It was assumed however that the "Lower Settlement" was the same area as the "English Settlement," and "St. Boniface" the same as the "Catholic Settlement," since in each census the Swampy Village, the Saulteaux Village, and Grantown were identified separately.

Another designation, the place of birth of the head of the household, also changed. In 1843, for example, the designation "Orkney" was dropped. More important, it became apparent that the place of birth was for many an ethnic and racial affiliation. A few English-speaking halfbreeds of social pretension, for example, put Scotland rather than Rupert's Land down as their place of birth, while some Métis who listed themselves as born in Canada in 1832, indicated Rupert's Land to the census taker by 1843. Considerable work remains to determine the extent to which this occurred and, more important, the extent to which the variable has been rendered useless.

In the SPSS analysis, of which this paper is a preliminary product, an endeavor was made to separate the English-speaking halfbreeds and the French-speaking halfbreeds. This was done by designating all those Protestant, living in the Lower Settlement and born in Rupert's Land, as English-speaking halfbreeds and all those of Catholic faith, living in St. Boniface or Grantown and born in Rupert's Land, as Métis. It is important to emphasize that no statistically supportable difference was found in the demography of the two groups. Family size and composition was for the most part the same. On the other hand, substantial economic differences did exist. The Métis were definitely found to be a hunting people and the English-speaking halfbreeds an emphatically agricultural people.

It has probably struck the reader that although the censuses included both English-speaking halfbreeds and Métis, the specific examples are entirely from the Protestant parishes. This is because many French parish registers were either unavailable or illegible. Consequently only the Protestant baptismal, burial, and marriage registers, all in the Provincial Archives of Manitoba, could be used to reconstruct 22 Red River families selected at random. They included the Gaddy, Cook, Flett, Bird, Bannerman, Sutherland, Garrioch, Hallet, Inkster, Corrigal, Favel, Tait, Cockran, and Ross families. The servants' lists and wills in the Hudson's Bay Company archives were also found to be an excellent source. It should be emphasized that the SPSS analysis and the family reconstructions produced mutually reinforcing results.

PART II
THE PERIOD OF SETTLEMENT

Canadianizing the West: The North-West Mounted Police as Agents of the National Policy, 1873-1905

R. C. Macleod

It has become one of the commonplaces of Canadian history to see the experience of the prairie west in terms of protest. Those aspects of Western history which have received the lion's share of attention all fall into this category - the Riel rebellions, the responsible government issue, the Manitoba schools question, the Winnipeg general strike, the Progressive movement, and Social Credit. The National Policy has been perceived almost exclusively as an instrument of economic injustice. The C.P.R., with much justification, becomes the oppressor of the farmer as soon as the heroic saga of its construction is over. It is no coincidence that Pierre Berton stops with the last spike. In his definition of the National Policy, R.C. Brown noted that,

> ...the spirit of the National Policy went much deeper than railways, immigrants and tariffs. Beneath these external manifestations was the will to build and maintain a separate Canadian nation on the North American continent.[1]

The fact that westerners have been deeply attached to the goals of the National Policy while being critical of specific policies has too often been overlooked by historians and others. Western protest certainly existed, but it existed in the context of efforts to reform the National Policy rather than to reject it. A letter to the editor of the Medicine Hat *Times* expressed the attitude very well:

> We would ask our Eastern friends to regard us as fellow Canadians who are prone to claim that they form a part of this great Dominion, and not as serfs.... Do not look upon us as a selfish, unsatisfied people who want the world, but rather as a people who are struggling for those rights and liberties so dear to themselves.[2]

Eastern observers who know a little about Western Canadian history tend to give Western separatism much more attention than it deserves and are often baffled by indications that the West really is part of Canada.

Such misunderstandings can have serious consequences and it is time historians, without forgetting the history of protest, began redressing the balance by exploring those forces which have counteracted Western regionalism and prevented it from becoming separatism. The prairie west had its political origins as a colony of Eastern Canada. As with other colonies, the development of the West was shaped in part by utopianism, in the sense of a desire to improve upon the original model. The West was created by people who sought to reproduce there what they believed to be the best characteristics of Eastern Canadian life. Difficult as it is to think of Sir John A. Macdonald and his colleagues as utopians, their intention in Western Canada was, if not to create a new Jerusalem, at least to build a better Ontario. Many of their designs failed, of course, but not all did. The North-West Mounted Police succeeded so well in transplanting Eastern Canadian institutions and ideas to the West that they became a part of the fabric of Western identity.

John A. would no doubt have appreciated the irony inherent in the recent furore in the West over the government's proposal to replace the letters R.C.M.P. with the word POLICE in the insignia of the force. When this seemingly innocent change was announced the West rose as one to object to Eastern tampering with Western traditions. The *Edmonton Journal* for a period of months kept a daily watch on R.C.M.P. headquarters in the city to see if the offending sign had been removed. Huge petitions descended upon the Solicitor-General, who seemed totally unprepared for the reaction. The West had risen again but this time to protect a federal police force run from Ottawa. In the course of a century an organization that began as one of the federal government's most clearly imperialistic ventures in the West had become a symbol of regional identity; one which represented not only the uniqueness of the West, but its historical ties to the rest of the country.

The Mounted Police were successful in ensuring that the imperatives of the National Policy were carried out and they managed to do it in such a way that their popularity among the citizenry of Western Canada never faded. There can be no doubt that the primary reason for the establishment of the policy was to ensure a peaceful occupation and exploitation of the West. Long before Canada acquired the former domain of the Hudson's Bay Company, Sir John A. Macdonald had decided that the logic of the National Policy would require some means of exercising direct federal control in the area of law enforcement.[3] The only possible Canadian West was a peaceful and orderly one; a wild west would certainly have bankrupted the government in short order. Canadian authorities were only too well aware that the United States government by 1870 was spending approximately 20 million dollars a year to subdue the Indians, more than the total Canadian budget. Obviously, too, the transcontinental railway would be much cheaper if the project was not hampered by either opposition from the Indians or excessive labor unrest among the workers. Immigrants would be more easily attracted to a non-violent West.

The idea that law enforcement should be a function of local government was deeply rooted in the British legal tradition and had been enshrined in the B.N.A. Act which placed it unequivocally in the hands of the provinces. Difficult as it was to break with this tradition, the alternative of leaving law enforcement in local hands in the North-West Territories seemed an invitation to disaster. There was the obvious example of the American West to discredit this alternative and the Canadian experience was hardly more encouraging. In spite of the emphasis in

Canadian mythology on peace, order, and good government, the country's law enforcement institutions at the time of Confederation were primitive and ineffective.[4] Political and religious violence occurred regularly and was regarded as normal, if not particularly desirable.[5] In the West itself the experience of the Hudson's Bay Company had demonstrated that local law enforcement institutions on the British model were even less effective on the frontier than in the settled regions of the East.[6] The uprising of 1869-1870 merely confirmed their total ineffectiveness. Reluctantly therefore, because the traditional system had the great advantage of not costing the federal government any money, Macdonald created the Mounted Police in 1873.

The primary task of the new force was to effectively occupy the West for Canada until the growth of population established Canadian ownership beyond any doubt. This meant avoiding by whatever means possible, conflicts between white settlers and native peoples. In this respect the police were outstandingly successful. Firmness, fair dealing, and compassion for the plight of the Indians were their basic tactics, supplemented where necessary by bluff and histrionics. In maintaining peace with the Indians, the most significant victories of the police were over other government departments, whose zeal to civilize the Indians often outstripped their commonsense. In 1881, for example, a group of Indians at Fort Walsh refused to accept their annual treaty payments until the government agreed to discuss some of their grievances with them. The Indian Agent in charge was infuriated and wanted to cut off their rations and starve them into submission. Fortunately for all concerned the Mounted Police refused to consider such action, negotiations were held, and the incident ended peacefully.[7] When an Indian named Standing Buffalo removed his sick child from a government Industrial School at Qu'Appelle in 1894, the principal asked the police to bring the boy back and arrest the father for stealing government property, namely the boy's clothes. Inspector Charles Constantine, in charge of the case, declined both requests and after citing some legal grounds for leaving the boy with his parents, reported:

> Whether these reasons are good or not, it would have been an inhuman act to have taken the boy away, to say nothing of the criminality attached to it should the child have died after his having been taken out in such cold weather.[8]

This list of similar confrontations could be extended for pages.

The police also had to cope with a settler population, many of whom believed that the only good Indian was a dead one.[9] Every cow that strayed was assumed to have been killed by the Indians. Under these difficult circumstances the police managed to tread the narrow path between the interests of the two groups and avoid confrontations. Ranchers and farmers were given to understand that the Indians had first priority. The treaties gave them unrestricted hunting rights and there was no legal justification for ordering Indians away from farms and ranches.[10] The Police responded by trying, usually with success, to persuade the Indians to return to their reserves. On the other hand white squatters were kept strictly away from Indian lands.[11] After 1885 police dealings with the Indians began to shift gradually away from persuasion toward coercion.[12] From the point of view of the National Policy, and therefore of the Mounted Police, the years between 1873 and 1885 were crucial. The treaties were negotiated in this period and relations with the Indians established on a firm enough basis that two great crises, Sitting Bull's sojourn in Canada and the 1885 rebellion, could be dealt with. Once the railway was complete, the Indians could safely be pushed to one side and forgotten, as indeed they were. The relationship based upon trust and mutual respect was never completely dissipated, however, and remained the dominant feature of the period up to the turn of the century.

The whole point of pacifying the Indians was to allow the unhampered construction of the C.P.R. The railway made more direct use of the police as well. Thousands of navvies had to be kept reasonably sober and on the job under working conditions that were frequently scandalous even for that unenlightened age. During the building of the C.P.R. main line, the Mounted Police allowed nothing to interfere with construction, even if it meant facing down angry mobs of strikers single-handed, as Sam Steele claims to have done in his memoirs, or strikebreaking by operating trains for the company.[13] Once again, however, 1885 marks an important change in police attitudes. After that date and during the construction of other railways less vital to the National Policy, such as the Crowsnest Pass Branch of the C.P.R., the Calgary and Edmonton Railway, and the two new transcontinental lines, the police were much less willing to give management a free hand. Construction was unquestionably aided by the strict enforcement of the Public Works Peace Preservation Act which prohibited the sale of liquor within 10 miles of the right of way. But in these later cases the police scrupulously avoided taking sides in labor disputes and in fact often went out of their way to ensure that the rights of the workers were protected. Police officers acted as mediators in countless disputes, persuaded construction bosses to make working and living conditions more tolerable, and assisted workers in extracting unpaid wages from reluctant contractors.[14] Relations between the police and labor were, on the whole, good between 1885 and 1905.

Settlement of the prairies was the indispensable corollary to the construction of railways. The police were as valuable to the government in carrying out this part of the National Policy as they had been in others. In the early years aid to settlers was direct. The police advised newcomers as to the most desirable locations, gave advice about crops and weather conditions, and even lent farm equipment. Such administrative services as there were prior to 1885 came largely from the police who in addition to their regular duties delivered mail, organized the fighting of prairie fires, and acted as health officers, to name only a few of their activities. Police officers gave conducted tours of the countryside to advance men for parties of prospective immigrants. Perhaps most important of all, police patrols attempted to visit every settler at regular intervals.[15] These patrols gave the isolated settler a sense of security and provided welcome relief from the loneliness of prairie life.

All these activities of the Mounted Police are well known and were of the greatest importance in the history of the Canadian West. Yet had police work been confined to supporting the institutional framework of the National Policy the force would long since have ceased to exist. What ensured the survival of the Mounted Police was the work done by the force in building and sustaining the informal National Policy in the West. There was little point in developing the West unless it became firmly a part of that independent North American nation the National Policy was intended to create. A West which existed only as an economic colony of Eastern Canada would be more trouble than it was worth. This meant, as far as the police were concerned, that the allegiance of Canadian settlers mut be reinforced. Immigrants, of course, would have to be integrated. Many institutions participated in this process; the most important of those overtly involved in integrating the immigrant being the churches, the schools, and the Department of the Interior.[16] For a number of reasons the police were more influential than any of these. Not everyone went to church and only the children went to school. Many of the churches, in any case, were imported along with the immigrants and tended to perpetuate the traditions of the old country.[17] More important still was the fact that while clergymen and teachers might have rather hazy ideas about what Canadianism was, the police had very firm convictions on the subject. Their own area of concern coincided with one of the primary Canadian national myths: the conviction that Canadian society was more orderly and law-abiding than others. The Mounted Police had no doubts about what set Canadians apart from other men and their determination to impose what they considered proper standards of behavior imparted to their day-to-day activities an almost missionary zeal.

The background of the personnel of the Mounted Police, especially the officers, ensured not only that they would take the task of educating the settlers in the correct political attitudes very seriously but that they would be heard with respect. Although there is a tradition perpetuated in all early writings on the Mounted Police that many officers were British, most were Canadian. At least 80 percent of the officers of the force were Canadian-born throughout the period under discussion.[18] The percentage of British-born in the non-commissioned ranks was much higher, rising from 33 percent in 1888 to a peak of 61 percent in 1895 and dropping off sharply thereafter.[19] Significantly, however, in spite of the steady increase in the numbers of promotions from the ranks, the percentage of British-born officers remained the same.

That the leadership of the force was solidly Canadian was of the utmost importance. Since Canada's military establishment was almost non-existent, the Mounted Police provided an opportunity for talented young men with military ambitions. Public hostility to the granting of police commissions to British individuals was intense. On one of the rare occasions when the government dared to make such an appointment the *Canadian Military Gazette* commented, "We could have understood the appointment of a graduate of the Royal Military College or of an officer with a record in the militia; but for this appointment of a rank outsider there can be no excuse."[20] The Ottawa *Free Press* reacted savagely to a suggestion by W.R. Grahame, an immigration official at Winnipeg who acted as a recruiting agent for the Mounted Police, that the force recruit in England.

> ...one would imagine that Captain Grahame could find plenty of recruits in Canada without importing English dudes. If we are to have 'Canada for the Canadians' why send to England for troopers when Canadians can be obtained? The recruiting of the Mounted Police Force with strangers who have no sympathy with Canada, who know nothing of the country and who imagine that all their follies and vices should be condoned because 'they are English don't cher know' has been a fruitful cause of trouble in the past, and if the management of the force is left to Captain Grahame and Mr. Herchmer the outlook for the future is not promising.[21]

By the late 1880s the pattern for recruiting officers was well established. Graduates of the Royal Military College at Kingston were considered the most desirable candidates and dominated the leadership of the force by the turn of the century.[22] Other officers came from the Active Militia and by promotions from within the force itself. The officers who emerged from this selection process were almost invariably upper-class, well educated, and well connected in Eastern Canadian society and politics. From the beginning they established themselves as social leaders in the growing settlements on the prairies and by the 1890s their status was taken for granted. Officers stationed at Calgary were entitled to membership in the exclusive Ranchmen's Club without having to pay the usual fees. Complaints were frequently heard that the officer without private means could not afford to do the entertaining expected of him.[23] Because the police associated with local opinion leaders on a basis of equality they were in an excellent position to influence the development of Western attitudes.

The origins of the other ranks in the Mounted Police were more diverse but they seem to have absorbed their officers' attitudes very thoroughly.[24] A large number of men from the force became settlers themselves and often leading figures in their community.[25] The opportunities for contact provided by the varied duties of the police and by their regular patrols were very great. For many settlers, the regular visits of the police were their most important source of information about the outside world. Rumors and neighborhood gossip could be verified and interpreted through such conversations. The police knew the importance of such contacts and used them in the short run to prevent any recourse to private justice and in the long run to encourage the 'correct' view of law and order.

While the police were constantly aware of the necessity to reinforce correct Canadian values concerning law and order, the arrival of substantial groups of non-Canadian immigrants brought forth a different response. The police considered it one of their primary functions to ensure the integration of these groups. Assimilation, it was assumed, would follow in due course. In a report of 1893 Commissioner Herchmer noted the problem as he saw it and outlined the steps necessary to deal with it.

A very large immigration, as you are aware, took place last year into the
Edmonton country, mostly from the Western States where law and order
are not rigidly enforced, and I am credibly informed that the flow this
year will greatly exceed all previous seasons, most of the immigrants
being drawn from Oregon and Washington States, and it will be necessary
to greatly increase our patrols in consequence, as the opinion these
people form of our administration of the laws on their first arrival, has
the greatest possible effect on their future conduct, and inability on our
part to impress them with the necessity of strictly obeying our laws,
will, in my opinion, be certain to lead to heavy expenses later on in the
administration of justice, the cost of which would greatly exceed that of
laying a good moral foundation at the start, through the activity and
vigilance of the police.[26]

Where large concentrations of European immigrants were present the police endeavored to establish a detachment as soon as a settlement was founded. If possible the
man selected for this duty would be one who spoke the language of the community;
if not, an interpreter was hired.[27] Sometimes these detachments were set up as a
result of pressure from other settlers in surrounding districts who harbored dire
suspicions about all foreigners. If no such request was forthcoming, the police
would establish a detachment anyway as a matter of principle.

Police outposts among colonies of European immigrants proved to have very little
to do in the way of actual law enforcement. With the single exception of the
Doukhobours, the police found European immigrants less prone to break the law
than the general population. This was partly due to the close supervision exercised
by the police and their concern to explain the law to the immigrants. It was also
partly due to the fact that the police got along well with them and were able to act
as a buffer against public and official nativism.

In one typical case a settler near Qu'Appelle by the name of D. Henry Starr
wrote an angry letter to the Minister of the Interior, accusing some German colonists who lived nearby of stealing his hay. Warming to his task, he went on to say
that the Germans,

...have turned out to be the very worst and lowest class of people under
the sun, who are considered quite a nuisance, and ought to be banished
from the country otherwise they will be the means of driving every
respectable settler out of the place.[28]

A corporal was despatched to investigate as soon as the charges reached the Mounted
Police. He discovered that all Starr's ideas were based on hearsay; he had had no
contact with the Germans since their arrival. By the time the corporal had finished
his questioning, Starr was ready to admit that no shred of evidence existed to connect the Germans with the theft. In forwarding the report to Ottawa, the Superintendent in charge of the case appended his own views. "I might add that our
experience of German settlers in different parts of the North West points to the

fact that they are law-abiding and good citizens and cause the police little trouble."[29]

A similar incident at the Ukrainian settlement of Edna, near Edmonton, involved Frank Oliver, M.P. for the district and no friend of the non-Anglo-Saxon immigrant. In June of 1899, Oliver wrote to the police demanding that something be done to curb thievery by the Ukrainians, otherwise the English-speaking settlers would be forced to take the law into their own hands. He added that, in addition to the crime wave, filthy conditions in the settlement had caused a smallpox epidemic which threatened surrounding communities.[30] A police investigation began at once. The smallpox epidemic turned out to be two cases of measles. No one could be found who had experienced theft from any source, but rumors of the larcenous propensities of the Ukrainians abounded. Inspector J.O. Wilson, who investigated the complaints, reported that both English-speaking and Ukrainian settlers were strongly in favor of the establishment of a detachment in the community. He urged that this be done at once to prevent rumor from getting out of hand in the future. For the Ukrainian settlers, he had only praise as hard-working and law-abiding individuals.[31]

It might be thought that the police were interested only in anglicizing the immigrants and indeed their frequent references to British law and justice lend some credence to this view. But a closer examination reveals that the Mounted Police sought to assimilate the immigrant to specifically Canadian values. The Commissioner issued the following orders concerning a group of English settlers who arrived in 1903. "The police must be especially active in aiding the new settlers to overcome their difficulties. They must establish friendly relations, carefully explain the law without resorting to harsh measures, and give them general advice."[32] American settlers, who had no linguistic differences to set them apart, received even more attention from the police than the Europeans did. To the police, American settlers, so like Canadians in other ways, differed in that they carried with them American political attitudes; the seeds of anarchy, disorder, and violence. Commissioner A. Bowen Perry was merely expressing the view of the force as a whole when he wrote to Comptroller White in 1903, "I suppose the peace of the Territories may seem assured to those who are in the East, and even to the people of the Territories who are accustomed to it. They little know of the reckless class of American outlaws to the South of us."[33] Although there is no evidence in the police records to indicate that Americans were any less law-abiding than other groups, the Mounted Police continued to think of themselves as engaged in a desperate struggle to preserve Canadian civilization in the West.

The police arrived in the North-West with very definite ideas about Americans and American society. Early contacts were confined mainly to whisky traders and deserters from the U.S. Army; men who tended to reinforce the stereotype of the lawless American. The police were constant and interested observers of the American scene across the border. The only observation which registered permanently, however, were those which provided opportunities to compare the quality of American life unfavorably with that of Canada. The police records are filled with lurid accounts of lynchings, mob violence, and general lawlessness garnered from American newspapers, hearsay, and observation of border towns. Sergeant G.W. Byrne, travelling in Montana on the trail of some cattle stolen in Canada, reported that he had been forced to pass himself off as a merchant because the town to which he traced the cattle was controlled by a gang of thieves.

> I might state here that the town of Culbertson consists of two stores, two gambling saloons, one boarding house and a couple of houses of ill fame. There are about 20 cowboys or horse thieves and gamblers who take turns watching our every movement, and immediately one of us leaves the town scouts are sent out in all directions to give the alarm.[34]

Construction of a railway across the border provided an even better opportunity to contrast the two ways of life.

> The detachment stationed at Sterling, the new town on the Boundary on the Soo R'way did good service in keeping the peace. The track laying gang on the American side was accompanied by a number of whisky sellers, gamblers and prostitutes. S/Sgt. McGinnis' report, which I have forwarded you, relates that great disorder prevailed on the American side -- serious rows, drunkenness and debauchery. On our side there was no trouble of any kind.[35]

It followed from these assumptions that if disorder existed in the North-West Territories, it was probably attributable to Americans, indirectly if not directly. The police were not slow to draw this conclusion and on several occasions blamed disturbances on Americans on no better evidence than the mere presence of American settlers in the neighborhood. When an angry crowd of trial spectators at Carlyle voiced their disapproval of a liquor conviction by shouting, "To hell with the red coats!" Superintendent J.O. Wilson offered the following explanation.

> The settlers and residents of Carlyle and Arcola are chiefly Americans, a large proportion of them being single men, who are imbued with the American western idea of law and order, and consequently will have to be taught that they cannot do as they like on this side of the line.[36]

As Superintendent Wilson's remarks indicate, the remedy was as obvious to the police as the complaint. Reporting on a small American settlement on the Canadian side of the international boundary, Superintendent R.B. Deane wrote,

> They live in Canada but get everything from the United States and most likely they still believe they are American citizens and do not intend to abide by Canadian laws unless they are told to. No doubt a detachment of N.W.M. Police at that point will soon settle the matter.[37]

When Major-General Selby-Smyth, commanding the Canadian Militia, inspected the Mounted Police in 1875, he noted that in spite of the exceedingly primitive conditions, the men of the force were generally contented. He believed that their satisfaction came from their future hopes for the region under their charge.

> ...above all they have the conscious knowledge that they are pioneers in a rich and fertile territory, magnificently spacious though still strangely solitary and silent, which at no distant time will re-echo with the busy life, of a numerous and prosperous population...[38]

This was a very perceptive observation. To the Mounted Police the West represented an opportunity to create a new and better version of Eastern Canadian society; a chance to prove that Canadian institutions were fundamentally better than those of the United States. The society they envisaged was to be orderly and hierarchical; not a lawless frontier democracy but a place where powerful institutions and a responsible and paternalistic upper class would ensure true liberty and justice. Here was the Upper Canadian Tory tradition in its purest form. The corresponding Reform tradition was almost totally absent. This was hardly surprising since entry into the force, and especially into the commissioned ranks, was strictly controlled by patronage.[39] With the exception of a very few officers appointed during the Mackenzie regime, the leadership of the Mounted Police until the turn of the century was solidly Conservative.

It is very difficult to assess accurately the extent to which the Mounted Police were successful in imposing their concept of the West. Perhaps the best evidence of the strength and permanence of their contribution lies in the fact that the force was very popular among all citizens of the region and in its continuing symbolic significance. When the Liberal government of Wilfrid Laurier took office in 1896, it was decided to eliminate the Mounted Police.[40] The West was now safe for the National Policy and the Liberals were understandably anxious to rid themselves of what they correctly considered a nest of Conservatives. The Liberals, in any case, had an ideological commitment to local self-government. These plans encountered such a storm of protest, even from Liberal party workers in the West, that they had to be abandoned.[41] When Alberta and Saskatchewan received provincial status in 1905, the federal government made another half-hearted attempt to persuade the new provinces to set up their own police and abandon the N.W.M.P., but it proved easier to work out an evasion of the B.N.A. Act which allowed the force to continue to operate under provincial control, than to do away with it.[42] Westerners by this time found it almost impossible to conceive of the region without the Mounted Police. The North-West Mounted Police and all that it stood for had become an important part of the way in which the West defined itself.

Contracting for the
Canadian Pacific Railway
T. D. Regehr

Despite an already enormous bibliography on the construction of the Canadian Pacific Railway[1] there is a surprising paucity of published information relating to the contractors who built the railway. The general impression to be gained from the published sources is that Canadian Pacific Railway officials and, more specifically, General Manager William C. Van Horne, were in charge of construction and followed a more or less consistent contracting policy from beginning to end.

This impression gives more prominence to Van Horne and less to the contractors who built the line than is justified. It obscures the sharp changes in contracting policy from year to year, and the fact that most of the early contracts were let to large American contracting outfits who brought with them many American sub-contractors, while the later Canadian Pacific Railway construction contracts tended to go to smaller Canadian contractors and sub-contractors. For these Canadian contractors the construction of the Canadian Pacific Railway was a remarkable entrepreneurial experience. A number subsequently rose to occupy dominant positions in the commercial and industrial affairs of Canada.

Contract work on the Canadian Pacific Railway mainline went through four quite distinct phases, with Canadian contractors only dominant in the last. The purpose of this paper is to examine contracts and contracting policies and procedures on the Canadian Pacific Railway through these four phases. The four phases are: the period of government contracts from 1873 to the end of 1881; the 1882 Langdon, Shepherd and Company contract; the 1883 contract with the North American Railway Contracting Company; and the smaller, mainly Canadian, contracts from 1884 through 1886.

Government Contracting, 1873-1881

In the 1870s both of Canada's major political parties believed that the promised railway to the Pacific could best be built by a private entrepreneurial syndicate enjoying substantial government support. Unfortunately the first attempt to sign an appropriate contract with a financial syndicate ended in 1873 in scandal and financial disaster. Alexander Mackenzie replaced Sir John A. Macdonald as Prime Minister, but Mackenzie could not, in the financially depressed years after 1873, find any financial group which would undertake construction of the proposed transcontinental railway. He really had no choice but to build the railway as a public work, if it was to be built at all. In this, however, the Prime Minister was seriously inhibited by the precarious state of the federal treasury. It seemed impossible to proceed immediately with the construction of the entire project.

Mackenzie and his cabinet colleagues decided to give priority to those sections of the new line which seemed most urgently needed. These were the sections where no practicable alternative mode of transportation was available. Specifically, the government devised a policy whereby water transport would be used wherever possible, and rail connections would be built to connect the available navigable water transport systems. The long term objective was still a transcontinental railway, but the short term objective was a mixed rail and water route.

Under Mackenzie's so-called "water stretches" policy the federal government called for tenders and let construction contracts on two important railway lines in the 1870s. These were the line from the head of shipping on the Great Lakes at Thunder Bay to Red River, hereinafter referred to as the Thunder Bay line; and the Pembina line from Winnipeg to the International Boundary at Pembina.

When the Conservatives regained political power in 1878 contracts for two further lines were let. The first of these was for the construction of a line from Winnipeg to Brandon, while the second called for the construction of a very difficult British Columbia section from Kamloops in the British Columbia interior to the Pacific Coast.

All these contracts were administered by the Department of Railways and Canals. The construction contracts themselves were let to a number of comparatively small contractors who really worked for the department as sub-contractors. The department itself undertook most of the responsibilities normally assigned to large general contracting firms which then sub-contracted much of the work. Most of the early contracts were comparatively small, with approximately 20 small contracting firms undertaking construction work of between 10 and 40 miles of the Thunder Bay line and approximately half that number engaged on the Pembina Line.[2]

The administration of construction contracts by the Department of Railways and Canals was not altogether satisfactory. Several factors led to serious difficulties. The first and probably the most time consuming was that contracts were generally let for specific work at specified rates, rather than simply for the complete construction of a particular portion of the new railway. Contractors were paid according to the amount of earth, rock, clay, hardpan, or other material moved in building the embankments and roadbeds. Different rates prevailed for different materials and different types of work done. This provided endless opportunities for disagreements when the actual amounts of materials handled had to be measured and classified. The contractors often brought forward one set of figures, departmental engineers and inspectors quite another. Payments by the government to the contractors could only be made after departmental engineers had measured, classified, and approved the work, and only according to the calculations made by those departmental officials. When these departmental calculations were at variance with those of the contractors whole batteries of lawyers were kept busy arguing the merits of the various claims and counter claims.

Aside from these costly and irritating disputes, now enshrined in intimidatingly bulky departmental files, the government encountered other and ultimately much more serious problems with the contractors. Tenders were called for on all the contracts, and the government felt it must award contracts to the lowest tender unless there were very obvious reasons not to do so. Prime Minister Mackenzie was determined that the railway contracts would be let and administered honestly, without favor or special considerations. This policy unfortunately interfered with efficiency. Many of the contractors were either too eager or too inexperienced to submit realistic tenders, and most lacked the financial backing to sustain losses which were inevitable if the contractor miscalculated when preparing a low tender, or was overtaken by an unexpected reverse while working his contract. The results were often chaotic.

Normally a general contractor, with substantial resources, was expected to stand behind his sub-contractors, if necessary taking over and completing their work. In the case of the early Canadian Pacific Railway contracts it was the Department of Railways and Canals that had to deal with any failures by its contractors. This it was ill equipped to do.

Sometimes it seemed best to departmental engineers and administrators to resort simply to rather generous measurements when assessing the work of an embarrassed but reasonably competent contractor. The department was apt to be particularly understanding if the contractor's difficulties were due to factors largely beyond his control. The primary objective of the department was to get the railway built, not to drive small contractors who had made a mistake into bankruptcy. It therefore became a widely accepted policy that honest and efficient contractors should not be relieved of their contracts if, for reasons beyond their control, they could not live up to all the terms of their contract. This policy certainly facilitated early completion of some important contracts, but it also deprived the department of its claim to absolute purity and honesty. Many of the better contractors received larger payments than a rigid application of the terms of their contract could justify.

Some contractors could not be saved by this device. They might be seriously underfinanced, inefficient, or even dishonest, and the department felt that in such cases no alternative was available but taking over the work of the delinquent contractor. The department, however, lacked the men and resources to complete such work itself. Usually a delinquent contract had to be let to another contractor who had the necessary men and supplies in the field already, but the cost was often much higher than that originally estimated and contracted. Speed was usually of the essence in such reassigned contracts since undue delays on one section inevitably affected work elsewhere. Consequently costs increased and some of the stronger contractors were able to extract handsome profits from the harassed department. The decision to cancel and take over a delinquent contract was never an easy one for the department. The harsh realities with which the Department of Railways and Canals had to deal often seemed quite unrelated to the absolute honesty and integrity promised by Alexander Mackenzie after the 1873 Pacific Scandal.

As the government gained experience it became more selective when granting contracts. The practical experience and financial resources of a prospective contractor were recognized as more important than a very low tender. Thus, when the government negotiated the contracts for the work on the western British Columbia section, considerations other than the tender price were accepted.

Originally the British Columbia work was divided into four separate contracts. An American contractor by the name of Andrew Onderdonk submitted tenders on all four contracts. He had already completed several large and difficult construction projects and was backed by very strong financial interests in Philadelphia. But his tender was not the lowest submitted on any of the four British Columbia contracts. Consequently the government let contracts to others who had bid lower than Onderdonk. None of the others, however, had the experience or financial backing of Onderdonk, and the government soon became very concerned about the ability of the successful contractors to carry the British Columbia work to completion. Difficulties with inexperienced and financially weak contractors on the Thunder Bay and Pembina lines added to the government's worries. Onderdonk, for his part, was willing to buy out the four contractors and then to carry on the work in accordance with the terms of his tenders, subject to further negotiations with the government. In effect Onderdonk offered to undertake general contracting responsibility, thus relieving the department of some of its most unpleasant obligations. Much of the work would be sub-contracted by Onderdonk, but he would have full responsibility for the sub-contracts. The government agreed, and the entire western section in British Columbia became the responsibility of Andrew Onderdonk.

The Onderdonk contracts, like all the others, were regularly inspected and the work measured and approved by officials of the Department of Railways and Canals. Disagreements arose from time to time, sometimes leading to litigation, but the unified management and the strong financial resources at Onderdonk's disposal made failures by sub-contractors in British Columbia less troublesome to the government than similar failures by small contractors on the Thunder Bay and Pembina lines.[3]

The "water stretches" policy of railway construction and the government contracts let under that policy were never regarded as more than a temporary expedient, made necessary by the economic depression following the 1873 crash. Both the Liberals and the Conservatives were eager to entrust the construction and operation of the Canadian Pacific Railway to a strong financial syndicate and get the government out of the railway contracting husiness. They were willing to provide very substantial government aid to any properly financed and organized syndicate which would build the railway in accordance with the government's general policies. In the 1870s they could find no suitable group of entrepreneurs, but after 1878 the Canadian economic outlook brightened somewhat. In 1880 a syndicate headed by the successful promoters of the St. Paul, Minneapolis and Manitoba Railroad in Minnesota was organized and began negotiations with the Canadian government. An agreement encompassing these objectives was signed and approved by the Canadian Parliament in 1881. Under the terms of this agreement the Canadian Pacific Railway syndicate assumed the contractual obligations entered into by the government prior to that date for the construction of portions of the new railway, and further committed themselves to completing the railway. By that time the Pembina line was completed, save for the settling of accounts submitted to arbitration or litigation. Contracts on the Thunder Bay line were well advanced and Onderdonk had completed the organization of his staff and was at work in British Columbia.

The 1881 agreement between the government and the Canadian Pacific Railway syndicate relieved the Department of Railways and Canals of the responsibility of dealing directly with difficult contractors and sub-contractors. The department still had to inspect, measure, and approve all construction work on the Canadian Pacific Railway, but after 1881 it dealt almost entirely with that company and not with its contractors and sub-contractors. Contracting on the Canadian Pacific Railway had entered a new era. The "water stretches" construction policy and government construction contracts had been replaced by general contracting agreements under the direction of the Canadian Pacific Railway syndicate.

The Langdon, Shepherd and Company Contract of 1882

The members of the Canadian Pacific Railway syndicate were promoters and financiers, not general construction contractors. They had no desire to duplicate the unfortunate experiences of the Department of Railways and Canals. Instead they looked immediately for a strong American contracting outfit which would undertake general responsibility for all aspects of the construction work.[4] Rather than negotiate a series of small contracts which would be administered by the railway company, members of the syndicate entered into a general construction contract with a Minnesota company for all the construction work to be done in 1882. The company which undertook this general responsibility was Langdon, Shepherd and Company. Langdon and Shepherd were expected to bring with them to Canada many experienced sub-contractors who had worked for them in Minnesota and other American states.

Langdon and Shepherd were well known to members of the Canadian Pacific Railway syndicate. They had held large construction contracts on the St. Paul, Minneapolis and Manitoba Railroad -- the road which the leading members of the Canadian Pacific Railway syndicate had promoted with great success in the 1870s. Langdon and Shepherd had the necessary experience, the financial resources, and the confidence of members of the Canadian Pacific Railway syndicate and on March 1, 1882 they signed a construction contract calling for not less than 500 miles of new railway on the Canadian prairies, all to be completed on or before January 1, 1883.

The Langdon, Shepherd and Company contract provided the specifications according to which the new line was to be built and set the rates for the various classes of work to be done. It also had several unusual clauses which probably reflected the influence of the Canadian Pacific Railway's new General Manager, William C. Van Horne, who had been recruited from the Chicago, Milwaukee and St. Paul Railroad only a few months before the Langdon, Shepherd and Company contract was signed. The contract clearly and repeatedly stated that the contractors would work under the general direction and supervision of the Canadian Pacific

Railway's Superintendent of Construction. The Superintendent of Construction could intervene and order changes at any time if he thought the progress of the work was not sufficient to ensure completion of the promised 500 miles of new track. He could also take over portions of the work or the entire contract if all the terms were not observed. In any dispute between the railway company and the contractors the Superintendent of Construction would serve as sole and final arbitor and umpire.

The Canadian Pacific Railway's Superintendent of Construction in 1881 was Alpheus B. Stickney. Stickney had held a similar position on the St. Paul, Minneapolis and Manitoba Railroad when Langdon and Shepherd held contracts on the road, and it seems clear that members of the Canadian Pacific Railway wanted to follow a precedent which had worked well on the American road. Unfortunately Stickney and Van Horne had a disagreement early in 1882 in connection with land speculations by Stickney and his Chief Engineer, General LaFayette Rosser. Both Stickney and Rosser were forced to leave the service of the Canadian Pacific Railway.[5] Consequently the company had no Superintendent of Construction when it signed the contract with Langdon and Shepherd under which the Superintendent of Construction would have almost unlimited power.

The departure of Stickney and Rosser left the Canadian Pacific Railway's management of the construction work on the prairies in an uncertain state. In 1882 John Egan, a divisional superintendent of the Chicago, Milwaukee and St. Paul Railroad, was appointed General Superintendent of the Western Division of the Canadian Pacific Railway. Egan's experience, however, had been in operating completed mileage, not in construction. Within months of his appointment Egan antagonized many of the construction men and his responsibility had to be carefully restricted to operations on the completed portions of the railway. Even there he was repeatedly instructed to respect fully all priorities assigned by the construction men.[6]

Egan was not the man the Canadian Pacific Railway needed as its Superintendent of Construction, but no one else was appointed to that position in 1882. As a result Van Horne, as General Manager, undertook many of the necessary responsibilities, working closely with several divisional engineers. Van Horne frequently visited the construction sites and tried to ensure that the work was properly planned and executed. He was ably assisted by Thomas Shaughnessy, another recruit from the Chicago, Milwaukee and St. Paul Railroad, who became general purchasing agent of the Canadian Pacific Railway in 1882, but the hard fact was that Van Horne simply could not do all the work that his office as General Manager required and also devote himself fully to the far-reaching duties of the Superintendent of Construction.

Van Horne is pictured by many writers as a kind of whirling dervish, darting to and fro, barking a command here, changing the planned route or overturning a cautious policy there, firing a less than dynamic employee on the spot somewhere else, and still taking time for the odd card game or a gargantuan meal; all this in addition to managing operations on the completed mileage.[7] Van Horne probably did do all those things in the busy year of 1882, but a detailed examination of the work completed and the costs incurred in that year clearly indicates that frenetic management of this kind also had its disadvantages. In fact the construction program of 1882 turned out to be something of a disappointment.

Van Horne had firmly set his goal for 1882. He had promised his directors 500 miles of new track on the prairies. A slow start in the spring due to heavy flooding undermined the construction program at the outset. That program, in any case, could only be completed if all essential supplies arrived on time and all sub-contractors completed their work on time. Both Van Horne and Langdon, Shepherd and Company poured enormous quantities of supplies into western Canada, and the supply and purchasing departments became models of efficiency. Langdon and Shepherd nevertheless brought in many supplies on their own, often at prices which Thomas Shaughnessy in Montreal considered too high. Most of these supplies had to be paid for by the Canadian Pacific Railway, but when time was of the greatest importance the economies preached by Shaughnessy from Montreal were often disregarded. As a result construction costs were higher than Shaughnessy thought they needed to be.

Costs were also increased by some of the temporary but quick construction expedients used. Difficult sections were circumvented by temporary track to avoid delays, but had to be completed later at additional cost. Trestles were used which had to be replaced almost immediately by permanent fills. Some of the ballasting was done before the graded roadbed had settled properly and later more fill, topped by more ballasting, had to be placed on these sections.

Further problems arose from the fact that some of Langdon and Shepherd's sub-contractors turned out to be less than satisfactory. Primary responsibility for the work of these sub-contractors was, of course, the responsibility of the general contractors. Unfortunately Langdon and Shepherd did not have immediately at hand the men and materials to complete quickly the work of ailing sub-contractors. Yet if that work was not completed on time the entire construction program could be disrupted and delayed. As a result Van Horne organized a special force of mobile construction workers who could be put to work, at Langdon and Shepherd's expense, on such sub-contracts at short notice. When not needed for such emergencies the special force built sidings or did secondary ballasting on the completed mileage.

At the constant urging of Van Horne and his divisional engineers, the contractors and their sub-contractors laid new steel on 417.91 miles of line, and had graded and ready for steel an additional 28 miles before the winter freeze-up forced them to close down construction for the year. The promised goal of 500 miles of new track had not been achieved and Canadian Pacific officials were determined that some of the frustrations of 1882 would not recur in 1883. The need for a Superintendent or Manager of Construction for the western section had become obvious[8] and the winter months provided the Canadian Pacific Railway officials with an opportunity both to review what had been done and to plan the construction work for the next year.

The review of the affairs of the Canadian Pacific Railway at the end of

1882 was not altogether encouraging. Certainly there had been good progress on the prairies, but the determination to build 500 miles had been expensive and had forced Van Horne and his assistants to do much of the work that should properly have been done by the general contractors. A review of the role and responsibilities of the contractors and the railway's construction staff was urgently needed.

Meanwhile progress on the Thunder Bay and Onderdonk contracts had been considerable, but on the Thunder Bay line the work had been supervised very closely by John Ross, the Canadian Pacific Railway's Superintendent of Construction, Eastern Section. Since the contracts for the Thunder Bay line had been negotiated before the syndicate took control there was little the company could do to change those arrangements, but John Ross ensured strict adherence to specifications and he was not troubled by the rigid timetables which had dominated all prairie construction in 1882. In British Columbia the Onderdonk contracts also seemed to be in good hands, particularly after one of the most experienced Canadian railway builders, Michael Haney, became Onderdonk's Superintendent of Construction.

East of Thunder Bay there was very little progress in 1882. The syndicate deliberately concentrated on the prairie section that year. That was where a new railway was needed most. With year round connections at Pembina, and Great Lakes shipping during the summer at Thunder Bay, western traffic had eastern connections, even if all Canadian railway construction north of Lake Superior was delayed. There was in fact no agreement among members of the syndicate when, if ever, the line north of Lake Superior should be built. Certainly very little was done on that line in 1882, and a few miles of new line that were built west of Callendar could fit into either the all-Canadian scheme or into an international railway system running south of Lake Superior via Pembina and Sault Ste Marie. It was the Canadian government that was most eager in 1882 to see substantial progress on the Lake Superior section.

Thus at the end of 1882 Canadian Pacific Railway officials had to review their contracting arrangements on the prairies, and make a basic decision about the importance of speedy construction north of Lake Superior. Both these matters, however, were overshadowed by serious financial problems. The syndicate's policy of paying for construction costs out of the proceeds of government subsidies and land and stock or share sales was not working. Neither the lands nor C.P.R. common shares were selling well, and it was clear that the pace of construction established in 1882 could not be sustained unless more funds became available. Consequently the granting of new construction contracts became intertwined with the financial problem, and in November of 1882 the Canadian Pacific Railway Company negotiated a major new contract which set both the financial and construction programs for 1883.

The North American Railway Contracting Company Contract, 1883

The construction contract of November 1882 was negotiated and signed in secrecy, and for many months there were rumors and suspicions of conspiratorial and nefarious activities. Under its contract with the federal government the Canadian Pacific Railway was required to table all its major construction contracts, but the company flatly refused to table the November 1882 contract when the Liberals in Parliament asked for it. The government supported the company, refusing to give even the name of the contracting company with which the new contract had been signed.[9] The contract was not in fact tabled in the House of Commons until March of 1884. By that time it had been taken over and rescinded by the Canadian Pacific Railway. Yet the entire 1883 construction program was carried out under the terms of that contract.[10]

The company with which the Canadian Pacific Railway dealt was the North American Railway Contracting Company.[11] It was incorporated in the State of New Jersey and allegedly had its head office in the Village of Walton, New Jersey. It had an authorized capitalization of $3,000,000 but began business when only $500,000 had been subscribed. On that only a call of ten percent, or $50,000 had been paid. The President and Secretary were James O. Bloss of New York City and Samuel Gwyn of Brooklyn, New York respectively. These two officers of the company and all their fellow directors, however, held little more than the minimum number of shares required for them to hold office. The bulk of the shares of the North American Railway Contracting Company were set aside for members of the Canadian Pacific Railway Company in proportion to their share holdings in the Canadian Pacific Railway. The North American Railway Contracting Company, in short, was apparently the Canadian Pacific Railway syndicate in another and foreign disguise.

This company signed a contract under the terms of which it agreed to build both the western (prairies to Kamloops, B.C.) and eastern (Callendar to Thunder Bay) sections of the Canadian Pacific Railway. The North American Railway Contracting Company also agreed to take over all obligations of the Canadian Pacific Railway to its contractors. Langdon, Shepherd and Company, and other contractors were expected to take large sub-contracts from the North American Railway Contracting Company. The contracting company had, in fact, signed a general contract to complete the entire mainline of the Canadian Pacific Railway. Some priority was to be given to the western section which was to be completed on or before December 31, 1885. The eastern section was to be completed one year later. In return for building the western section the North American Railway Contracting Company was to receive the sum of $17,880,000 in cash and $25,000,000 (par value) in ordinary paid up shares of the Canadian Pacific Railway. The payment for the eastern section was to be $14,099,979 in cash and $20,000,000 (par value) in Canadian Pacific Railway shares.[12]

The key to this construction contract was the fact that under its terms the Canadian Pacific Railway Company could pay for a part of its construction costs in common shares rather than in cash. Instead of taking the risks of disposing of its own shares on the open market the Canadian Pacific Railway transferred that responsibility to the contracting company. The authorized capitalization of the Canadian Pacific Railway was increased from $65,000,000 to $100,000,000 shortly before the construction contract was signed. This scheme, it was hoped, would assure adequate financing to complete the construction work. The profits to be earned, or the losses incurred, by the contracting company would be determined by the price they could get for the common stock. Canadian Pacific and North American Railway Contracting Company officials estimated that they would need to realize at least 50 and possibly 60 percent of par value when selling the Canadian Pacific Railway shares if they were to break even on the entire construction contract.[13]

As soon as the construction contract was signed the North American Railway Contracting Company established contacts with the financial firms of Drexel, Morgan & Co.; Winslow, Lanier & Co.; Kuhn, Loeb & Co.; and Seligman & Co., all of New York City, and with Mr. William L. Scott of Erie; Messrs Boissevain & Co.; and Messrs Oyens & Co. of Amsterdam. Each of these, and a number of other financial firms, were expected to take substantial allotments of Canadian Pacific Railway shares from the North American Railway Contracting Company. The financial firms, of course, were only interested if they in turn could dispose of the stock to private investors at a profit. Unfortunately the market value of Canadian Pacific Railway shares fell below the expected levels before the North American Railway Contracting Company was even properly organized and the market did not substantially improve for Canadian Pacific Railway shares throughout 1883. Thus, if the North American Railway Contracting Company received payment in the form of shares, as stipulated in their contract, it could only sell these to the New York financial firms and underwriters at a loss. This the contractors were understandably loth to do, and they simply did not have the financial strength to continue construction work, taking partial payment in shares but holding those shares until the market improved. Instead officials of the North American Railway Contracting Company requested that they be paid in cash only for all construction expenditures. Such an arrangement really rendered the North American Railway Contracting Company entirely redundant, and the Canadian Pacific Railway Company officials decided that they would pay suppliers and sub-contractors directly, without even the fiction of bookkeeping entries for the North American Railway Contracting Company. Canadian Pacific officials in effect became contractors dealing directly with the sub-contractors. The North American Railway Contracting Company contract was clearly a failure. It certainly brought no substantial new financial resources to the Canadian Pacific Railway and did nothing to ease the railway's financial problems.[14]

The construction work in 1883 was not seriously disrupted by the failure of the North American Railway Contracting Company. In fact the organization of construction work on the prairies in 1883 was better than it had been in 1882. This was largely attributable to two North American Railway Contracting Company employees -- the only two employees that company had in western Canada. They were James Ross, Construction Manager, and Herbert Holt, his assistant, who was sometimes also referred to as the Construction Manager. Both men officially worked for the North American Railway Contracting Company, although their salaries were paid from the beginning by the Canadian Pacific Railway.

Both Ross and Holt had gained their early railway experience in Ontario on railways which were purchased by the Canadian Pacific Railway in 1882. Ross had been the contractor who built the Credit Valley Railway, and the construction superintendent on the Ontario and Quebec Railway. Holt had been construction engineer and later chief operating officer on the Credit Valley Railway. He was also engineer in charge of the drafting office of the Ontario and Quebec Railway. Both men were under 40 years of age, had enormous confidence in their own abilities, and were ruthless in completing tasks given to them. They worked best when separated by at least 500 miles from one another and 1,000 miles from Van Horne. Yet each had enormous respect for the other. Each understood what was needed to get the new railway built and each demanded that he be evaluated by the results achieved, not by the excuses he could muster for his failures. They kept one another fully informed about their activities, but each had his own work in which he asked for no help and tolerated no interference. Van Horne as General Manager was responsible for co-ordinating all work on the Canadian Pacific, including the difficult problems of maintaining harmony between the construction and the operating departments. Ross, as Construction Manager, worked out of Winnipeg arranging supplies, negotiating with sub-contractors, arranging for the manpower requirements at the construction sites, and generally dealing with any problems and inadequacies in the construction work. Holt, on the other hand, worked at the end of track and in the various work camps in advance of the end of track. He visited, inspected, and reported on work done. He was Ross's eyes and ears in the front lines. Holt's frequent reports to Ross are among the best accounts available of conditions and problems in the various construction camps, and of the attitude of the new construction managers to their diverse contractors. They are, unfortunately, strictly businesslike, with little or no anecdotal or humorous materials.[15]

One of the sentiments that emerges from Holt's reports, and also from Ross's reports to Van Horne, is the comparative disillusionment with the large American contracting outfits and a growing respect for many of the smaller but often very reliable Canadian contractors. Outfits like Langdon and Shepherd reflected the attitudes and practices prevalent on the American roads where violence, political influence, and a more relaxed attitude toward morals and liquor prevailed. Some of the American sub-contractors also found it difficult to take direction from the young managers with their inflated egos. Canadian contractors, on the other hand, seemed better suited to the temperament of the new construction managers. Indeed, both Ross and Holt took pains to persuade some of their former friends and associates on the Ontario railways to take Canadian Pacific contracts in 1883 and later. These were men of limited financial resources but eager for contracts, and many did their work well.

The main reason for bringing in Langdon and Shepherd in 1882 had been that they and other large American outfits had the necessary experience and would bring with them reliable sub-contractors. To some extent the American outfits did this, but the Ontario men proved at least as competent. In 1883, moreover, there was much construction work available on American railroads, particularly the Northern Pacific, and it was generally conceded that contractors with the right connections did better there than on the Canadian Pacific Railway. Furthermore, once Ross and Holt got firmly into the saddle, the Canadian Pacific no longer needed the service of other general contractors to handle and co-ordinate the work of the sub-contractors. As a result more and more Canadians obtained work building the national railway. This Canadianization was begun by the two managers of the North American Railway Contracting Company of New Jersey.

Small Canadian Contracts, 1884-1886

The North American Railway Contracting Company did nothing to solve the financial problems plaguing the Canadian Pacific Railway, and very little to relieve the railway's General Manager of the trouble of dealing with both general contractors and, indirectly, with a multitude of small sub-contractors. Van Horne, Ross, and Holt looked after contracting details in 1883, and Holt was right when he told one of his employees that, in effect, the North American Railway Contracting Company was a subsidiary of the Canadian Pacific Railway.[16] He might have added that with the failure of the 1883 financing arrangements it was an altogether unnecessary subsidiary. When the Canadian Pacific Railway was forced, in 1883, to ask for huge loans and stock guarantees from the federal government these were provided, but only if the agreement with the North American Railway Contracting Company and in particular the proposed stock transfers, were rescinded and cancelled. An appropriate deed of cancellation was signed on November 21, under the terms of which the contracting company was paid in cash but only for expenditures actually incurred.

After November of 1883 Canadian Pacific Railway officials assumed full control of all construction contracts and sub-contracts. In practice this meant nothing more than that James Ross and Herbert Holt continued to exercise the authority and implement the policies they had begun in 1883 on the western section, while John Ross did the same on the eastern section. They ceased, in 1884, to deal with large general contractors such as Langdon and Shepherd. Instead they split the construction work into its several basic and distinct components -- location work, clearing of rights of way, building embankments, roadbeds, and tunnels, making rock cuts, laying track on prepared roadbed, ballasting, and building snowsheds and station facilities.

Splitting the work into its component parts and letting contracts directly to smaller contractors for such work cut costs for the Canadian Pacific Railway and was well suited to the abilities and resources of a number of Canadian railway contractors. The large general contracting outfits always expected that there would be a profit for them on sub-contracted work, even if the sub-contractor did all the work and Canadian Pacific Railway officials made the necessary inspections, measurements, and calculations. After 1883 the Canadian Pacific Railway men were their own contractors, dispensing with that intermediary service by others. The smaller contractors henceforth got their contracts directly from the railway company, resulting in savings which could be shared by the company and the contractors.

Many of the sub-contractors more or less attached to the large American outfits either left or were outbid by local Canadian contractors when the contracts for 1884 were put up for tender. The Canadian Pacific Railway, moreover, had no reservations about rejecting a very low tender if the contractor had a bad record of completions or seemed underfinanced. Many Canadians had held small sub-contracts in 1882 and 1883, but in 1884 they began to pick up larger and substantially more profitable contracts. Where formerly the preference was to subcontract with Americans associated with the general contractors, the preference shifted after 1883 to Canadian contractors.

It was perhaps a sign of the improved conditions for Canadian contractors that several eastern contractors moved their operations to the Rocky Mountains.[17] One of those doing so early in 1884 was William Mackenzie of Kirkfield, Ontario, who had completed a few very small contracts of the Credit Valley Railway. Also, Herbert Holt, Assistant Construction Manager of the Canadian Pacific Railway and a tough, self-confident but very cautious man, decided in 1884 that there was more money to be made from Canadian Pacific Railway contracts than from his safe and steady salary with the railway. A series of difficult contracts for mountain work, including the construction of several tunnels through shifting rock formations, had to be let in 1884. The initial call for tenders produced no satisfactory response, largely because the fixed rates for different classes of work were not suited to the prospective work in which unusual difficulties were certain to arise. Negotiations were then opened with two of the most experienced contractors and these were persuaded to take up some of the most difficult work at rates substantially higher than those normally paid by the company. The concern of the construction managers at the time was that this essential but difficult work be done efficiently and on time. The terms offered promised substantial remuneration for anyone who could do the work successfully.

The first two contracts thus negotiated convinced Holt, who had done much of the negotiating for the Canadian Pacific Railway, that the contractors were getting a good deal. When more work of this nature had to be contracted Holt asked James Ross for permission to take it up on the same special rates granted the other contractors. Ross agreed, and Holt left the employ of the Canadian Pacific Railway to become a contractor.[18] Holt knew the work well, had calculated all the costs to be incurred, had the proven organizational and managerial skills, and was on his way to a handsome profit. Indeed, after more than 10 years as a professional employee Holt found contracting so profitable and challenging that he spent the next 10 years building railways as a contractor, first in the Rockies, then in Maine, in the Canadian Northwest Territories, and in Ontario and Quebec. In time he and a number of other Canadian contractors who got their first big opportunity on the Canadian Pacific Railway in 1884 employed their own sub-contractors. As sub-contractors or as construction managers in 1882 and 1883 they had learned and learned well the entrepreneurial and management skills which carried them to great heights in the business world later.

The Canadian Pacific Railway was planned and supported by Sir John A. Macdonald as a great national highway which would tie together the diverse regions of a sparcely populated land. To Macdonald Canadian nationalism was always fueled by a large measure of anti-American sentiment. It was therefore ironic that the men responsible for the financing and building of the railway in 1881, 1882, and 1883 should be Americans, or Canadians who had made most of their money and their business reputations in the United States. Equally ironic is the fact that the increased prominence of Canadians among the contractors after 1883 was achieved without the benefit of discernible pressure from the government.

The men who rose to high positions in the service of the company after 1883 did so on their own merits. The experience they gained, and the money they earned proved invaluable to many of these men later. Anyone who survived and made substantial profits on Canadian Pacific Railway construction contracts had passed the hardest tests in the country's most difficult business school. It was not easy for any contractors to draw praise from men like Thomas Shaughnessy, but several received letters of recommendation as follows:

> I take pleasure in saying to you that the very large amount of work which you performed under contracts with this company was in every instance completed to the satisfaction of the Company, and without quibbling when the time came for final settlement.

The man who wrote that letter, and those who received it, were regarded by senior American railroad officials "like the rest of them, only perhaps a little abler than the management of many roads on the American side."[20] These were the Canadians, ready and able to undertake enormous enterprises in the twentieth century. They became the leaders who tried to implement the dream of the Canadian Prime Minister who proclaimed, "The twentieth century shall be the century of Canada and of Canadian development."[21]

The North Saskatchewan River Settlement Claims, 1883-1884

E. A. Mitchener

In 1873 the federal government established the Department of the Interior to regulate the development of the newly purchased Northwest Territories. One of the major problems facing the department was the allocation of the Territories' vast treasury of untouched physical resources -- in particular the farmlands of the Plains Region. However, before any division of land could be made, surveys would have to be carried out to aid in the land registration and a policy struck towards those people already on the Plains. Though in possession of farms and town lots, those people were in effect squatters and subject to the possible loss of their holdings through want of title.

As it evolved, the government's western land policy was basically simple. All those who could prove residence prior to July 15, 1870, the date of transfer of the Northwest Territory from the Hudson's Bay Company to the Government of Canada, had their land holdings confirmed. Those who had taken up land after that time were considered trespassers on the public domain and subject to government regulation. Before the latter could receive title to their lands they would have to meet the requirements of the Homestead Act and if they had inadvertently squatted on lands set aside for other purposes, such as Indian Reserves or railway land grants, they would have to move. The possibility of settlers taking up lands that had been withdrawn from settlement would be eliminated with the completion of the settlement surveys.

As far as the settlers were concerned the surveys could not be carried out soon enough. In an agrarian society where land is equated with wealth the matter of land title is of paramount importance. Petitions came from all quarters to have surveys done in particular areas first. But, of necessity, priority had to be given the region with the greatest need. This was seen to be along the proposed route of the main line of the Canadian Pacific Railway whose trains would bring hundreds of thousands of immigrants into the West, touching off a massive land boom. Initially this route was to pass through the fertile crescent that bordered the North Saskatchewan River and link a number of isolated frontier communities. To this end, in 1876, the Special Survey advanced along the proposed route establishing base lines and prime meridians.

The communities along the North Saskatchewan River eagerly awaited the advance of the surveys. Their settlements had sprung from mission stations and fur trade posts in the 1870s and had since grown in anticipation of the construction of the C.P.R. Most of the settlers and townsmen had waited over a decade to gain title to their lands. However, the lack of title did not hamper their land deals during the period of the northern land boom between 1881 and 1883, although it did cast an aura of uncertainty over eventual ownership. Under these circumstances each community took particular pains to safeguard its holdings against newcomers and speculators until patents were forthcoming.

Then, just at the height of the land boom when the surveyors were rumored to be quickly converging on their communities and real estate activity had reached frenzied proportions, news came of the decision to build the railway in the south. The change in route, designed to forestall the northward advance of the American railway frontier, also drew the surveyors with it. Overnight the northern land boom collapsed and the districts faced economic ruin. As dreams and aspirations were destroyed the mood of the settlers became ugly.

Policemen, justices of the peace, and federal agents were assaulted in the streets and some cases brought before the courts were forcibly adjourned by mob action. The Lieutenant-Governor of the Northwest Territories, Edgar Dewdney, warned Prime Minister Macdonald that where there was smoke there was fire and most of the smoke on the frontier came from the English-speaking settlers at Prince Albert, angered by their inability to obtain land patents.[1]

Fearful of the implications for his administration of any unrest in the West Macdonald ordered the immediate settlement of the land claims of the Prince Albert settlers "lest they all become Grits."[2] He now considered the delay in processing land patents in Prince Albert as scandalous and ordered the Department of the Interior to rush ahead settlement of the long standing claims. He was particularly sensitive to the possibility that the unexplained delay in registering the northern land claims would result in public indignation over what appeared to be the obvious inability of the Department of the Interior to handle a simple routine matter. It would at the same time tend to confirm Liberal charges made in the House of Commons of incompetence and maladministration within the Department of the Interior.

Macdonald's directive was passed on to the Dominion Lands Board, which informed the Prime Minister that they could not undertake the adjudication of the Prince Albert land claims until 1884. Not till then would they have township maps for the North Saskatchewan River regions. And even this was assuming that the surveyors would complete the extension of the survey grid northward during 1883. Nothing could be done by the Lands Branch by way of processing land claims until the surveys were completed and the maps drawn up. In any case the members of the Board were far too busily engaged in the south where, in addition to land claims, they were engaged in the matter of the C.P.R.'s 25-million-acre land grant. The northern land claims would have to wait until the following year.

This casual attitude to the demands of the Prince Albert settlers was due to many factors. The Lands Board had heard the same complaints from settlers all over the frontier and thus complaints from the north did not cause them undue concern. And when the land office was opened at Prince Albert there had been little business to occupy the agent. In 1882, from a district with a population of some 5,000, only

10 applications for patent were received and in 1883 there were only 75.[3] This belied the need for urgency.

The proposed date of 1884 for the Lands Board investigation was not suitable to Macdonald who chose the occasion of the reorganization of the Department of the Interior, in 1883, to create a special commission to settle the northern land claims. Lindsay Russell, the Surveyor-General, was asked to proceed to the region and summarily settle all the land disputes in the district. He was given the power to predate land claims to the date of actual entry and he was to make immediate patent recommendations where required.[4] He was to go to Prince Albert in the summer of 1883 and settle the land problems as efficiently and as quietly as possible. Macdonald, who viewed the growing unrest as primarily a political problem, knew that the Liberal party would be certain to take up the cause of the western settlers and relate it to his administration's record in the West. This he was determined to avoid.

Russell was prepared to leave immediately, and as the survey grid was being extended northward that summer, all augured well for his mission. Unfortunately he became ill and could not go. In his place the commission was given to William Pearce, the Inspector of Lands Agencies with the Dominion Lands Board. After Russell, whose illness was shortly to lead to his resignation, Pearce was the obvious choice for the task because of his wide experience in land matters. Indeed his supervision of the southern land rush made him the most qualified government agent available.

Macdonald agreed to the proposal,[5] but added certain provisos to Pearce's commission that further delayed the settlement of the claims. Whereas Russell's position as Surveyor-General would have enabled him to settle the claims summarily, Pearce, because of bureaucratic protocol, was required to forward his findings through the Commissioner for Dominion Lands, Acquila Walsh.

Pearce's task was still further complicated by the injunction that, whereas Russell had been expected only to deal with Prince Albert, he was to include in his investigation the settlements at Victoria, Edmonton, Fort Saskatchewan, and Lac St. Anne. The decision of the Minister of the Interior to expand the terms of reference of Pearce's commission would result in all the outstanding land disputes along the North Saskatchewan River being settled by the end of the 1884 season.

Pearce had made a routine inspection of the Prince Albert Registry Office in the course of his duties in 1883. Because township maps were not then available he had been satisfied to leave land matters pending, but he made it his business to meet as many people as possible and to assure them of the Board's good will. Of particular concern to the settlers on the South Branch were the actions of the Prince Albert Colonization Company and the fear that they would be removed from the Company's eight township tract.[6] Pearce assured them that he would intercede on their behalf and arrange for an exchange of lands where required. He also instructed Land Agent Duck and his assistant, Gavreau, to take a census of the French Métis on the South Branch and to make an inventory of the improvements to their lands, though on no account were they to imply that individual claims were granted. They were aided in this work by Father Andre and other members of the French-speaking Catholic clergy. They were also to urge the Métis at St. Laurent to make entry for their lands. This the hunter groups refused to do on the pretext that they might have to pay taxes on them, while others argued they would be forced to take up arms to defend the government from unspecified enemies.[7]

Pearce did not believe their reasons, as he had been informed by Duck and others that they had been advised by prominent citizens not to enter their lands but, by withholding entry, force the government to make larger concessions at a later date.

Now, despite the urgency of the situation, Pearce was in no hurry to proceed to Prince Albert because the township maps were not yet ready and without them he could accomplish little by way of settling individual claims. When all the township maps, except those for the South Branch, were ready he left Winnipeg on January 7, 1884 and arrived in Prince Albert on the 15th of that month.

It is ironic that after all the frenzied efforts of Macdonald and the Department of the Interior to hasten the investigation of land claims at Prince Albert, the investigation was to begin only a few weeks before the date originally set by the Lands Board. Even this insignificant gain in time was the result of Pearce proceeding to the district without the township maps of the South Branch. These were supposed to be forwarded to him during the course of his work, but they did not reach Prince Albert until March. By then he had returned to Winnipeg, leaving the land claims on the South Branch untouched. Had he waited a few more weeks before starting his work he would have had all the maps in his possession. He could then have adjudicated the Métis' claims in their communities at Batoche and St. Laurent. Had he done so the Metis leaders could not have used his inability to settle their land claims to incite their people to insurrection. The government authorities committed a serious error in insisting on unnecessary haste when the delay of a few more weeks would have permitted a complete investigation.

Immediately upon Pearce's arrival at Prince Albert he was faced by a major scandal involving one of the land guides, a forest ranger, and a prominent citizen. Van Luven, a townsman, claimed that Charles Patrick Moore, the local forest ranger, had approached him with the proposal that for $100 he could arrange to have land guide Robert Evans give him a good homestead report[8] so that Van Luven would get patent to certain parcels of land. Van Luven was afraid that because he was a townsman and could be on his lands only on the weekends and had therefore not met homestead residence requirements he would lose the land. When the previous November Van Luven had reported the bribe to Pearce, both government agents were suspended from their posts. The case had kept the settlement up in arms all winter and confirmed the townsmen's opinion of the character of government agents in general.[9]

When Pearce questioned the townsmen about the case he discovered that they were at first reluctant to give evidence as they felt all government agents, including Pearce, were corruptible and they were afraid to give evidence because they felt they would only jeopardize their own claims. When they did talk he found their evidence conflicting. Testimony taken under oath could gain him no insight into the matter as the three men continued to besiege him with corroborative evidence based upon the testimony of their friends. There had obviously been considerable community involvement in the affair; it appeared to Pearce that the entire settlement had taken sides in the matter.

The fundamental difficulty in deciding on a course of action was Pearce's inability to get at the truth. To him all three men involved were capable of the misdemeanours with which each charged the other. Unable to establish the rights of the matter, his main concern was to ensure that such a situation would not again arise. He reinstated Evans as a land guide on the proviso he report to Duck at least once a week and he reprimanded Moore and his superior, Crown Timber Agent Waggoner, for not putting a stop to the rumors. Moore was to be reinstated and recommended for service at another agency with the proviso he never again serve under Waggoner.

Pearce's rulings officially closed the case, but the damage done to the reputation of government agents in the district was irretrievable. It is little wonder that under these circumstances the settlers were uneasy over the future of their land claims. It is also understandable that in view of the calibre of government agents already in Prince Albert they should question the reliability of Pearce and the character of his investigations. Pearce would have to demonstrate his integrity before they would trust him. The actions of the local government agents had helped to undermine the authority of the Department of the Interior at a critical period in the history of the settlement and had contributed greatly to the unstable nature of the community.

Turning to land matters, Pearce had assumed that he would be able to resolve the outstanding claims without delay. He estimated that it was unlikely there would be more than 400 cases for disposal and with his power to predate land patent applications he was certain that he would be able to satisfy all parties.[10] His optimism, however, soon turned to despair as it was immediately obvious that land claims in the district were hopelessly confused. Many of the original squatters had sold "their" lands before obtaining title while subsequent "owners" had in turn sold to others. In effect they had sold land belonging to the public domain without title, and legally Pearce was required to seize the land. He realized that such a course of action would be both impractical and contrary to the settlement policies of the government. He decided that because they were all squatters he would treat each of the claimants equally and that he would accept the *status quo* of ownership claims. In the absence of corroborative witnesses he would have to assume that the present occupant did indeed have the right to the land. As there were no precedents dealing with such a situation he decided to proceed with each claim on its own merit in an attempt to satisfy both the settler and government policy.

Further complications arising from the character of the settlers denied any expedition in his work. The only three dates the settlers were likely to remember and to which they related their lives were the Riel Rebellion of 1870, the smallpox epidemic of 1871, and the flooding of the Saskatchewan River in 1875. In an effort to be fair to each claimant he devised a 40-question personal data sheet that each settler was required to fill out and sign. The questions were designed to outline each settler's claim and they were to add any other circumstance which might support their petition.

Pearce took over 1,000 affidavits in the course of his investigation of some 700 land claims. He was ready to concede that much of the evidence taken was not accurate but he felt it was honestly givern,[11] and therefore it could assist in the settlement of the claims particularly as the present allocation of lands seemed to be acceptable to the community as a whole. Where the settler was a *bona fide* farmer and gave evidence by his improvements and the length of his residence that he had every intention of developing the land, Pearce was prepared to be as lenient as possible consistent with his responsibilities under the Dominion Lands Act. Claims to homestead lands by townsmen or government employees he would deny. All claims could be predated to the date actual entry was made on the lands and the terms of settlement would be those of the Dominion Lands Act in force at that date. Where the settler needed to meet improvement requirements he would assess the value of improvements at the price rate of 1882, the height of the land boom when prices and wages were at a premium, no matter when the improvements had actually been made. He would also take into account the settler's time in making the improvements and credit him with labor costs calculated at the rate when hourly labor was at its peak. In this way the settler would be given the maximum credit for his improvements. He also decided to grant settlers the widest latitude possible in respect to the date of change in the pre-emption price from $1 to $2 an acre. This was to have come into effect on October 9, 1879, but the uncertainty of the mails and the time lag in receiving this information persuaded Pearce to set June 1, 1880 as the effective date of the price increase in this district.

Such leniency in dealing with the settlers placed most of his decisions outside the letter of the law. This meant that the Justice Department would not approve automatically his patent recommendations. Of particular concern was the fact that the majority of claims rested solely on the current resident swearing an affidavit that he was in fact the rightful owner. Unease over Pearce's actions were set to rest in April when word came from the Minister of the Interior that he had approved Pearce's recommendations and that the Lands Board could begin processing the individual claims along Pearce's guidelines.

The results of Pearce's investigation satisfied all but a few of the people in the Prince Albert district. In six weeks he had done much to remove the most acute grievances of the settlers, except in the French-speaking Métis settlements on the South Branch. He had been unable to examine land claims there because the promised township maps had never arrived.[12]

He had considered visiting these outlying settlements, but because he realized that he could not take any action there until he had the maps he decided nothing would be gained by such a visit. Without the maps he could not locate the boundary whose rear lines would be certain to interfere with the Indian reservation if, as he was sure it would, his examination lent validity to them. Another reason for not going to Batoche was that he was not certain of the government's policy regarding claims to river lots made by the Métis. He knew that the accepted policy was to permit claims to river lots in any area where they were made on the basis of entry prior to the grid survey being carried out. Land claims made after the square grid was drawn up would have to conform to it and if settlers wished to obtain river lots they would have to resort to a process of legal subdivision. The Batoche area had been surveyed in 1883 and this meant that anyone who settled there subsequently would have to take up lands on the sectional system. Pearce had been informed by

Duck that most of the claimants at Batoche were not really settlers but hunters and that they had recently arrived in the district from Montana and Manitoba after the extension of the grid. This meant that they were not eligible for river lots. But Father Vegreville and Charles Nolin had waited upon Pearce during his investigations and informed him that they had been assured by past promises of the Minister of the Interior and the Surveyor-General, E. Deville, that river lots would be available.[13]

Pearce cautioned Nolin and Vegreville against assuming that all those at Batoche would receive river lots as had their brothers at St. Laurent, where settlement had been prior to the surveys. The expenditure of $2,000[14] to carry out such a re-survey at Batoche would be entirely out of proportion to the handful of individuals involved, particularly as it could not be proven that these Métis were in fact intent upon settling. He warned them that the promises by the Surveyor-General to recommend river lots for the new arrivals were considerably outside his jurisdiction and were indiscreet. Pearce promised them he would forward their request to the Minister of the Interior but he held out little hope their wish would be met.

One of the reasons the Lands Board would look upon their request unfavorably was because at least two of the settlers on the South Branch had indicated a desire to take up sectional parcels of land. They had done so in the face of the determined opposition of their neighbors[15] who were demanding river lots. Such applications and the neighbors' reaction to them would not go unnoticed by the authorities. Pearce was not himself disposed towards a river lot survey merely to satisfy the temporary wants of the hunter group.

Without the township maps and a definite statement of government policy on the river lots at Batoche, Pearce felt he had no choice but to hold the matter in abeyance. In any case he did not speak the French language and would have had difficulty in taking their evidence. Both Duck and Gavreau were French-speaking and as they had assisted him in the past few weeks he did not hesitate to leave the work of the South Branch to them to be completed when the maps arrived. Unfortunately some of the Métis took his failure to visit them as a slight upon their race and further evidence of government indifference to their plight.

Pearce had planned to proceed directly to Edmonton after he had completed his work at Prince Albert, but as those township maps were not ready he knew his trip would be pointless. He therefore returned to Winnipeg and began the task of organizing the Prince Albert claims for ministerial approval. At the same time Duck informed Pearce that the township maps for St. Laurent and Batoche had arrived and that he and Gavreau had investigated all but 50 of the claims on the South Branch. The delay in examining the remainder was the result of the difficulty in defining One Arrow's Reserve which interfered with their back lines.[16] Secure in this knowledge Pearce pushed the thoughts of the South Branch land claims from his mind.

Most of the settlers were satisfied with the results of Pearce's investigation. Of more than 700 claims he examined, less than five percent of the claimants were unhappy with his recommendations. His liberal treatment of the settlers had ensured that his work would be generally well received.

Pearce's visit to the other settlements was put off due to an inspection of the West by the Deputy Minister of the Interior, A.M. Burgess. Burgess was intent on establishing a Superintendent of Mines in Calgary to control what was anticipated as being a major mining boom touched off by the C.P.R.'s penetration of the Eastern Rockies. Because of his work with the Lands Board and his investigation at Prince Albert, whose results Burgess heartily endorsed, Pearce was offered and accepted the position.

As Burgess returned to Ottawa, Pearce left for Edmonton to complete his inspection of the settlement claims there prior to assuming his duties as Superintendent of Mines. He arrived in Edmonton on July 1 and found that he would have to deal with about 240 cases of which only 30 involved disputes over boundaries. Here, as in Prince Albert, Pearce was surprised to find so little disagreement over actual land ownership as the community had kept its members' land rights inviolable until title could be granted.[17]

In 1882, Mr. M. Deane, D.L.S., had carried out the first official settlement survey of Edmonton. He had been ordered to consult Pearce for advice on how the survey should be conducted. Pearce suggested he should not make a definitive survey but merely locate the improvements made by the settlers so that when the Lands Board investigated the townsite to make final land allocations, equity could be taken into account. In no case was Deane to give the impression that the survey implied government recognition of a claim or the grant of title to land. Urged on by local townsmen, Deane exceeded his authority with the result that the townsmen concluded they had in fact been assured of title to the land they occupied and many of them promptly subdivided their holdings into town lots and sold them. When Pearce arrived in 1884 to adjudicate the original land claims the process of subdivision had been carried to the point where in most cases it was irreversible and he had no alternative to accepting the *status quo*.

Despite Deane's bungling there were only two major instances of disputed claims, both of which were to prove a dilemma for Pearce. These were boundary disputes between the Hudson's Bay Company and the settlers on lots 6-18 east of the Hudson's Bay Company Reserve on the north bank of the Saskatchewan River and between the claimants to lots 7-11 on the south bank.

The dispute on the north bank arose from the positioning of the lot lines. Whereas the Hudson's Bay Company had insisted upon their right under law to north-south boundary lines the claimants to lots 6-18 had placed their front line on a north-east angle roughly paralleling the river's course.[18] In the spring of 1872 the settlers had marked off seven claims, ten chains wide, along the river bank. They then ran the side lines of their claims in a north-west direction, perpendicular to the river's course. When the Hudson's Bay Company asserted their right to north-south lines in March, 1873 the lots adjacent to the reserve were cut off. It would have been simple then to merely rearrange all the lot lines north and south but this was not done and subsequent subdivision had placed buildings and other improvements across the recognized north-south boundaries. In 1875 William McGillivray, the original claimant to lot 12, gave up his claim and Richard Hardisty on lot 10 and Donald McLeod on lot 14 divided their lots equally. Hardisty, the Hudson's Bay Company Factor, wanted the division to be made along north-south lines, but McLeod would not agree to the rearrangement as it would push much of Donald McDonald's land on lot 20 into the river. The matter remained unresolved. In 1878, W.F. King of the Special Survey noted that most of the claimants were now agreeable to a north-south survey. But in 1881, when the claimants contracted for a private survey of the land, the Rowlands, on lots 16 and 18, would not accept this and refused to pay their share of the survey because it was not certified by the government. That fall the land boom started in Edmonton and the Hudson's Bay Company lots were sold during April and May of 1882. In the heat of the land rush it is understandable why the original claimants demanded a certified survey that would permit subdivision of their claims into town lots and enable them to join in the frenzied land speculation. They had persuaded Deane to run the survey despite Pearce's advice to leave the matter for the jurisdiction of a land court. Deane used the original north-west lot lines. As a result the settlers believed the original lines were officially recognized and began to sell parcels of land.

As it stood in 1884, Pearce wisely decided to change as few of the lot lines as possible. But he could only do this if all the claimants would agree on their boundaries. If any one of them insisted upon the legal boundary lines he would be bound to recognize their wishes. He hoped he would not be placed in the quandary of having to decide the direction of the original lot lines, as a realignment along north-south lines would throw the settlement into hopeless confusion. His decision to accept the *status quo* was practical and it almost worked. But John McDougall, acting as trustee for the Methodist Mission and his brother David, claimant to lot 8, although not insistent upon north-south lines, demanded an equal area of land to that given to those on lots 10-18 to bolster the areas of the McDougall lots. To do this Pearce used Rat Creek as cutoff for the rear lines behind which the regular grid survey had been made. He was able to accomplish this without further complaints as he found the claimants did not care so much for their rear areas as all they really desired was title to the valuable town lots fronting on the river.

Pearce was prepared to recommend immediate patent for the claimants of the disputed lots if agreement on the boundary lines could be reached. This would have given legal status to the subdivision into town lots and permitted subsequent land transactions which now held no status under law as long as patents were denied. The stubborness of the McDougalls in not accepting Pearce's plan forced the Lands Board to set their lot boundaries arbitrarily. Pearce's decision was to cause continued appeals by the McDougalls which carried on long after Pearce left the government's service in 1904.

The south bank dispute centered about rival claims to the area encompassed by lots 7, 9, and 11. Although the existing arrangement under Deane's survey, whereby John Walter had been allocated only 120.88 acres compared to 235 acres for McDonald and 269 acres for Garneau, had satisfied the three claimants, Pearce was determined not to let Walter be denied an amount of land equal to that claimed by the others. They were all technically guilty of squatting on public lands and thus they had no prior claim to these lots. Pearce was therefore determined they would share the land equally. None of the three claimants to these river lots could in any way have been considered settlers,[19] but they had all contributed so much to the development of the settlement that Pearce was willing to hear their claims. They had taken up their lands at the same time, in 1870, but the value of improvements Walter had made to his lot since then was double that of either of his neighbors.[20] If the value of improvements was to be used as the criterion for land claims then his lot should not be smaller than the others but double their size.

At the time of Deane's survey, however, the three men had signed a document agreeing to the unequal acreages. Walter made no fuss over the unequal disbursement after Deane hold him that he was lucky to get what he did as he certainly was not a *bona fide* settler in the eyes of the Lands Board officials.[21] Walter, an easygoing, good natured and hardworking man, told Pearce he had always felt the government would do him justice and get him his 160 acres in the end. In the meantime he had not questioned Deane's decision lest the Lands Board investigate the matter, with the probability that it would cancel all three claims for noncompliance with regulations.

To complicate matters further Garneau had ceded five acres of his large claim to the Roman Catholic Mission. This land was at the top of the hill on his south-east line next to Walter's claim. Pearce took this as evidence that Garneau had far more land than he in fact needed. Garneau, he reasoned, could therefore afford to give Walter some of his land to balance the areas. Pearce decided to take four chains from Garneau's eastern border and put it onto Walter's lot to raise it to 155 acres and reduce Garneau's total claim to 235 acres, the same size as McDonald's. In no way would the transfer interfere with the mission's lands, but Father Leduc, the business manager for the Roman Catholic Church in Alberta for the region south of the Athabasca River, jumped to the conclusion that the church was to lose its title to the land through Pearce's interference. A warm controversy ensued between him and Pearce over this misunderstanding. At one point Leduc charged Pearce with racial prejudice in favor of the Scotsman Walter against the halfbreed Garneau and complained to the Department of the Interior.

The remaining 227 claims were of a routine nature. For these Pearce used the same criteria he had used at Prince Albert except that the effective date of change in pre-emption price was set back an additional month to July 1 because of the greater distance Edmonton was from Winnipeg. By the end of July Pearce had taken evidence on most of the Edmonton claims and in the company of the Edmonton Lands Agent Gavreau[22] he prepared to leave for Battleford.

Again much to his disgust he discovered that the township maps promised him were not yet available. He wired Ottawa to forward the Battleford plans post haste as well as those for the outlying districts in the Edmonton region at St. Albert, Lac St. Anne, and Fort Saskatchewan. He proposed to visit the latter settlements on his return from Battleford and in this way complete the work of his commission before the fall.

Pearce and Gavreau arrived at the Battleford settlement, situated at the junction of the North Saskatchewan and Battle Rivers, on August 7. The settlement had been established by an Order-in-Council February 20, 1876 when a townsite reserve of 16 square miles was established on the south bank of the

Battle River at Telegraph Flats. At that time all land for a distance of two miles
from the telegraph office had been reserved from homestead settlement. In addition railway reserves of some 20 miles on either side of what was then the proposed
main line of the Pacific Railway were made along the telegraph route which was
assumed to precede the railway. These reserves were withdrawn in 1879 as a result
of a change in government policy towards financing the Canadian Pacific.

The actual settlement remained small owing to the better agricultural capabilities
of lands to the northwest.23 As the total number of claimants in the townsite was
therefore limited, Pearce decided to proceed using a map drawn up by Mr. R.C.
Laurie, D.L.S., a townsman. There were only three types of claims to be judged;
those of settlement prior to the railway belt and townsite reserves made in 1876,
which were valid; those of illegal squatters on the reserves during the time of their
existence, which were therefore not valid; and those of claimants to reserved land
occupied after the reserves were withdrawn in 1879. In the case of those who had
settled prior to or subsequent to the period of the reserves it was merely a matter
of identifying their claims and recommending they be recognized. But the claims
of those who squatted on the reserves when law-abiding settlers had moved off were
not to be denied.

When the townsite reserve was made, most of the squatters had moved two
miles distant from the telegraph office. There they took up the usual homestead
and pre-emption claims. Only six men took up lands within the townsite boundaries
during the period of the reserve, trusting in a benevolent government to give them
title to these choice lands at a future date.24 These were A. McDonald, general
merchant; Scott Robertson, general merchant; N. Antrobus, N.W.M.P. officer; W.M.
Herchmer, N.W.M.P. officer; W.J. Scott, telegrapher and postman; and Hayter Reed,
Indian Agent. In March, 1882, three years after the cancellation of the reserves,
they entered into a plan to gather the remaining lands between the forks of the
rivers into their hands for a new townsite. This land was well within the original
government townsite reserve. Some said the new townsite came about as the
result of a keg party where the stipendary magistrate, Colonel Richardson, had
blessed their scheme and jokingly given the conspirators the right to sue for
trespass on their imaginary townsite. After the party the six men, faced by the
prospect of the ridicule of the settlement, decided not to back down but to
proceed with their plans.25

They promptly laid out their townsite in town lots 100 feet long and 50 feet
wide which they put up for sale at $50 each with the proviso that whoever bought
one lot and placed a house on it would receive the adjacent lot free. Fortune
favored them when that spring the Battle River flooded the low lying lands at
Telegraph Flats. This resulted in most of the townsmen moving to the higher
ground of the new townsite and purchasing lots from the speculators. Scott
used the flood as an excuse to move his telegraph office onto the new townsite
and as his office was also the post office his move brought most of the businessmen with him. This effectively captured the townsite for the conspirators. Then
to further consolidate their coup they gave five acres of land to each of the Roman
Catholic and Protestant churches and to E.A. Prince and Company for a grist mill.

It appeared that their promotion would now bear fruit as the government would be faced with a *fait accompli* and would not dare to change their arrangements.

In 1883 government surveyors working on the township grid arrived and sub-divided the lands within the old and new township along the recognized north-south lines. This gave the government 1,000 lots at the old townsite at Telegraph Flats and 5,200 lots between the forks of the river. The government surveys cut across the conspirators' lot lines and placed newly constructed town buildings on streets and lanes. The government survey placed all the holdings in the new town-site in jeopardy. The conspirators had made a concerted effort to persuade the citizens to ignore the government surveys, but Pearce was determined that the group would not profit from their actions. He had recognized the *status quo* of the town lots in Edmonton because the original claimants were *bona fide* settlers, but four of these Battleford claimants had been and still were government agents. By their actions they had brought the government service into disrepute. They had taken up squatters' claims within the townsite reserve in full knowledge that their course of action was illegal. Pearce would not tolerate a situation in which these men would make financial gain at the expense of those who had obeyed the government's original removal orders.

Pearce, however, recognized that the new townsite was superior to that at Telegraph Flats and in their efforts to sell their lots the conspirators had in fact been of service to the community. He also recognized that some of the conspi-rators had made improvements to their lands that were worthy of notice. Macdonald had erected buildings valued at over $5,500 and had put in $100 in fencing while each of the others had made improvements worth approximately $600. In addition, the six had put a considerable sum into having their townsite surveyed. Despite his personal feelings towards them, Pearce gave them credit for what good they had done in making his decisions regarding their claims.

In his report Pearce recommended that Macdonald receive 24 town lots free, Scott three free lots, and the others one lot each except for Hayter Reed who, because of lack of improvements, was not to receive a free grant. Their claims to the townsite were completely denied. The townsite was government property and it would be the government who would gain financially from the sale of town lots. As to the townsmen who had purchased lots in the new townsite, Pearce recom-mended they were to receive title to their lots at half the government upset price provided they had made at least $250 improvements on them. This concession was made because some of them had already paid the conspirators and Pearce did not want them to suffer unduly for their ill-advised action. Although their houses were now on what were streets and lanes according to the government survey, Pearce told the townsmen not to worry over having to move their buildings as, from his observations, most would need reconstruction before any boundary dis-putes would arise. They were to make certain that when they rebuilt they would align themselves with the government survey. When he left Battleford on August 17 all parties appeared to agree that the government survey would stand, but Pearce urged the government to arrange to sell as many town lots as possible in the near future to prevent the conspirators from reversing this agreement in Pearce's absence.

He and Gavreau returned to Edmonton to find the north bank dispute un-resolved. Pearce still preferred an amicable agreement among the claimants to an imposed settlement by the Lands Board, but he now found the parties to the dispute further apart than before. While he was in Battleford, Frank Oliver, editor of the *Edmonton Bulletin* and a leading western Liberal, had become personally involved in the north bank dispute. When Pearce had set Rat Creek as the back line for the disputed lots he had divided the rear lines on the creek into segments proportional to the frontage of lots 6-18. Then he had drawn the side lines back to the creek. This had resulted in minor shifts of the side lines and small changes in the acreages of the original lots. One of the lots affected by this shift was Oliver's, and he protested the shift in line as interfering with his improvements. He expected the government to protect his property rights and told Pearce that as his improvements had been put up with the concurrence of McLeod on lot 14 he supposed that Pearce would recognize them. Pearce said he would try to arrange an understanding with the others involved, but failing this Oliver would have to remove his fence from what was now McLeod's land.[26]

Oliver, who had purchased the first town lot in Edmonton for $25 in 1878, felt he was the aggrieved party and demanded that Pearce uphold the rights of settlers such as himself.[27] In 1882 he had been instrumental in establishing a vigilante committee to protect the townsmen's property rights. Its efforts had resulted in at least one claim jumper's shack being set on fire and then pushed into the North Saskatchewan River. Now, after all of his efforts to keep property rights inviolate, he was being asked by a government bureaucrat, who had no stake in the community, to take down his fencing. At the same time Oliver, though not a farmer, had applied to homestead and pre-empt farm lands outside the Edmonton townsite. Because he was not a farmer Pearce recommended he not be granted any free homestead nor was he to receive any of the school lands he had taken up. Like the other townsmen he could pay $2 an acre for lands he desired.[28]

Oliver was incensed at Pearce's decision. Since the first issue of the *Bulletin* in 1880 he had been a critic of the Conservative government's western policies. He opposed the monopoly clauses of the Canadian Pacific Railway's charter and the railway's large land reserves because he did not believe that the Northwest Territories should alone bear the burden of Macdonald's National Policy. He began a crusade to uphold the rights of the squatters against eastern business and the government bureaucracy. He demanded a free choice of lands for all westerners and he attacked the Dominion Lands policy with unrestrained vigor.

Now he had personal experience at the hands of one William Pearce of the government's arbitrary disposition. It did not concern him that Pearce's recom-mendations conformed to established principles. Oliver saw himself not only as another western settler abused by the government but as one who, right or wrong, had the means to make the weight of his opinion felt. Through his newspaper Oliver set out to make life as disagreeable as possible for Pearce. He quickly became a thorn in Pearce's side and from this point on he used the power of his paper to seek his dismissal from the civil service. Through his editorial comments in *The Bulletin* he was able to enlist the sympathy of other townsmen who felt that a garden patch and a tent or shanty should give them homestead rights. His campaign was aimed at changing the government's homestead policy and forcing Pearce to resign from the Lands Board.

Pearce was sensitive to Oliver's press attacks. He placed the highest value on his own integrity. Now, because he proposed that the settlers on the north bank settle their boundaries amicably amongst themselves rather than by a settlement imposed upon them, Oliver was accusing him of incompetence and maladministration. To Pearce those of Oliver's class were the worst white poeple one could meet on Canadian soil.[29] He wrote that there was more whiskey drunk per head in Edmonton than anwhere else in the Dominion, while the chief occupation of the townsmen appeared to be causing trouble with one another and stirring up rival elements in the community. He termed the Edmonton townsmen toughs who made things "nasty for the few nice people." These ruffians seemed to him to be bent on becoming unreasonably boorish. Oliver's outrageous demand that every westerner should receive free one square mile of land as a reward for venturing beyond the frontier could not in any way be entertained.

Publicly Pearce chose to ignore Oliver's diatribe. In the latter part of August he set about completing the work of his commission by investigating the land claims at St. Albert and Fort Saskatchewan.[30] At St. Albert he was aided in his work by the Roman Catholic priests. In both places his work went so smoothly that he was ready to leave the Edmonton district early in September.

On September 15 Pearce returned to Calgary to prepare the schedules of the claims arising from his investigations and then to take up his duties as the Superintendent of Mines. In the past eight months he had investigated all the long standing land claims on the periphery of the plains apart from the isolated settlements at Lac La Biche and Fort Victoria. Every case had been fully documented in a special file and each claimant had been subjected to a thorough examination so that in effect a detailed personal history of each individual had been taken and signed. The effort involved in compiling these personal histories was great but in future the files were to prove their worth to Pearce in defending himself from an ever-increasing volume of abuse from the western press as well as criticism from some of his superiors.

Throughout his investigations Pearce had been consistently liberal in his interpretations of the lands regulations towards claims put forward by the *bona fide* settler and his rapport with the settlers was excellent. The same could not be said for his relationship with the townsmen. But even here he was as liberal in handling their claims as his conscience would allow. He would not, however, tolerate either the irresponsible actions of government agents involved in land speculations or other individual attempts to make illegal profit from the public domain. Because of his resolve to deny unearned profits to the speculative elements on the frontier he had run afoul of the more aggressive and most vocal newcomers, men capable of exerting pressure on Pearce through the western press and government lobbies.

To the credit of the Department of the Interior and of Pearce himself such pressure was in the long run ineffective. Initially, however, continuing criticism of Pearce and the Lands Board in the press caused the Prime Minister some concern. To the extent that the western press created public opinion, its active opposition to the operations of government agencies such as the Lands Board could diminish popular support for the Conservative Party. Although Macdonald knew that Pearce was carrying out his work with energy and efficiency, he could not help but deplore his lack of tact in dealing with the public.[31] He should have put down these men firmly but kindly, he said, and Macdonald cautioned H.H. Smith, who replaced Pearce as the Inspector of Lands Agencies, to try to maintain better public relations with the townsmen so that he would not provide ammunition for the Liberal opposition and thus become an embarrassment to the government.

Pearce was aware of Macdonald's criticism of his methods. He also knew the fate of civil servants who became a political liability. In deference to the Prime Minister he promised to watch his ways and to moderate his gruff manner in his approach to the press. However, his character was such that he quickly resumed his old ways.

Although the matter of land claims was to become a factor in the Saskatchewan Rebellion of 1885, had Pearce not carried out his commission to the extent that he did the matter would have taken an even more serious turn. The settlement of the long-standing land claims on the North Saskatchewan River in 1884 was the result more of the personal action of William Pearce, the Inspector of Dominion Lands Agencies, than of sound government planning.

The Turner Thesis and the Canadian West: A Closer Look at the Ranching Frontier

David H. Breen

In his monumental paper delivered to assembled historians at Chicago in 1893, Wisconsin historian Frederick Jackson Turner presented his colleagues with the thesis that "what the Mediterranean Sea was to the Greeks, breaking the bond of custom, offering new experiences, calling out new institutions and activities, that, and more, the ever retreating frontier has been to the United States...."[1] His conception of the frontier as a crucible from which emerged a distinctly North American society has had a lesser, but none the less considerable impact on Canadian historiography. Turner's Canadian disciples were not deterred by the fact that the phenomenon of a continuous geographical and chronological frontier experience in the American pattern was not apparent in Canada. Canadian historians proceeded to identify frontiers compressed and separated in both time and space. While each of these frontiers; the Maritime, French Canadian, Upper Canadian, Prairie, and Pacific West, have had their Turnerian apologists,[2] for the most part they have had to yield their position over the past two decades. The arguments and attention of the few remaining Turnerians and environmentalists now are mainly focused on the prairie west. In this region they claim to see evidence of the more equalitarian ethos and of the institutional corrosion described by Turner. Stating his belief in the regenerative quality of the prairie environment one senior Canadian historian has asserted "On the prairies Ontario's sturdy yeoman was born anew."[3] Most frequently the still persistent third party political tradition in the west is cited as a manifestation of frontierist influences.[4]

But even with regard to the prairie west, the application of the Turner thesis, at least in the direct sense, is rendered difficult on several grounds, the most important being the different time period in which the last "frontier stage," the farmers' frontier, occurred. General settlement of the Canadian prairie west was essentially a twentieth century phenomenon and technology thus assured that the character of this settlement would vary considerably from the nineteenth century frontier described by Turner. The western Canadian prairie was occupied within the incredibly short span of twenty years and the personal and institutional isolation so important in Turner's frontier setting was almost unknown. In light of this problem, and in order to achieve the advantage of a more direct comparison in time and place with the nineteenth century American frontier, perhaps it would be fruitful to focus upon one of Turner's earlier frontier stages. There are two disparate possibilities -- the fur trader's Red

River Colony and the cattlemen's emergent empire along the foothills of the Rocky Mountains. The former offers the attractive advantage of a longer period of isolated development to be assessed, but while the unique character of the society does seem to suggest a great deal about the significance of the frontier environment on social formation in the Canadian setting, a truly comparable community is not to be found on the American frontier.[5] With the cattlemen's frontier, on the other hand, developments on either side of the border are directly comparable.

Traditional historiography has asserted in fact that the ranching frontier in Canada was the most "American" of all Canadian frontiers. This would seem to be conceded even by those who would perhaps challenge the frontierist's interpretation of the subsequent farmers' frontier.[6] One work dealing with the social aspect of prairie settlement has characterized the development of the Canadian cattle country as simply a "...cultural diffusion northward."[7] In elaboration it is explained that "the practice of ranching brought to Western Canada a picturesque type of frontier settlement which was noted for [the] relatively free and unconventional mode of existence" reminiscent of Texas.[8] In another, more recent, account of the Canadian cattle kingdom, the author similarly has observed that: "Ranchland traditions were inherited from the south. The stock-saddle, and all that went with it, followed the ranch herds north from Texas, across Montana, and over the border into Canada."[9] In keeping with this interpretation, the typical cowboy of the Canadian west, like his American counterpart, is identified as a man whose rough exterior masked a sterling character.

> The law of the range, born of necessity, said that he had to fight to defend himself, his boss's property, and the honour of the ranch. Often in the early years he was armed, and he knew that carrying a gun was a huge folly unless he could shoot straight and shoot fast. He learned to do both.[10]

The standard then, has been for Canadian scholars to view the ranching frontier in continental terms, to observe the unities of time, geography, and economic organization. Of particular importance is the inclination to ascribe a social or culture homogeneity to the region, resting on the assumption that the population on the Canadian side, like the cattle, were largely of American origin. In consequence of this widely held belief that the cattlemen's frontier in Canada, to a greater extent than any other stage in western Canadian development, was in form and spirit an integral part of the American west, it is hardly surprising that the dominant frontierist arguments delineating the character of the American cattle kingdom were also accepted. Thus the term "American," as it appears in the literature, usually comes with strong Turnerian overtones. This being the case, it is clear that an important part of any evaluation of the frontierist interpretation of the ranching frontier in Canada must include an examination of the alleged demographic unity of the region.

In looking at the initial movement into the cattle country on either side of the boundary one is immediately impressed with a phenomenon, the significance of which the continentalists perhaps have not fully appreciated, or at least have played down. On the northern side the stockmen pushed into a region already pacified by the North-West Mounted Police who arrived in the southwest in 1874. The significance of their presence, however, is more than simply one of degree -- more law and order on one side and less on the other. What is especially important is the attitude manifest in the act of sending the police west. The police symbolized the government's full commitment to the region and functioned as the cutting edge of a pervasive and unrelenting metropolitan domination.

While it is essential to see the police in the broad context of overall federal com-mitment, their specific contribution to the territory's development should not be neglected. In the immediate context the police were successful in negotiating with the powerful and much feared blackfoot Confederacy, the peaceful transfer of indigenous land title to the dominion, and then ensuring the peaceful co-existence between the natives and incoming whites. This meant that the cattlemen pushing into the foothill valleys in the later seventies did not fight the Indians to gain pos-session. Thus it was the northern tradition of the Hudson's Bay Company and the fur trade; the tradition of paternalism and co-existence that remained unbroken. The armed struggle that Turner described as part of the American frontier experience was not characteristic of the ranching frontier in Canada.[11] A "conquest of the west" theme is not present in Canadian historiography.

On the Canadian frontier the relationship that developed between the federal police and the cattlemen was remarkably close. After the solution of the Indian "problem" the paramount concern in ranch country was the protection of property. The rancher's cattle, representing almost his entire capital investment, wandered freely over a vast expanse with only the most limited supervision. American cattle-men therefore took the initiative, as seems to befit the frontier model, to come together to structure their own associations for the express purpose of supervising the conduct of their industry and providing organized protection for their herds. In this manner cattlemen were prepared to, and frequently did, interpret and ad-minister the law as they saw fit. In the Canadian west cattlemen's associations were also active but law enforcement was left strictly to the North-West Mounted Police, and in this regard the ranchers were well served. Police posts and patrols were constantly increased to keep pace with the expansion of the ranchers' domain. By 1889 a vast surveillance network thoroughly covered the southwest. Daily patrols and irregular "flying patrols" kept careful watch, the coming and going of strangers was closely checked, and most ranchers and settlers were visited at regular intervals.[12]

While the numerous detachments scattered throughout the cattle country were not intended to be simply guardians of the ranchers' interests, despite the contrary view of many would-be settlers,[13] and did spend much of their time on routine police duties, it is apparent that their single most important function after the maintenance of peace and order was to prevent the killing and stealing of livestock. The thoroughness of their activity is indicated by the numerous reports in police files, some of which run to hundreds of pages, on cases which involved only a few head of livestock. Even more important than the thorough-going character of their investigations was simply the preventive effect of this formidable network of posts and patrols which kept cattle theft to a minimum before 1896. Each of the four largest ranches had a police detachment stationed within a few miles of its home ranch. On no other frontier was the cattleman afforded such protection as he established his herds, and it is hardly surprising that the ranchers were among the staunchest defenders of the force when it was occasionally confronted with proposals of reduction or elimination urged by economy-minded parliamentarians in Ottawa.[14]

The presence of the police, coupled with their firm insistence that they alone were the sole agents of Her Majesty's law, ensured that "frontier justice" did not gain currency, and that the extra-legal voluntary associations described by Turner were not only vigorously discouraged but were also unnecessary. Violence in the Canadian cattle country was most uncommon. Between 1878 and 1883 only five murder cases were brought before the courts.[15] An incident in December 1895 in which the Texas foreman of the Walrond Ranch beat an adversary to the draw and shot him in the stomach caused the editor of the *Fort Macleod Gazette* to call attention to the rarity of such incidents, with the observation that this was only the second time since the paper was established in 1882 that it had been able to report a gun fight.[16] The police vigorously discouraged the carrying of side arms and the mere pointing of a revolver was sufficient to bring imprisonment.[17] The "law and order" ethos of the Canadian range assured that the myth of sociological jurisprudence could not gain root. In contrast to the idea that administration of the law was a local responsibility and hence should be administered and directed by the citizenry below, the inhabitants of the Canadian range country by and large accepted the premise that the law should be formulated and imposed from above. Violence and disruption were looked upon as unwanted "American" characteristics and southwestern newspapers missed few opportunities to compare favorably their west with its "British justice" to the seemingly chaotic American west.[18]

In the despatch of the North-West Mounted Police to the western frontier can be seen the determination of the central authority to reach out and integrate the new territory into the established institutional framework. The police clearly were the direct agents of national policy. With this enforcement body came the full panoply of federal law and authority. And among those laws of most immediate and long term impact on the region's development, were those governing the use and disposal of western lands. From the standpoint of the Turner analysis this is of particular significance, for as Turner writes, "...the fundamental fact in regard to this new society was the relation to the land."[19] Speaking further of the American experience he explained

> ...the public land policy was developed by laws which subordinated the revenue idea to the idea of the upbuilding of a democracy of small landholders. The squatters of the Ohio Valley forced the passage of preemption laws and these laws in their turn led to the homestead agitation. There has been no single element more influential in shaping American democracy and ideals than this land policy.[20]

The doctrine, well articulated by Senator Thomas Hart Benton, that since the national resources belonged to the people any person had a moral right to appropriate public land for his individual use, gained wide acceptance in the United States. After 1820 squatting grew steadily as public policy came more and more to accord preferential treatment of squatters.[21] This attitude toward public land is amply demonstrated in the "free grass" ethos of the grazing country. Here squatter sovereignty was based upon the recognized custom of priority; the stockman who first drove cattle into a likely valley was understood to have gained a kind of prescriptive right to that range.[22]

In contrast, on the Canadian side, the venturesome squatter was largely unknown, the idea of squatter sovereignty never gained significant support, and the free use of public lands for grazing purposes was never sanctioned. In the north the attitude toward public land was demonstrably different, as is subtly suggested in the preferred Canadian term -- Crown land as opposed to public land. From the moment of purchase of the western interior from the Hudson's Bay Company, the Canadian government viewed its new estate in an imperial manner. Judging westward expansion as an urgent national necessity, the new Dominion determined therefore, that unlike the original provinces of the Federation, control of lands in the prairie west would be retained even after provincehood, and administered by the Government of Canada for what were termed "the purposes of the Dominion."[23] In this way the first prairie province, Manitoba, and later, Saskatchewan and Alberta, were relegated to an inferior colonial status and until federal control of lands and natural resources was relinquished in 1930 this remained the touchstone of western alienation.

In keeping with this philosophy and with an eye to the American example, the Canadian government adopted the principle that users of the range land should pay a rent. To accomplish this end and to encourage eastern investment capital, a comprehensive lease policy was devised and presented in December 1881. Grazing leases of up to 100,000 acres were offered for 21 years at the rate of 10 dollars per 1,000 acres -- or one cent per acre per year.[24] In light of later developments, perhaps the most significant feature of the new lease policy was the provision that excluded all except the lessee from the right of immediate homestead entry. The lease system was the foundation upon which the ranching empire in Canada was built and it meant that the Canadian range developed in a manner significantly different from the American pattern. By leasing the public domain rather than allowing it to be used as common pasture, the Canadian government maintained a much more direct control of land use, and by establishing a clear basis of legal ownership, helped prevent the range wars that occasionally developed in the American west among ranchers disputing one another's rights to a particular range. The legal position of the Canadian leaseholder was explicitly defined by statute and this, with a federal police force at hand to uphold the provisions of national laws, provided a security that the American rancher dependent upon "range rights" did not possess. Those who squatted on the extensive leaseholds did so only at the sufferance of the leaseholder and more often than not were summarily evicted by the rancher and his cowhands or by the police.[25] While the lease system fostered economic and political stability as well as the superior husbanding of the land's resources, it also restricted greatly the activities of the small or beginning cattlemen who could not afford to buy or lease land, and in this sense was one of the factors influencing the region's evolving social milieu.

The federal presence in the ranch country as manifest in the lease system with its concomitant ranch inspectors was characteristic of the government's supervisory commitment towards the use and disposal of western lands in general. The wide-ranging activities of the department entrusted with this supervisory function in fact, soon gave the Department of the Interior a central and field bureaucracy that made it the largest and perhaps the most dynamic of all government departments. The actual perspective is readily apparent when weighed in the national balance. As one historian has recently asserted, "from 1870 to 1930 the administration of public lands was the most important and far-reaching activity in which the federal government was engaged during the period, with the sole exception of the prosecution of the First World War."[26]

Not only does expansion into the Canadian west occur within the tight grip of central authority, but the character of the incoming population to the cattle country further enhanced the metropolitan presence. Since in the Canadian setting the phenomenon of a continuous settlement frontier is not to be observed, one does not find in newly settled regions a significant vanguard of indigenous frontiersmen "conditioned" by several generations exposure and experience on the advancing edge of settlement. Thus, by virtue of their small number, the contribution made by this group to the evolving social and political environment was small. Though some of the first ranchers in the Canadian southwest were American, they were always a small minority and as a body they carried practically no social or political weight. Even by 1890 most of the cowboys were of Canadian or British origin.[27] The few Canadian frontiersmen who were among the earliest arrivals were often ex-Hudson's Bay Company men of a somewhat different temperament than their American counterparts. By far the majority of the early ranchers were former members of the North-West Mounted Police, and given their eastern and general middle class backgrounds, they contributed a special quality to the early settlement that immeasurably strengthened the community's law and order ethos.[28] A third identifiable group of Canadians in the grazing country were from the Eastern townships of Quebec who brought with them a sound knowledge of the stock raising industry and in general strengthened the region's eastward and Canadian orientation. Added to these groups was a host of immigrants from the British Isles who very often wrote "gentleman" under the heading "previous occupation" on their homestead applications. These prospective ranchers invariably possessed sufficient capital to establish ranches of their own and were drawn generally from the ranks of the lesser landed gentry and military families. The English character of the ranching fraternity and the presence of so many Englishmen "of good family" was consistently reported by visitors to the region before the turn of the century.[29] The men sent west to manage the large company ranches were very much of the same cast. In terms of their cultural and educational backgrounds, the management of western ranch companies was simply a transplanted part of the eastern managerial class. The Canadian range was never in the hands of "wild and woolly" Westerners,[30] either American or Canadian.

The officer and directorship lists of the early stock associations indicate very clearly who comprised the economic and political leadership of the ranch community and the names of the small stockmen or the enterprising frontiersmen are noticeable by their absence.

Though the squirarchy or "race of 'ranch patriarchs'" which Professor W. Brown of the Agricultural College at Guelph felt should be established in the pastoral regions of the southwest,[31] did not quite develop, a distinctive society peculiar to the Canadian cattle kingdom did evolve. At the apex of the region's social pyramid was a wealthy and politically powerful elite composed principally of Britons and Eastern Canadians. The vast majority of this population was not part of an advancing frontier that moved slowly westward. They were instead representatives of the metropolitan culture of the east, or of the stratified society of rural Britain, and their social orientation was eastward rather than southward.

Of interest are some of the outward manifestations of this society, including among other things the fox hunt, in which the lowly coyote was the unhappy substitute for the fox; a polo league of international calibre; Chinese cooks; governesses; schools in the "Old Country" and eastern Canada; and winters in Calgary, Victoria, or Great Britain, depending on financial means. What is observed here is not a community of innovators seeking a release from the restraints of traditional ways, but rather a society vigorously attempting, and with general success, to recreate the kind of community in which they had been nurtured and had found congenial. After the police barracks the next building of prominence to appear in the foothill ranch communities was the Anglican church, and with the support of this institutional foundation the conservative cattlemen endeavored to maintain the *status quo*.[32] And in the defence of tradition, the economic structure of the cattle industry was especially well suited. In the first place the character of the industry itself had gone far in determining the class base from which the original population was drawn. Stock raising, unlike farming, demanded an initial capital investment that was substantial and therefore tended to eliminate those of lesser means.[33] In addition, the lease system made it difficult for the small operator to get established. This difficulty was compounded further by the federal government's partisan attitude towards lease disposal which meant that the would-be leaseholder had to be a known supporter of the government, or at least have friends in Parliament. In the period before 1896 leaseholders, and this meant practically all of the ranchers of consequence, were stalwart supporters of the Conservative party.[34] In the second place, once the proprietor had established his ranch, the operational structure was particularly suitable for the support of the English country estate ethos. Cattle ranching permitted the retention of the manager-employer relationship as well as a leisured life style, and in this manner actually assisted in the perpetuation of an imported social system that helped to set the ranch community apart from the general social development of the agrarian frontier. Cereal agriculture, in contrast, was unable to support the rural establishment desired by the European landowner. Few persons wanted to take employment on a gentleman's farm or become tenant farmers, in a region where they might easily acquire land of their own.[35] Ranch labor on the other hand was seldom in short supply.

Beyond this, British ranchers for the most part found congenial entry into a society that itself displayed a marked attachment to things British. The "British way" as it was termed by the contemporary press was not the alien cultural force that it was on the American frontier. There small groups of British ranchers were culturally isolated. To be socially accepted they were obliged to make substantial concessions to the dominant social pattern or to hope fondly as did one forlorn chatelaine in Montana, that "...in time, perhaps, the country may get more thickly settled with English people, or a better class of Americans from the older States."36 Even the very prominent and respected Scottish born managers of the huge Texas based Matador Land and Cattle Company, were sensitive to the imperial bond that gave the Briton a place north of the boundary that he did not enjoy in the United States.37

In place of the almost wholly absent backwoods or frontier tradition in this emergent community, an aggressive, confident and competing tradition existed. The environmental forces were rendered much less effective because the population did not seek its identity in the land, its spiritual home was elsewhere and existent technology facilitated continued nourishment from distant quarters. Far from being isolationists, the cattlemen's horizons, Canadian and British born, were as broad as the far reaches of the empire where many of them had done service and where many of their sons and grandsons would later follow.38 The ranch country's imperial sentiment is readily demonstrated in its response to every royal or semi-regal visit, to all the pageants and imperial crises of the pre-World War I period, and is strikingly evident in the region's South African and First World War enlistment statistics.39

Just as the cattlemen were prepared directly to maintain the Empire abroad, they were equally prepared, and were remarkably effective in resisting change at home. The stockmen are noticeable by their absence in the ranks of those engaged in the struggle for responsible government in the Territories. The intimate character of their metropolitan links provided them with a most effective political voice -- the directorship lists of the big cattle companies read like a "who's who" in the Canadian business world and the influence that this lobby was able to assert assured the ranchers' preferred position.40 When, for example, under strong public pressure, the government was finally forced to abandon its closed lease policy, a conclave of the most powerful members of the ranch establishment extracted a promise from the Minister of the Interior to expand greatly the system of public water reservations that would enable the cattlemen to maintain their control of the land in a less direct but still most effective way.41 The ranchers clearly preferred Ottawa's direct administration of the region and when at last, provincehood became inevitable, the cattlemen expressed their preference for a north-south division of the territory that would sever the more populous northern farming region and thereby enhance their own regional strength.42 Temperament and motives of political practicality combined to bind the ranchers to the Conservative party almost to a man and the bond continued through the difficult years of Liberal rule from 1896 to 1911.43

The stockmen's most concerted effort to maintain the *status quo* naturally came in their resistance to farm settlement. The powerful Canadian cattlemen, no less

than their American counterparts, were determined to protect their large and profitable holdings. But added to this was a social dimension that colored the essentially
economic character of this contest. The majority of the farmers moving into the dry
country after the turn of the century were American. This new population was not
prepared for the most part to become British-Canadians, or even Canadians unless
on their terms. They were proud of their own democratic tradition and republican
institutions and viewed themselves as the agents of "progress," and in some cases of
manifest destiny, in the Canadian west. As the noted student of North American
migration, Marcus Lee Hansen, has observed, the people who found their way northward were used to moving where opportunity seemed to beckon, these people
"...viewed the continent as a whole" and for them the border held no real meaning.[44]
When the stockmen's favored solicitor and later Prime Minister of Canada, R.B. Bennett, warned the Canadian Club in Montreal of the threat to British institutions posed
by this vast influx of Americans, he echoed the sentiments of many of his fellow
members of the Ranchmen's Club in Calgary.[45] Such concern regarding the rapidly
growing American population which developed after the turn of the century grew
easily from the anti-American bias that had existed in the region from the arrival of
the North-West Mounted Police. The idea was widely held amongst the original
ranch population that they were building a British-Canadian west and to many of
those remaining, the fear of cultural assimilation was second only to the economic
threat posed by the arrival of thousands of American farmers.[46] Conscious of the
fact that they had become a minority within their own region, some among their
number proposed to redress the social imbalance through the foundation of a
"Ranch School" designed to draw new blood from amongst the public school
population in Great Britain, and preferably from Eton, Harrow, Winchester, and
Westminster.[47] While the "Ranch School" that did eventually emerge, the
Bradfield College Ranch, was just comfortably established when the First Great
War intervened to draw all of the pupils back to the mother country, it is clear
that a small increment of young men from a single public school could have done
little to affect the changing demographic balance.[48]

This sentiment serves to underline the fact that the ranching frontier in the
Canadian and American west can hardly be described as culturally homogeneous.
Further, it is apparent that while there is a certain unity of time and physical
environment as well as a common economic enterprise, social and political patterns developed with marked differences on either side of the boundary. This
dissimilar development, and the seemingly minor impact of the frontier environment on the Canadian side would seem essentially to be the consequence of two
factors -- the character of the in-coming population and the degree of the central
government's administrative control. And in the pervasive influence of the central
authority, one sees a continuity in western Canadian development that flows through
the earlier fur trade period to the closing years of western settlement.

Given the strength of established authority and institutions, and a population
confident in its own tradition with little or no inclination to tamper with the existing social or political milieu, democratization of the political process is not an
observable phenomenon on the Canadian range. New men were not created, a

local or indigenous leadership did not emerge. Institutional modification similarly is circumscribed and the limited social disorder that is apparent was never a threat to existing structures. The traditionally ascribed levelling power of the frontier environment also seems weak in this setting. The would-be squirarchy in fact appears more at ease in the cattle country than perhaps on any other nineteenth century Canadian frontier.[49] Ironically, the old Canadian cattle kingdom, usually considered to have been simply an economic and social adjunct of the American west, was in fact one of the main bulwarks of "British" tradition in the south-western prairie region. The cattlemen and their community least of all English-speaking groups to settle in the prairie west exhibited those characteristics commonly imputed to the Turnerian stereotype.

The Emergence and Role of the Elite in the Franco-Albertan Community to 1914

Edward J. Hart

La Survivance, a dominant feature and objective of French-Canadian life, has manifested itself in many forms in the two hundred odd years since the Conquest. These forms are now well known to scholars of Canadian history with relation to the French-speaking communities of Quebec and to some extent those of the Maritime provinces. However, until recently, little probing had been done into the situations of the relatively small communities of western Canada, probably since they hardly seemed important enough to warrant the attention. But once the task was undertaken some interesting aspects of *la survivance* in these communities began to become apparent, aspects which have added to the rich ethnic fabric woven into the area's history. The purpose of this essay is to examine a major factor in the Alberta community's success in retaining its identity during its early years of existence -- the emergence and effective functioning of an elite. As the study will show, this interesting group not only played an important part in the community's life but was largely responsible for its survival, even to the present day.

The original *raison d'etre* for a French-speaking presence in the lands which in 1905 became the Province of Alberta was, of course, the fur trade. By 1795 when Edmonton was established as a fur post on the Saskatchewan the area north of the river was already being hotly contested by the chartered Hudson's Bay Company and its interloper rival the North West Company. Hudson's Bay Company policy called for the employment of servants brought out from the British Isles, particularly Orkneymen, while on the other hand the North West Company preferred French-Canadian *voyageurs* recruited in Quebec. The latter were noted for their hardiness, bravery, and perseverance during the long and hazardous canoe trips of the fur brigades from Lachine into the up-country with supplies and back again with the fur packs. In addition they had a great faculty for learning Indian languages and were amenable to marriage with Indian women, valuable factors in the keen competition for the various tribes' trading patronage. Because of these considerations and an increasing difficulty in attracting Orkneymen to their service, after 1804 the Hudson's Bay Company began to recruit French-Canadians as well.

At the same time a further French-speaking element began to make an appearance in the ranks of both companies, an element that within a short period would begin to predominate as a source of manpower. These were the mixed bloods or Métis, the products of the aforementioned marriages between the *voyageurs* and Indian women. In the case of the North West Company, servants could take Indian wives with the permission of the *bourgeois* and these wives and their children were supported at the expense of the post. This was allowed because by virtue of the ties the Métis off-spring had with the various Indian tribes, as well as their facility in speaking the Indian tongues, they became equally if not more valuable to the trade than their French-Canadian fathers. Therefore, after the amalgamation of the rival fur companies into the new Hudson's Bay Company in 1821 the posts within the future lands of Alberta were called upon to support large numbers of these people. For example, in 1833 Edmonton House had to assume responsibility for 18 Métis men, 28 women and 71 children.[1] Overall the preponderance of the French-speaking Métis and their French-Canadian progenitors in the Company's service resulted in French being the universally accepted language of the trade right up until the middle of the nineteenth century.

Despite this fact the early French-speaking fur trade population was not to form the basis of or bear any real relationship to the community which would appear towards the end of the century. However, it did play a role in the very existence of that future community. During the second half of the nineteenth century the fur trade entered a period of decline and it is very likely that French, both oral and written, would have disappeared altogether as a language of use in the area had not a new element, the French-speaking Catholic missionary, appeared on the scene. Not only did these individuals provide a link between the old fur trade community and the future basically agricultural one but, as will be shown, they were actually the instigators of the latter. The primary importance of the early French-speaking fur trade inhabitants was, therefore, not only their establishment of an historical basis for the French language and rights in the area but the attraction they helped provide for this second element, the clergy.

The first missionaries to enter the lands of Alberta were the Reverend Fathers Norbert Blanchet and Modeste Demers who paused at Edmonton House in September 1838 on their way to open missions around Fort Vancouver. But it was not until 1842, after the appearance of the Wesleyan Reverend Robert T. Rundle at Edmonton, that an appeal from a Métis convinced Bishop J.N. Provencher, auxiliary to the Bishop of Quebec, that he best send a permanent French-speaking missionary to the region if it were not to be irrevocably lost to the English Protestants. Provencher's choice fell upon Father Jean-Baptiste Thibault who during his first summer on the Saskatchewan performed 353 baptisms and 18 marriages, mostly among the French-Canadians and Métis.[2] In 1843 Thibault decided upon a site for a permanent mission at Lac Ste. Anne 50 miles west of Edmonton House, and in 1844 was joined there by Father Joseph Bourassa. Worn out by the exigencies of their missionary efforts, these two returned to Saint Boniface in 1852 and 1853 respectively and Bishop Alexander Taché, O.M.I., appointed coadjutor with Bishop Prevencher on June 14, 1850, was forced to find an immediate replacement for the mission. Although the Oblates of Mary Immaculate, a French religious order, had been procured in 1845 to provide supplementation to the few secular priests on the prairies, they were not as yet present in sufficient numbers to alleviate all shortages. As a result, Taché had to turn to a young priest who after spending two years among the Red River Métis had just returned to Montreal with the intention of joining the Oblates. This was Father Albert Lacombe whose name was to become synonomous with the missions of the whole Saskatchewan River district for the next half century. Due to his energy and perseverance the missions began to flourish shortly after his arrival. In 1854 he and Bishop Taché initiated a mission dedicated to Saint Joachim within the confines of Edmonton House, the first church being constructed in 1859, and in 1861 they founded on the banks of the Sturgeon River north of Edmonton, the site for the new Saint Albert mission. By 1871 this had become the seat of the Episcopal See of Saint Albert with Monseigneur Vital Grandin, O.M.I., as its first Bishop.[3]

To this point the entire thrust of the clergy's work had been directed towards the Indians, Métis, and French-Canadians associated with the fur trade. This missionary zeal was to continue on into the twentieth century but at the same time there began to be a gradual shifting of emphasis towards other work as well. Initially the clergy themselves may not even have been aware of this change, but with the initiation of settlement at Edmonton outside the fort it was nonetheless taking place.

Beginning around 1870 several buildings had begun to appear in the Edmonton townsite, including the McDougall Mission, Donald Ross's hotel, and the houses of a few individuals, mostly ex-employees of the Company, who chose to live outside the fort. With this development Chief Factor William Christie decided that it was no longer necessary to provide space for Saint Joachim's mission on the Company's property and in 1876 demanded that it be removed. Although the clergy opposed this action, Christie's order ultimately proved beneficial and may even be said to have marked the birth of Alberta's French-speaking community as it exists today. Forced to find a new location, Bishop Grandin gratefully accepted the donation of a piece of land by Malcolm Groat, a former Company man himself, and constructed a new Saint Joachim's Church which was formally dedicated by his nephew the Reverend Father Henri Grandin, O.M.I., on January 4, 1877. Although at the outset this new edifice attracted few new faces other than its normal complement from the old mission, after 1880 its patronage began to undergo a gradual change. This was attributable to the appearance of several recent French-speaking arrivals, mainly Quebeckers of middle class backgrounds, who had come to test their luck in the budding economic life of the new settlement -- men such as Xavier St. Jean who started out as a cabinet maker and later became a major building contractor and Stanislas LaRue who, although originally only a surveyor's assistant, eventually became one of the town's leading general merchants. The new Saint Joachim's provided a nucleus around which these and other French-speaking newcomers to Edmonton could establish themselves and tended to act as a focal point for their religious and social activities. It was the clergy, of course, who originally came forward to foster these tendencies by holding special services and gatherings on French-Canadian feastdays and holidays and by arranging *soirées* and other social events. By so doing they were no longer acting strictly in a missionary capacity but more in the manner of a *curé* in a typical French-Canadian parish. In effect they had begun to fulfil the traditional role of the Quebec clergy as one of the integral parts of a small group of the French-speaking community who saw it as their duty, in this case their sacred duty, to provide an example and guide the rest of the community in the fight to maintain the French language and culture as well as the Catholic faith. Very soon thereafter it would begin to become increasingly more apparent that there was a vital need for them to perform exactly this type of elitist function.

As late as 1885 the French-speaking majority among Alberta's non-Indian population, especially that north of Edmonton, remained intact. The *Census of the Three Provisional Districts of the North-West Territories 1884-85* showed that in the sub-district of Edmonton, one of three in the Provisional District of Alberta, there were 582 whites and 940 Métis of French racial origin out of a total non-Indian population of 2,599.[4] However, in the years after the Riel Rebellion the region's population began a slow but steady growth and most of this tended to be composed of English-speaking settlers attracted by the excellent agricultural possibilities of the Edmonton vicinity. Edmonton itself underwent a similar type of growth although a few of its new inhabitants were French-speaking, again mostly middle class men who engaged in construction or the retail trades. The clergy, aware that the French and Catholic majority was gradually being eroded, made every effort to make life in the new environment attractive to these new arrivals in the hope that this would in turn attract more of them. A new and larger Saint Joachim's Church was constructed in 1886 and in the same year a Mr. Saint-Cyr was hired to teach school on a regular basis. During 1883 this situation was improved upon when Bishop Grandin persuaded some of the Sisters of the Faithful Companions of Jesus to establish a convent and open a school in Edmonton. This success was followed by what the clergy regarded as the greatest victory to date -- the formation of Saint Joachim's Roman Catholic Separate School District, No. 7, after a petition was sent to the Educational Council at Regina by the town's Roman Catholic population.[5]

Although these measures made the area secure for Catholics, be they French or English, they did little to solve the problem of maintaining the French-speaking proportion of the population. A more far-reaching policy had to be pursued if the possibility of attaining that objective was to be entertained. Fortunately one policy that the clergy throughout the West had been attempting to implement, more or less unsuccessfully for the past twenty years, was finally beginning to bear fruit around 1890. This was organized French-Catholic colonization of the vast agricultural lands of the West, and it had been unsuccessful for three main reasons: (1) a general lack of confidence in the lands of the West probably caused by the reports of early failures who returned to Quebec and by the adverse reports circulated by the clergy prior to 1870 in an attempt to discourage colonization, thereby protecting the Indians and Métis from the conceptions of white society; (2) a feeling that it was not safe for a French-Canadian to live outside the Province of Quebec due mainly to the amnesty question after 1870 and later by the fate of Riel after 1885; (3) a feeling that by going from Quebec to live in Manitoba or the North-West Territories one was going into exile from one's own kind.[6] In spite of the fact that these attitudes were not easily dispelled, through persistence and hard work, the clergy had been fairly successful in eradicating them by 1890. This was largely accomplished by *les missionnaries-colonisateurs,* or colonization priests, who were stationed in Quebec and the eastern United States with the intention of disseminating information on the West and organizing prospective groups of colonists. Father Jean-Baptiste Morin, one such priest attached to the Canadian Immigration Bureau in Montreal, succeeded in organizing a group in 1891 after consulting with the local clergy and acquainting himself with the excellent agricultural opportunities to be had in the Edmonton-Saint Albert area. Since the most productive lands in the vicinity of the Saint Albert mission were already under cultivation this first group took up land immediately to the north in the area subsequently known as Morinville. Success in 1891 spurred Father Morin to even greater efforts in the following years and by 1894 he was able to report to the Department of the Interior that he had established several new French-Canadian agricultural colonies in the Edmonton district which could, including Edmonton itself, boast a total population of some 466 families comprised of 1,987 souls.[7] By 1899, when he retired, the total had increased to eight distinct colonies, with the opening up of the Rivière-qu-Barre, Legal, Beaumont, and Vegreville districts, containing some 620 families or 2,479 individuals.[8]

As in the case of Saint Joachim's in Edmonton the clergy serving these new colonies took on the functions of an elite leading the community in the maintenance of their French outlook. Indeed through their work in the local parish they made it their primary objective to minimize the difference between the old Quebec environment and the new western one, feeling that this would help protect their flocks. Although the outside influences were many, through the constant organization of religious and social activities at the parish level they were fairly successful. Part of this success stemmed from the utilization of every opportunity to encourage the traditional resistance of French-Canadians to assimilation through the integrating of religion and race consciousness. Examples of this were legion, but a particularly vivid one was provided in a speech by Bishop Langevin to French-Catholics assembled in Edmonton to celebrate the golden anniversary of Father Lacombe's ordination in September, 1899:

> Restez français, de coeur, de pensée, parlez votre belle langue francaise, conservez précieusement cette portion de notre héritage a nous légue par nos pères. La langue française est la langue des rois; le diplomates de tous les pays se réunissent-ils pour decider les questions politiques et internationales, c'est en français que les délibérations ont lieu.
>
> Parlez le francais non seulement dans vos relations d'affaires, mais aussi dans vos familles. Nous sommes un peuple qui a une mission à remplir sur ce continent, nous avons des traditions de foi et de langue, conservons-les et pour les conserver il faut marcher avec notre clergé la main dans la main. Qui dit canadien-français dit catholique et la prospérité nationale de notre fidélité à notre religion. "L'une ne va pas sans l'autre".[9]

Despite the unflagging efforts of the colonization priests and the local clergy it became increasingly more obvious as the decade of the nineties progressed that their efforts, be they aimed at bringing out new French-speaking colonists or attending to their needs once on the scene, were not in themselves sufficient to ensure preservation of the French identity in the area. The proportion of the French element in the total population continued to decline as the trickle of homesteaders onto the prairies at the decade's beginning turned to a veritable flood at its end with the implementations of the Laurier government's aggressive immigration policies. Soon the French-speaking population's predominant position to the north of Edmonton gave way to the English-speaking English-Irish-Scots group and was almost immediately to be threatened further by a massive influx of Europeans. Such a turn of events placed the French-speaking community in jeopardy from two directions, both internally and externally. On the one hand there was the possibility that as their numbers declined relatively there would be a corresponding tendency for them to falter in their racial consciousness and bé absorbed into a melting pot of English-speaking peoples. On the other hand the decline of their position from a pre-eminent one in the fur trade era to a minority one in the new agricultural situation could possibly lead to that old bugbear of French-Canadians, an assault on their cultural and religious rights. Given these circumstances it was obvious that the clergy could not bear the mantle of leadership alone for any length of time.

Fortunately, while the above developments were taking place, a non-religious segment of the elite was gradually beginning to emerge. Interestingly this was almost entirely an urban phenomenon with the Edmonton community providing its base, a circumstance which upon examination is not as strange as it, perhaps, may seem. As previously pointed out, a few French-speaking arrivals in Edmonton after 1880 had succeeded in establishing themselves in the town's slowly developing economic community, a pattern which continued until the decade of the nineties. At that time several new factors came into play which helped to accelerate and even broaden the scope of the French-speaking involvement in the town's life to the extent that they were soon well entrenched in its business and professional circles. Certainly the clergy's colonization policies played a role in this, as some of those brought out ostensibly as agricultural colonists actually came from educated, urban backgrounds and understandably wished to settle in the town. Another impetus for such people's appearance at this time was the Klondike gold rush which brought several French-Canadian business and professional men as far as Edmonton where they thought better of the fabulous stories of fortunes to be made in the Yukon and opted to remain where they were. Whatever their reasons for settling in Edmonton, and undoubtedly there were others, businessmen such as J.H. Gariépy, J.H. Picard, and P.E. Lessard as well as professional men such as Dr. Philippe Roy, Dr. Aristride Blais, Antonio Prince, Frederic Villeneuve, and Jean-L. Côté were well established by the turn of the century and had begun to come to the fore in all aspects of the promotion and protection of the French language and culture. This was not surprising since they possessed all the prerequisites for the formation of an elite similar to that then prevailing in Quebec's French-Canadian society. In addition to its religious sector, the clergy, the social category of the elite in Quebec also contained a non-religious sector evolving on one hand from the political leaders, which several of the aforementioned men were soon to become in Alberta, and on the other from professional men such as doctors and lawyers with many being members of both groups. Added to these were the businessmen of Quebec who towards the end of the nineteenth century had begun to acquire sufficient import-ance to be identified as a group in the elite producing process.[10]

As the Edmonton based elite began to emerge, their existence became manifest in their activities and the influence they wielded. To meet the internal threat of a decline in the community's racial consciousness it was quickly realized that the clergy would need support in keeping the population in close contact with one another and aware of their linguistic rights. One means of achieving this goal was through the establishment of a French language organization such as the popular Saint-Jean-Baptiste Society which had originated in Montreal in 1834. Its objec-tive was to bind the French-Canadian masses together with the elite and to awaken within the former a spirit of nationalism, exactly the combination which the leading lights of Edmonton's community realized was needed in their own situation. Not surprisingly, therefore, on April 8, 1894 *la Société Saint-Jean-Baptiste d'Edmonton* came into existence with the community's leaders firmly fixed in its executive positions. At the founding meeting the hope was expressed that the rural com-munities would follow the example and create their own societies and that these would in turn participate with the Edmonton group in an annual holiday which would be proclaimed every year on or about June 24, the feast day of Saint-Jean-Baptiste. This in fact did occur and a description in the *Edmonton Bulletin* of the first of these celebrations to be held showed the great enthusiasm with which they were greeted by members of the community:

> ...At an early hour the people began to arrive from a distance to take part in the procession. The Columbia Hotel of Joseph Brunelle at which the muster took place was decorated for the occasion with flags and evergreens. Promptly at 10 o'clock the procession started and moved along Jasper Avenue to Saint Joachim's Church in the following order: Major J. Brunelle mounted; Union Jack; Edmonton brass band in uniform; banner of the Fort Saskatchewan society between two mounted men; carriage with four mounted men carry-ing the emblem of the society, and a little boy -- the son of R. Duplessis -- holding aloft a cross with a lamb beside him. Then the flag of the Edmonton society followed by the members of the Society on foot. Then a carriage in which were the president, Georges Roy, vice-president, J.H. Gariépy and Mayor McCaulay and a number of other vehicles occupied by friends of the society, including a large proportion of ladies. Mass was celebrated in Saint Joachim's Church and the picnic is now in progress. Dance tonight at Robertson Hall.[11]

Once the Saint-Jean-Baptiste Society was well established, other measures to continue the process of keeping the community in touch and the rest of the population aware of the French-speaking presence in the area were undertaken by the elite. Perhaps the most noteworthy of these was the beginning of the French-language weekly newspaper *l'Ouest Canadien* in February 1898. Originally conceived by and published under the auspices of *la Société de la Colonisation d'Edmonton,* an organization created by Father Morin with the objective of promoting French-Catholic colonization of the Edmonton district, its influence soon outstripped its original goal of making known colonization prospects. Under the guidance of a management committee composed of Frederic Villeneuve, a young Edmonton lawyer; Joseph E. Laurencelle, the manager of the Banque Jacques Cartier in Edmonton; and Joseph Cartier, a well-known local accountant, its soon became the medium through which individuals could keep track of the social, economic, religious and political activities of the entire community. The paper achieved modest success under the editorship of Villeneuve until February 1900 when increasing financial difficulties finally forced it to cease publication. However, the value of such an organ was not lost on community leaders and it was not many years before a successor, *Le Courrier de l'Ouest,* took up the gauntlet in the French cause.

While the foregoing steps went a long way towards alleviating the internal threat to the community's existence, their significance in combatting the external threat imposed by its minority position were slight. In terms of protecting their cultural and religious rights, the French language, and separate schools, influence, and participation in politics and educational matters were of the utmost necessity. Here the clergy depended even more heavily on the lay elite to fill the breach and once more it tended to be the members of the Edmonton community who came to the fore.

The questions affecting the future of the entire French-speaking community would ultimately be decided in the field of politics and it was therefore not surprising that politics would quickly become a key factor in the emergence of the elite. At the local level it was felt that it was necessary to uphold the interests of the local community, and in Edmonton J.H. Picard provided an excellent example for the rural communities by first being elected to the Municipal Council of Edmonton in 1893 and serving, with only one brief interlude, until 1907 when he was defeated in a bid for the mayoralty. But it was in the councils of the Territorial Government where the real battles over French-Catholic rights were fought, rights which were basically embodied in three pieces of legislation. These three, *The North-West Territories Acts of 1875 and 1877* and a further ordinance respecting education in 1884, essentially guaranteed the right to separate schools and the right to have French used in the debates, records, journals, and ordinances of the North-West Territories Council and in proceedings before the Courts.[12] While this legislation was being respected the community could feel secure, but the moment it began to be undermined the need for vigorous political activity was immediately recognized.

In 1889 Dalton McCarthy proposed legislation in the federal Parliament aimed at abolishing the use of the French language in the North-West Territories. After bitter debate a compromise was reached in *The North-West Territories Amendment Act, 1891* which provided that after the next general election of the Legislative Assembly it could regulate its proceedings and the manner of recording and publishing them. Therefore, the election of 1891 marked the beginning of a crucial period in the attempts of the community to maintain what it felt were its legitimate rights, and Antonio Prince, a lawyer and a leading figure in the Edmonton community, decided to run in the constituency of Saint Albert. Prince campaigned on a platform of protection for the French language and separate schools and his victory over a local English-speaking candidate marked the inauguration of a trend which was to continually reappear in the political history of the French-speaking community of Alberta -- the election of a member of the elite of Edmonton's community to represent a predominantly French rural constituency.

In the course of the session of 1892 the need for a representative in the Legislative Assembly became increasingly apparent as Prince was called upon to take a stand on two issues of vital importance. These were Frederick Haultain's motion that the debates of the Legislative Assembly should be recorded and published only in the English language and an ordinance which provided for the replacement of the individual Protestant and Roman Catholic Board of Education by a Council of Public Instruction on which the denominational representatives had no vote. Prince moved amendments on both of these issues, but to no avail, and the remainder of his term of office was spent in attempting to have modifications made in these two pieces of legislation. He was unsuccessful and the despondency of the French-speaking voters in the constituency was such that Prince was defeated in the election of 1894 by an English candidate. It was not until 1898 that there was again a real awakening of interest in the community, probably at least partially due to the exhortations of the Saint-Jean-Baptiste Society and *l'Ouest Canadien.* At the Saint-Jean-Baptiste celebrations of 1898 a resolution was passed which resolved that it was the duty of French-Canadians to demand the publication of ordinances in French and a hope was expressed that a candidate would be elected to represent the French element of the population.[13] Shortly afterward Frederic Villeneuve, the lawyer-newspaper editor from Edmonton, was nominated to oppose the local candidate Dan Maloney in the election. Campaigning much in the same vein as had his predecessor Prince, Villeneuve concentrated on the issues of French and Catholic rights and was able to achieve a comfortable majority at the polls. During his years as a member the major piece of legislation was the Ordinance of 1901 which was found to be quite acceptable to the community as it stated that the schools were to be under the control of a Commissioner of Education assisted by an Educational Council of five persons, at least two of whom were to be Catholics. Most importantly, though, it allowed for a primary grade to be taught in French and for the hiring of those competent to teach it.[14]

Meanwhile, the question of provincial autonomy for Alberta and Saskatchewan was beginning to come to the fore and Villeneuve supported the idea provided that due consideration would be given to the rights of each segment of the population, a theme that remained the main contention of the French community throughout the struggle for provincial status. Villeneuve decided not to run in the election of May 1902 but his replacement in Saint Albert was the equally able L.J.A. Lambert who continued to fight for their historic rights in the forthcoming Autonomy Bills. In this endeavor he was vociferously backed by the Saint-Jean-Baptiste Society of Edmonton which in February 1904 sent a communication to Prime Minister Laurier urging that the government preserve the legitimate rights of French-Canadians and even going as far as to suggest that French should have official language status in the new province.[15] The eventual settlement of the Autonomy Bills crisis by Laurier's compromise of continuing the system then in force under the Ordinance of 1901 did not fulfil this hope but, on the whole, the French community realized that they were being fairly treated and accepted the Bills with good grace.[16]

Educational matters were held to be as vital as politics in the eyes of the community's leaders but, as is made evident by the foregoing, they were often so closely related as to be inextricable. However, apart from their political concern that the right to separate schools and the teaching of classes in French be upheld, the elite tried to ensure that the schools they did have were properly run. Such a goal entailed adequate representation on the School Board and again the Edmonton community provided an excellent example for their rural counterparts. Of the three original trustees on the Separate School Board in 1888 two of them, Georges Roy and Antonio Prince, adequately upheld the interests of the French community. This number of representatives became the community's goal in subsequent elections and it was reasonably successful in achieving it. In fact between 1901 and 1905 the two French-speaking trustees, J.H. Picard and J.H. Gariépy, were complemented by Lucien Dubuc, a young French-Canadian lawyer, who served as the Board's secretary.

By 1905, then, on the eve of the creation of the Province of Alberta, it is obvious that a well defined elite, both religious and lay, had emerged within the French-speaking community; that for very good reasons the lay segment of the elite was almost entirely drawn from the Edmonton community's members; and that in spite of some fairly substantial odds against it the elite had been largely successful in maintaining the community's identity and protecting its rights. It now remains to briefly examine the elite during the period from 1905 to the outbreak of the First World War when both it and the community it represented reached their apogee.

As in the past the elite continued to retain both its internal and external functions during the 1905 to 1914 period. Internally the parish remained the focal point of community life with the clergy continuing to promote the traditional forms of religious and social contact. Supporting and aiding these efforts were the Saint-Jean-Baptiste Society and a plethora of new social-religious groups which made their appearance during these years. Included among these were: *l'Alliance Nationale* and *les Artisans Canadiens-français*, both parts of Quebec federative groups designed to unify the moral and material interests of all French-Catholics in America; *l'Association Catholique de la Jeunesse Canadienne-française*, an organization for the community's youth; *le Cercle 'Jeanne d'Arc,'* an Edmonton based dramatic society; and *le Club National* and *l'Union Française de l'Alberta*, both loosely formed benevolent groups. With this proliferation of organizations there were inevitably those who began to envisage a general organization of the entire French-speaking population of the province. This idea was first expressed in a resolution of the Saint-Jean-Baptiste Society of Edmonton in May 1909, calling for a convention of all the French-Canadians of Alberta on June 24, 1910. Although the general convention was not held on that date a preliminary assembly took place and it set up an organizational committee to explore further action. Thus the proposed general convention would undoubtedly eventually have been held had it not been for the appearance of a new organization in 1911 which largely usurped its proposed role. This organization known as *la Société du Parler Français au Canada* had been founded in Quebec in 1902 but was not until 1911 that an attempt was made to enrol western groups in order that they might participate in a convention of all French-Canadians to be held in Quebec in 1912. Throughout Alberta's French-speaking districts there was tremendous enthusiasm for this convention and during a meeting held at Edmonton in May 1912, parish delegates from across the province elected Wilfrid Gariepy, an Edmonton lawyer, as their representative to it. Although no concrete results were achieved at the Quebec convention, *la Société du Parler Français* continued to hold an annual convention in Alberta. Eventually it might even have achieved the creation of a provincial organization had not the exigencies of the First World War intervened and caused its demise. As it transpired it was not until July 1926 that the work of an organizational committee appointed at a convention of Franco-Albertans held in December 1925 and attended by 400 delegates culminated in the creation of a truly provincial body, *l'Association Canadienne-Française de l'Alberta* (A.C.F.A.).[17]

In terms of the lay elite the great increase in the number of organizations provided a fertile field for their further development as leaders in the community. The membership lists of the above-named organizations showed that the same group of men were constantly being called upon or were volunteering to fill the executive offices. Such was particularly the case with respect to the most popular and important groups; the Saint-Jean-Baptiste Society, *la Société du Parler Français* and later *l'Association Canadienne-Française de l'Alberta;* whose executive lists read like a social register of the French-speaking population. In fact the Saint-Jean-Baptiste Society gave tacit admission to its elitist outlook in 1908 when it inserted in its constitution a clause calling for the appointment of an honorary president who was "le Canadien-francais de la Province ayant la position sociale le plus élévée."[18]

Apart from their support of the clergy's attempts to reinforce community identity through their work in these various organizations, the lay elite provided aid in an area of concern that had formerly been left entirely to the clergy to deal with, that of colonization. Of course, *les missionnaires-colonisateurs* remained as the primary agents of promotion and organization, but as time progressed they received very welcome assistance through the personal efforts of other community members. Some took upon themselves the task of promoting Alberta during the course of their numerous travels to Quebec, the eastern United States, and France. Similarly, those who controlled the French language press devoted the columns of their newspapers to the cause of French-Catholic colonization. On one occasion

Le Courrier de l'Ouest, initiated by Dr. Philippe Roy and P.E. Lessard in 1905, published 1,500 extra copies of a colonization special issue and distributed them free to the major French-speaking centres of the United States.[19] To second these individual efforts a new organization *la Société de la Colonisation de l'Alberta* was created in 1912 under the direction of J.H. Picard, P.E. Lessard, and L.A. Giroux. Immediately this organization set to work to create an information office and in February 1913, *le Bureau de la Colonisation de l'Alberta,* located on Edmonton's Jasper Avenue, opened its doors. Overall the efforts by both segments of the elite resulted in the appearance of several new colonies, particularly in the Saint Paul-Bonnyville region, and substantial increases in the French-speaking population of the province. According to the *Census of the Prairie Provinces, 1916* there were 24,286 people of French origin out of a total population of 496,525[20], although this again represented a substantial percentage decrease from the previous census.

Because of this continuing decrease, the external threat to the community's existence remained a very real consideration and necessitated a redoubling of the elite's efforts in the protection of its rights. As previously the closely related fields of politics and education continued to demand the most attention and correspondingly produced the most obvious results. In provincial politics the French community made the best possible political choice upon the creation of the province in its predominantly staunch support of the Liberals, who formed the first government. Support stemmed from a feeling that the Liberals would best maintain their rights, from loyalty to Laurier as a French-Canadian and upholder of the French position in the Manitoba schools question and the Autonomy Bills, and from the astute realization that identification with the strongest party held the best hope for the future. In return for their loyalty the community expected the government to include a French-speaking representative in the Cabinet whenever possible, a stipulation the government was apparently willing to accept as it made verbal promises to that effect.[21]

To a great degree the representatives during this period tended to be, like their predecessors in the Legislative Assembly of the North-West Territories, members of the Edmonton elite representing predominantly French rural constituencies. None were elected in the first provincial election of 1905 but by 1909 the community was better organized politically and succeeded in gaining two members, P.E. Lessard and Lucien Boudreau. Representation reached its peak in the election of 1913 when five French-speaking M.L.A.s were elected to the 56 seat house. The five, all Liberals, included P.E. Lessard in Saint Paul, Wilfrid Gariépy in Beaver River, Jean-L. Côté in Grouard, Lucien Boudreau in Saint Albert, and J.G. Turgeon in Ribstone. The promised Cabinet appointment first went to P.E. Lessard who became Minister Without Portfolio in October 1909 and later on to Wilfrid Gariépy who received the portfolio of Minister of Municipal Affairs in December 1913.

Even though the representatives in the provincial Legislature were highly successful, the dominant political personality of the community was Dr. Philippe Roy. Roy, a graduate of Laval University, had come to Edmonton in 1898 and had soon built up a thriving medical practice. Intensely interested in politics, he had played a major part in the organization of the Liberal Party of Alberta and had been suitably rewarded in September 1905 with his appointment as Senator representing Northern Alberta. He retained this position until May 1911 at which time he was named to the important post of Commissioner-General of Canada in Paris. The prestige of his position as a Senator made him the most influential and respected member of the entire Franco-Albertan community, a fact which he realized and attempted to put to good use. Constantly underscoring his many speeches to the French population were the twin themes of the necessity of their taking positive political action to gain and protect their rights and the necessity of close relations with the rest of the population, particularly in the political sense, so that they would accept the community's ideas. Many of the elite, heeding his suggestions, served on the executives of the Edmonton and Alberta Liberal Associations and eventually created their own vehicle, *le Club Laurier,* to represent the community as a separate entity within the ranks of the Liberal party.[22]

Attesting to the effectiveness of the community's political representation was the fact that throughout the entire 1905 to 1914 period not one major issue regarded as being prejudicial to French-speaking Catholics came to the fore. Of course, education continued to be the main area of concern, and at the beginning of the war the rights guaranteed in the Autonomy Bills remained intact. In fact in 1914 these rights were actually enhanced when it was announced by the Minister of Education that under certain circumstances teaching diplomas from Quebec would be recognized in Alberta schools.[23]

Another development in education which was regarded as a significant victory was the appearance of a truly bilingual educational institution in Edmonton. The idea of building a bilingual classical college had first come to light in 1904 but it was not until the Jesuit priest Father T. Hudon arrived in the city in 1912 to begin construction of a Jesuit College that the community's hopes were realized. Largely financed through the monetary pledges of the elite, the college was completed in 1913 and classes begun with 40 students divided into four elementary classes, two each in English and French.[24] The creation of this college fulfilled a real need in the Franco-Albertan community since parents who desired their children to have a classical education in the French language no longer had to send them east, which many could not afford. In addition it was felt that the college would become a training ground for the elite who would lead the community in the future, a bit of foresight which would ultimately prove true.

Before leaving the subject of the elite's attempts to protect the community's rights one further though much less obvious aspect of them must be examined. This is the effect that their social and business contacts with influential members of the English-speaking community had on the course of events. Particularly in the case of the earlier French-speaking inhabitants of Edmonton, there tended to be active social exchanges with "important" English-speaking residents and some members of the community attained exalted positions in "society" circles. Similarly the ties of marriage went a long way towards bridging the gap between French and English and during these years marriages between members of the elite and

English women of noteworthy families became fairly common. An excellent example was the marriage of Dr. Philippe Roy to Helen Young, daughter of one of the leading Hudson's Bay Company men in Edmonton, through which he established ties with the McDougall and Lougheed families. Equally important as liaisons established on the social level were those forged through contact in business and professional affairs. Many prominent French-speaking businessmen were partners with some of the province's leading financiers in the large-scale real estate, resource, and industrial developments that were common to the age. At the professional level many French-speaking doctors and lawyers were partners in some of the most prestigious medical and legal practices existing in the city. While the direct results of such contacts are rather intangible it is certain that at the least they went a long way towards eradicating ignorance of the French community's aspirations among an important segment of the English community and at the best convinced them that these aspirations were legitimate.

It has not been the intention of this study to deny the existence of nor disparage the role of the leaders of the individual local French-speaking communities of Alberta. As pointed out the parish priests were a major influence, and it is undeniable that in certain situations there were local people who played a very active part in the fight for the French cause. But it is also undeniable that as a rule the rural population tended to look to the elite of the Edmonton community for their examples and for the leadership at the levels where the future would necessarily be decided. For their part the elite could count upon the rural population to act as a sort of ethnic hinterland from which they could draw support when the need arose. Generally speaking, there tended to be very little democracy attached to this situation as the elite rarely asked for guidance in the path they should follow towards their ultimate goals and the general populace rarely offered any advice, trusting that their leaders knew the best way to achieve them. Of course, neither this situation nor the position achieved by the Franco-Albertan community prior to World War I could last indefinitely. For reasons which are beyond the scope of this study both the elite and the community as a whole entered into a period of decline following the war. However, it was not a decline to oblivion as is witnessed by the fact that even to the present day the elite has played an important part in the life of the community and the community in the life of Alberta.

Farm Politics in an Urban Age: The Decline of the United Farmers of Alberta After 1921

Carl F. Betke

Certain recent articles on the role of the metropolis in Canadian history have emphasized fundamental differences between "town and country," or the metropolis and the hinterland.[1] These articles may reflect a Canadian (though not uniquely Canadian) preoccupation with the contrast between old (interpreted as rural) and new (interpreted as urban) Canadian social organization or, in other words, with what appears to be a process of urbanization in Canada. A view of the farmer's place in society which exhibits an awareness of the urban features of early twentieth century North America can be discovered in the thought of one Canadian agrarian leader, Alberta's Henry Wise Wood. Wood transcended the simple town-country dichotomy in his own more sophisticated characterization of farmers as only one economic group among several, farmers happening to require spacious land area as most others do not. His ideas would accord well with an expanded interpretation of urbanization as the necessity for humanity to resolve potential and real inter-individual and inter-group conflicts in favor of the increasingly complex community of economic specialists, who must of course share their unique contributions in order to maintain their life-styles.[2] Wood's social analysis was, however, only imperfectly translated into a practical plan of independent political action for farmers, largely because, as he correctly believed, farmers could not make public policy independently of related, even if sometimes conflicting, interests. If his own social philosophy was more or less correct, then the political theory on which he campaigned during 1921 was impossible of implementation, as he was quick to acknowledge.

Direct political intercession was nevertheless wildly popular among Alberta farmers in the immediate post-First World War period, leading Wood to devise his proposal for "group government" to legitimize the political effort. That Wood's ideas could not work has been noted at length;[3] that they were temporarily popular, though, demonstrates an aspect of urbanization -- responses to perceived lack of benefit from urban interrelations -- which makes the appeal of Aberhart in 1935, not only to farmers, fascinatingly comprehensible. The United Farmers of Alberta organization was not, as one student falsely infers from incomplete statistics, suddenly replaced in popularity by that of Social Credit in 1935.[4] The decline of the U.F.A. actually took place in the early 1920s, despite the persistence of a U.F.A. government between 1921 and 1935, and in the nature of that decline may be found some explanation for the political success of Social Credit during the depression. It is true that Aberhart in 1935 spoke to all Albertans while Wood in 1921 reserved his message for farmers alone, yet in another respect they were similar: both appealed to the economically disenchanted, those who seemed to gain no benefit from the network of urban specialists. On the other hand, the nature of the U.F.A. decline made it impossible for the U.F.A. government to regain the political support of economically disenchanted farmers in 1935, for it had long since given up representing only the aggrieved among the farming population, dedicating itself instead to the maintenance of successful urban integration. By the mid-1920s the U.F.A. government had firmly rejected Wood's recommendation of stubborn farmer solidarity in politics in favor of the implications of his social theory: that modern urban society required a balance of a multitude of interests, among whom farmers represented only one.

I

Henry Wise Wood's concept of government was developed after national events in 1918 undermined his original efforts to keep Alberta farmers free of direct political activity. For a farmer to be active in a political party representing members of all or several economic groups would be, thought Wood, to disperse his energy in premature support of interests opposed to the farmer's and, therefore, to deaden his impact. Far better that farmers should concentrate on unity, man with man to form a local union, and local with local to support a central organization narrowly representative of the farmers' consolidated voice. Far better that farmers should continue the traditional U.F.A. practice of exerting lobby pressure upon governments, an approach consistent with Wood's notion that social order depended upon strong expression of each of a number of economic interests, including those of finance, labor and professionals as well as agriculture. The first aim was respect for farmers as for other groups; the ultimate aim through mutual respect was "an equilibrium of interests."[5]

But the substantial response stimulated among Alberta farmers by a new "Farmers' Platform" (known as the "New National Policy") issued by the Canadian Council of Agriculture in November 1918[6] forced Wood, if he was to sustain the unanimity of the province's farmers, to translate his concept of economic group organization into political terms. If the U.F.A. was to enter politics, he pointed out,

> the solidarity of our organization must be maintained, its strength increased, and its thought mobilized....For this reason I would strongly advise that the U.F.A. be the only door through which admission can be had to our political organization.

Those engaged in other than farming enterprises might vote with them, and cooperation was not ruled out, but only after election of special farmer representatives, so as not to confuse the group's principles. "The first stage of democratic organization," he reminded, "is to bring the individuals of a group together in organization. The second stage is to gradually [sic] bring the several organized groups together toward cooperation."[7] Throughout 1919 Wood's views rapidly won favor within the U.F.A. despite some minority opposition.[8] At the same time membership totals increased at an astonishing rate, from 18,000 in 1918 to 28,784 in 1919 and over 32,000 in 1920.[9] The scope of U.F.A. activities expanded at a similar rate,[10] the developing spirit of agrarian unity coinciding with the approach of the 1921 provincial election.

During the ensuing campaign, new U.F.A. constituency organizations conducted their own affairs, but with the help of a suggested "Reconstructive Legislative Program" supplied for use at their discretion by a special U.F.A. central committee. The accompanying "Declaration of Principles" of the U.F.A. placed blame for many of the unsettled conditions on the political institutions, so vulnerable to control by a powerful few, and declared the best system for representation of all individual citizens to be "the vehicle of systematically organized groups." The U.F.A. was therefore taking the first step toward that reorganization of society:

> We are a group of citizens going into political action as an organization. Our elected representatives are at all times answerable to the organization. Each elected representative is answerable directly to the organization in the constituency that elected him.[11]

The basis of the U.F.A. campaign was this proposal of instructed delegation, with government administration, in the ideal situation, to be conducted by a selected number of legislators chosen proportionally from all economic groups represented.[12] Materials printed by the U.F.A. included far more copies of pamphlets entitled "Co-operation Between [sic] Organized Democratic Groups" and "How Groups function in Manitoba Legislature" than of anything else.[13]

Such an approach was roundly criticized by the Liberal press. Farmers were urged to open their eyes and realize that the U.F.A. stood for "Bolshevik" organization, whereas the Liberal administration had given the farmers continuously good service. The *Edmonton Bulletin* unleashed vitriolic attacks on a number of imported speakers (including J.S. Woodsworth) as "Bolshevik spellbinders" who would deliver the farmers' property to be administered "by a Soviet under the Lenin system." At the same time the *Bulletin* took comfort from the fact that "no very emphatic criticism is being offered as to the manner in which the affairs of the province are being conducted by the Stewart administration."[14] The *Lethbridge Herald* was assured that "with all that the Stewart government has done in the interests of the farmer, the 'U.F.A. over all,' in what appears to be the present attitude in the holding of conventions to name candidates to oppose the government, is not one which will find general favour." The editor of the *Vegreville Observer* thought he had found the fallacy of the U.F.A. approach:

> ...this article is not aimed at the United Farmers of Alberta, a strong organization, which in its economic and social sense has proven its

worth. It is aimed at what appears to us to be the impracticable theory that the political activities of the organization can be successfully conducted under a plan which has its bedrock in selfishness.

Furthermore, if a candidate "places his resignation in the hands of any committee whatsoever, he ceases immediately to be a member of the constituency and is a member for that committee only."[15] Unfortunately for the *Observer,* what was meant to be a telling blow was only an accurate appraisal of the attraction the U.F.A. program held for most farmers, particularly during a time of economic difficulty.

Meanwhile U.F.A. and Labor candidates ran mutually supportive campaigns. The Labor candidates appeared especially anxious to identify themselves with the U.F.A., going so far as to sponsor an advertisement in the *Edmonton Journal* announcing "The Labor U.F.A. Candidates" and claiming that "the next Government will be a Farmer-Labor Government."[16] The U.F.A., for their part, emphasized the principle of co-operation between the farmer and Labor candidates *after* their election. Wood softened his attitude only very slightly, allowing that the non-farmer should be permitted to join the U.F.A. "if his viewpoint is known to be in harmony with ours, but if it is not in harmony with ours, the only object he could have in trying to come through the door would be to do the organization harm."[17] The U.F.A. left little doubt about the identity of the enemy in this farmer crusade: a *Western Independent* cartoon showed the burden of "Profiteer," "Grit," and "Tory" held dangling over a cliff by a rope supported by "Middle Class Worker," "Farmer," and "Labor", with the "Organized Farmer" about to axe the supporting cord and exclaiming gleefully, "It's time to drop 'em, Boys!"[18]

The result, of course, was that U.F.A. candidates polled over 62 percent of the vote in the rural ridings in which they campaigned, with the shocking consequence that 38 novice farmer legislators commanded a majority in the 61 seat Assembly.[19] It was at this point that the wisdom of Wood's original concept of modern social organization became obvious at the expense of his political formula. How could the government of Alberta be conducted on the basis of occupational group meetings in the legislature? The 1921 federal census lists for Alberta substantial employment in each of the following major categories and more: business owners, managers, foremen, factory laborers, miners, office employees, farm owners, farm laborers, tradesmen, construction workers, transportation employees, wholesale and retail merchants, salespersons, financiers (including insurance and real estate salesmen), government and other service employees, including assorted professionals.[20] Farmers were in the ascendancy, to be sure, but how could the other significant contributors to the Alberta economy be represented adequately by "group government" when farmers so clearly dominated the legislature and most other groups were completely without representation? Farmers had enthusiastically espoused Wood's political doctrines because they emphasized the proud isolation of farmers in difficult times, a stance which could only be symbolically sustained in an election campaign, not practically embodied in the government of a successful urban society. U.F.A. leaders scarcely questioned the normal parliamentary requirement that a cabinet be formed from the majority caucus in the legislature.[21]

Significantly, support for the parent organization dwindled rapidly. Several factors may have contributed. For one thing, it is possible to argue that election fever sustained exceptionally great agrarian interest in 1921 which simply dropped off with the passing of the elections.[22] For another, the economic situation of Alberta farmers, which had worsened drastically after 1918,[23] improved for many after 1921. And thirdly, the formation of the Alberta Wheat Pool in mid-1923 may have had far-reaching effects. There can be no doubt that the attraction held for farmers by co-operative marketing pools dispersed their energies over a wider field of organizational interests than had been the case previously and, insofar as they were successful, the pools rendered membership in the U.F.A. less necessary. In 1924 a Livestock Pool, a Dairy Pool, and an Egg and Poultry Pool supplemented the operations of the Wheat Pool in Alberta, while the 1923 and 1924 membership in all branches of the U.F.A. sank to around 15,000.[24]

At the same time, though, the style of the U.F.A. government was to recognize implicitly the urban nature of Alberta society, in which every moderately success-ful participant was happily interdependent with an array of other specialists. The U.F.A. administration made its decisions on the basis of expert advice, referring regularly to the trust which farmers must necessarily place in such traditionally alien authorities as financiers. During the early 1920s, however, a substantial portion of the farming population continued to press complaints. In the frame-work of Wood's theory of economic groups, the dissatisfied element might be characterized as that continuing to perceive no benefit from the interdependence. Prior to the 1921 election, that fragment had included the majority of Alberta farmers; after the election, it would have been surprising indeed had satisfaction been abrupt. In the early 1920s the U.F.A. government worked to reconcile farmers to the realities of an urban age, but this process also eliminated the U.F.A. as a political mouthpiece for any future dislocated group of failing agriculturalists. The U.F.A. in government ceased to have the Woodsian estranged agrarian image and began immediately to display its commitment to urban integration.

II

No sooner did Herbert Greenfield occupy the Premier's office than he was besieged by resolutions from U.F.A. branches. The most persistent badgering came from southern Alberta. A typical resolution read:

> Whereas this district has gone through five years of Drought placing many people in a destitute condition and whereas something has to be done immediately to alleviate the hardships that are inevitable, therefore be it resolved that Haig Local U.F.A. petition the Provincial Government to assist the people either in giving work on the roads in our municipality or relief, and it is important that something be done immediately.[25]

The U.F.A. central executive, too, seemed initially prepared to exact results of its newly elected government: its members wished an immediate investigation of the effect of current high freight rates on agriculture and other industries, to be followed by appropriate representations to the Board of Railway Commissioners.[26] One U.F.A. local member telegraphed rather overexpectantly: "U.F.A. Stock yards completely destroyed by Fire Need $4000 to rebuild at once Wire reply."[27] There was, in short, considerable feeling that as the organized farmers had elected their special representatives to the legislature, they now had a right to expect some direct special benefits from those representatives. Some U.F.A. adherents were persuaded that U.F.A. representatives ought to secure the best possible conditions for the farmers of their constituencies, without regard for any other section of the population.

The U.F.A. legislators did not entirely share that opinion, preferring the broader philosophy "that city men should represent the cities and farmers the rural sections, all meeting together at the legislature in a business way to draft legislation applicable to all..."[28] Such dedication to co-operation between farmers and non-farmers failed to dispel every confusion, though, about the ideal relationship between the backbenchers and the cabinet. Many backbenchers continued to believe that their voting decisions should not be "controlled" in advance by the cabinet through the use of group caucuses. Co-operation should be voluntary. Alex Moore, member for Cochrane, created a sensation on the very first day of the 1922 session of the legislature by taking exception to the selection of O.L. McPherson as Speaker. After Greenfield, seconded by Attorney-General Brownlee, had nominated McPherson, Moore, seconded by Samuel Brown, nominated J.S. Stewart, Independent Conservative member for Lethbridge. Stewart declined the nomination, thereby averting a potentially critical situation for the government, but Moore regretted Stewart's decision. He had no doubt that McPherson would be a good Speaker, but he claimed the support of at least half a dozen U.F.A. backbenchers in objecting "to the machine of government selecting a speaker and asking the private members merely to act as its rubber stamp."[29] He was to continue to insist on the integrity of each farmer representative in the decisions reached in the legislature.

Moore made another attempt to resurrect the governmental principles of the U.F.A. election campaign when, seconded by Russell Love (U.F.A. member for Wainwright), he proposed an exact replica of a 1920 motion by two dissident Liberals. At the time declared out of order by the Speaker, the 1920 motion had resolved that an adverse vote on a government measure was not sufficient reason for the government's resignation, unless the motion be one of direct want of confidence. Moore's reiteration of the motion remained on the order sheet from February 17 until March 3, while the U.F.A. members apparently discussed it among themselves. Finally, on March 3, with Moore's motion still on the order sheet, a substitute motion sponsored by N.S. Smith and seconded by G.A. Forster replaced it, making a significant change. According to the substitute motion, the government should not "be bound" to resign in the event of an adverse vote; the implication, of course, was that it should not be expected to carry on either, contrary to the intent of Moore's original motion. Greenfield stated during the debate that it would probably be plain when the government lacked the confidence of the assembly and that he meant to live up to the traditions of British parliamentary procedure.[30] The very motion calculated eventually to eliminate the government's dependence on the caucus system was thus evaded by the government's judicious use of caucus discussions.

But other private members apparently still felt it their duty to express in the legislature whatever sincere criticisms of government policies they had, rather than to confine their remarks to support for every government proposal. Caucus meetings proved distasteful to members reared on scathing denunciations of the corruption inherent in such a means of controlling representatives' performances in the interest of government solidarity. The climactic episode came when a Dairymen's Bill, introduced by George Hoadley in his role as Minister of Agriculture, passed third reading without difficulty, only to arouse at that inopportune moment the protests of certain U.F.A. backbenchers. C.O.F. Wright, U.F.A. member for Ribstone, rejected the Speaker's decision that the bill had passed and called for a vote. The hitherto silent Liberal opposition members were perfectly willing to support the dissident U.F.A. faction. When the vote was called, only the support of the five Labor and Independent members saved the government from defeat.[31]

The U.F.A. ministers had no desire to experience repetition of this unsettling incident and a meeting of the U.F.A. group was called to discuss future procedure. Attorney-General Brownlee, at the request of Greenfield, explained the government's position. Each member, he declared, had the right to vote as his conscience dictated when a question was before the house, but the government had no wish to be embarrassed in introducing a bill which did not have the general support of the U.F.A. membership. Therefore caucus meetings would be valuable to determine the attitude of the membership; if members were opposed to a proposition, the government would not introduce it in the house. This explanation proved acceptable to most, particularly as some had already realized that any unforeseen U.F.A. dissension in the house was certain to prompt a concerted effort by political opponents to embarrass the government and its supporters.[32] It was generally accepted that individual representative integrity in the legislature without prior U.F.A. consultation was unworkable in the presence of determined opposition by disciplined political parties. Thereafter, private meetings of the U.F.A. group were standard procedure, and the disillusioned consoled themselves with the assurance that these meetings were "conferences" or "legislative U.F.A. local gatherings" for the airing of opinions rather than for the repression of individual wills. In any event they were sure that the business of government administration was being kept entirely separate from political affairs in the constituencies and that the government therefore could have no ulterior motives for overruling decisions of backbenchers.[33]

After this agreement upon an amicable line of procedure, there were still occasions on which isolated criticisms were expressed by individual U.F.A. members in the house, but none threatened to develop into a defeat of the government. Divisions would commonly be ironed out before bills appeared in the house or insolubly contentious issues would not appear at all. Deviations in debate caused scarcely a ripple of concern and soon ceased to occur.

J.C. Buckley was presently identifiable as the government "ship," functioning similarly to his counterparts in the traditional political parties.[34] The cabinet would not again be disconcertingly surprised by its supporters in the legislature, and would therefore not risk the undermining of judicious policies by legislative demonstrations of peculiar local agrarian demands.

III

The elimination of embarrassing agrarian independence from public legislative debate was accompanied by a gradual decline in the frequency of attempts by individual farmers outside the legislature to influence government policy. As a result of U.F.A. election rhetoric, many U.F.A. adherents originally believed the new government would respond without question to instructions from its legitimate supporters. In 1921 and 1922, and to a reduced extent in 1923, the government was deluged with resolutions from U.F.A. local unions and letters from individual paid-up members. Almost all of these petitions were from farmers in trouble; that is, farmers for whom the cabinet's dedication to co-operation among the variety of economic contributors appeared not to be working, farmers with little or no stake in the existing economic integration. By far the greatest volume of correspondence dealt with solutions proposed for the plight of farmers in areas of southern Alberta, where crops had been repeatedly stricken by drought. The farmers had discussed their favorite remedies for this dilemma for years; here finally was a government elected to respond to their desires.

The preceding Liberal government had years previously instituted a policy of relief to destitute farmers, and one of Greenfield's first moves was to have a Provincial Director of Relief appointed to oversee the continuing program.[35] Many farmers, however, sought a more drastic solution. The Chinook U.F.A. local was only one of many to insist "that the Government of Alberta be asked to protect the farmers in the dried out areas from foreclosure by mortgage companies, from judgments and seizures for debts until the fall of 1922....[and] from having lands forfeited under tax sale proceedings." Appeals were frequently made on the assumption that "we look to you as Farmer Premier, put into power through the efforts of our U.F.A. to do something and do it quick to protect a large percentage of the agricultural classes from utter ruin."[36] Should the government fail to extend the redemption period on farms seized in lieu of 1920 and 1921 tax payments, warned W.C. Smith, M.L.A. for Redcliff, "you will hit our U.F.A. movement in Redcliff constituency a blow, the bad effects of which should not be underestimated." Smith had himself been inundated with letters from constituents who expected a stay in proceedings.[37] The financial situations of some farmers became more critical as the winter progressed. The Coronation U.F.A. Provincial Political Association unanimously carried a resolution declaring that as "we must have help if we are going to carry on, therefore be it resolved that this convention demand that the Provincial Government declare a moratorium [on taxes and mortgage company foreclosures] to take effect immediately and until after the House meets."[38]

The government naturally preferred to investigate more constructive possibilities, such as the extensive planting of fall rye in dried-out areas.[39] Government leaders were not prepared to alienate loan and mortgage companies by peremptorily issuing orders which might have the effect of jeopardizing all rural credit. Nor did they feel financially strong enough to provide cheaper credit by implementation of the 1917 Farm Loan Act. Instead Hoadley, Brownlee, and Provincial Treasurer R.G. Reid were despatched to Calgary in September for conferences with representatives of banks and mortgage companies in a co-operative effort to find some arrangement by which the fullest possible leniency could be shown to farmer debtors in bad circumstances because of crop failures. Greenfield was prepared to accept that the financiers were demonstrating a fair attitude; they were fully aware, he thought, that the eventual success of farmer debtors was their only redeemable asset. A moratorium on debt liability, in the opinion of the government, "should only be established as a last resort. Experience has shown that the effects of a moratorium are not good." The government would go only so far as to press leniency on the part of creditors and judges.[40]

For the time being the 1921 crop failure in south-eastern Alberta forced the government to continue the previous administration's relief policy, however reluctantly. In late October the provincial government entered into an agreement with the federal government to share the cost of provisions and fuel to be advanced by the provincial government to needy settlers owning or holding land under entry from the dominion of Canada.[41] The resulting relief work involved municipal officials, the Red Cross, and even volunteer assistance by U.F.A. and U.F.W.A. local unions.

Because provincial authorities were not finding it easy to collect on advances made during the previous winter, the government was eager to find a more satisfactory alternative. As early as September some sort of government sponsored survey of the situation was anticipated. On November 22 an Order-in-Council appointed a four-member survey board, chaired by C.A. Magrath, to study the drought problem in Southern Alberta and to recommend solutions. Public hearings were held at Medicine Hat, Lethbridge, Enchant, Macleod, Youngstown, Hanna, and Jenner in late November and December. Informal conferences were also held with committees of the Canadian Bankers' Association and the Dominion Mortgage and Investments Association and with officers of member banks and companies. The board's report, submitted on January 21, 1922, included recommendations for continued provincial government guarantee of advances for purchase of seed grain, cautious assistance to irrigation projects, agricultural education for the young and dissemination of information about better dry-farming techniques. It did not recommend any drastic interference by the government with the financial affairs of farmers, referring only briefly to alleged cases of inequitable taxation.[42]

It was not, therefore, calculated to draw accolades from the more desperate farmers, who were suspicious from the start. Even before the board initiated its study the Brutus and Blue Grass U.F.A. Locals (at Alderson) were apprehensive lest hearings be held in places relatively inaccessible to most farmers; it was, indeed, more important to them to be assured of immediate assistance to the needy than of a survey. They held a stormy meeting. One member reported

that "some of our supporters and very strong members are commencing to
ponder as to whether we really worked in our best interests in changing Govt.,"
as their urgent demands for road relief work, food and fuel relief, and a moratorium on foreclosures were apparently largely ignored. In a more pertinent criticism, the Medicine Hat U.F.A. District Association expressed concern at the
lack of farmers on the board and recommended a substitute commission of
"elected members" from the defined drought area. One U.F.A. local hoped
at least one practical farmer would be added to the board, since "a representative of one class is unable to truly represent other classes...." Still others
were irritated that bank managers rather than municipal or U.F.A. organizations were asked to prepare the lists of farmers to give evidence. Clearly the
venture lacked that "almost universal commendation" claimed for it by Greenfield; just as obviously was universal rather than narrowly agrarian commendation
the goal.[43]

The 1922 session of the legislature indicated to farmers which solutions to
farming difficulties the government was prepared to implement. A new "Tax
Recovery Act" to replace that of 1919 was not accompanied by any extension
of the temporary suspension on land tax recovery procedures. The Liberal
government's suspension until April 1, 1922 in the old act was merely tran-
ferred to the new act. Legislation to provide for another year of the traditional
government guarantees to creditors on behalf of farmers seeking advances to
obtain seed grain and the necessities of life was supplemented by the "Drought
Area Relief Act" which would continue in effect until June 1,1923. The measure
permitted the Lieutenant-Governor-in-Council to define an area excessively affected
by drought which would receive the attention of a commissioner. This official
would have the power to adjust financial affairs between creditor and debtor in
order to ease the farmer's burden in an arrangement still satisfactory to the finan-
cier. In addition the indebted farmer would be permitted to arrange for up to
$500 worth of seed, twine, farm labor, food and clothing in return for the right to
first claim on the coming crop.[44] In debate on this measure in the legislature it
was referred to as a "semi-moratorium."[45]

These remedies, designed to assist not only farmers but also creditors, were in-
sufficient for a great many farmers who continued to bombard the government
with their petitions for immediate relief of one kind or another. One suggestion
struck a sympathetic chord in the administation. A growing number of farmers
felt that the southeastern part of Alberta had been given more than a fair trial
for agricultural enterprise, and that it was time for the government to abandon
efforts there and to relocate settlers elsewhere.[46] These farmers were quite
bitter that the government relief program had created a number of parasites
who exhibited every intention to subsist indefinitely on the relief roll with no
endeavor ever to repay the advances.[47] The provincial government was particularly sensitive to this allegation but, burdened with years of accumulated debt,
naturally felt that the dominion government must at least share the responsibility
for any permanent relocation of settlers. As an interim measure, the feasibility
of having demands for harvest help in other parts of Alberta supplied from the

drought area was studied, without very encouraging findings. While the government turned to negotiate with Ottawa, indications of yet another crop failure for the 1922 season increased the urgency of requests to move. By early August the Alberta government had made an arrangement under which the dominion government would grant a second right to file for a homestead upon the recommendation of the provincial government. But it was the end of September before the provincial government, the dominion government, and the C.P.R. were able to agree on a formula to divide equally the cost of transportation of farmers relocating in Alberta.[48] The delay, that is to say, was caused by the necessity for negotiations to involve not just the provincial government and farmers, but also additional interested parties. Farmers were not the only concern.

The 1922 crop yield was light in many parts of Alberta other than the south, occasioning requests for assistance in a less welcome form. For example, it was suggested that the government underwrite reduced freight rates for the movement of feed grain and stock from areas of plenty to areas of scarce supply. The new Liberal federal administration was exhibiting a strong disinclination to contribute to such assistance, reducing the likelihood that much direct relief would be carried on at all in light of the provincial treasury's accumulated deficit. Besides, the Greenfield administration was loth to undermine the hardy pioneer spirit! Wrote Greenfield to one applicant:

> The tendency to look for Government assistance in any time of stress has been growing rapidly in the last few years and, in my judgment, has been responded to too freely by Governments, with the result that the morale of many of the people of Western Canada has been weakened, and the old spirit of "get in there in spite of set-backs" is rapidly disappearing.[49]

It was with considerable satisfaction that Greenfield, during the 1923 session of the legislature, announced the discontinuance of the costly policy of seed grain advances inherited from the preceding Liberal regime, despite the contrary desires of the U.F.A. convention in January.[50] The wishes of no one group, not even farmers, could be fulfilled at the cost of significant injury to related economic interests.

IV

The replacement of the agrarian wisdom of the U.F.A. by the expertise of special consultants was epitomized by the fate of the various U.F.A. propositions for the revision of monetary policy. At U.F.A. conventions prior to 1922 the welter of suggestions had usually been shaped into resolutions calling for a national central bank, a measure which did not require provincial government attention. But at the 1922 convention delegates decided to take advantage of their new U.F.A. administration in Edmonton and passed a resolution (with a large majority) calling on the Alberta government to "cause to be secured a Bank Charter, in accordance with the Federal Bank Act" in order to "do a general banking business and proceed to take full advantage of the right to issue paper currency...."[51] This was supported by petitions from a number of U.F.A. locals in the early part of 1922 which elicited the response from Greenfield that the subject was under investigation, but only with a view to requesting amendments to the Dominion Bank Act. "In my judgment," confided Greenfield, "public opinion in this Province is not ready for a Provincial Bank at the present time."[52] "Public opinion" presumably referred to the collective wisdom of the broader community to which farmers contributed.

Instead the government once again sought expert opinion. Greenfield and Brownlee undertook to secure the services of D.A. MacGibbon, Professor of Economics at The University of Alberta, to act as a one-man Commission on Banking and Credit with respect to agricultural enterprise in Alberta.[53] While Professor MacGibbon researched, *The U.F.A.* carried several reviews of books written by C.H. Douglas, an English crusader on behalf of an unorthodox monetary system known as "Social Credit."[54] The government procrastinated all year in replying to the resolutions of the January U.F.A. convention, but in June the U.F.A. executive received some indication from Attorney-General Brownlee of the government attitude to the resolution recommending a provincial bank. The government, revealed Brownlee, "did not consider it advisable or practicable at the present time to establish a Provincial Bank, and had decided to concentrate its efforts upon securing all the information it could to assist in making suggestions for the revision of the Bank Act, when it came up for re-enactment, in the Dominion House, next session."[55] In December, when Greenfield was finally able to gather together the answers of the various ministers to the January U.F.A. convention resolutions and submit the government positions on each to the U.F.A. executive, he indicated merely that Professor MacGibbon's report was now under study.[56]

With no firm declaration of government intentions before them, the delegates at the U.F.A. convention in January 1923 reiterated unanimously their request of the previous year for a provincial bank. The U.F.A. Committee on Banking and Credit, for which George Bevington was the chief spokesman, also submitted a separate resolution asking the Alberta government to obtain the authority of the legislature to issue provincial bonds to liquidate farmers' debts under a funding plan and to negotiate with the federal government for the issue of dominion treasury notes to be loaned to the debtors at cost to cover the provincial bonds. Brownlee was called upon to comment; he took particular exception to the latter resolution, claiming that the government had all it could do to sell enough bonds on the markets of the world merely to raise the money necessary to begin to replace past borrowings. Farmers did not act in a financial vacuum. He suggested darkly that the government was receiving undue pressure on these matters from the U.F.A.

> The Attorney-General appealed to the Convention to place faith in the Government, and leave it to the Government to see how far they could go. He added: "I am not speaking lightly, but I do say that there is a possibility of this Government being faced with a program next year, as a result of certain resolutions that have been passed today, and per-

haps this resolution, in which we may find it a very serious problem to carry on the Government at all for another year."

Brownlee was persuasive: the resolution in question failed by a decisive majority.[57]

The resolution favoring a provincial bank was, nevertheless, once again submitted for government consideration at a meeting of the government with U.F.A. executive members on February 3. In the confused discussion, Bevington sought vainly to convince Greenfield and Brownlee that a provincial bank could avoid losses alleged by the existing banks for their Alberta operations. Greenfield's paramount concern was that the provincial government's financial position was such that "bond houses and those who deal in our securities are beginning to ask some very awkward questions." Therefore, whether or not the government was opposed to the idea, "We must get a very clear grasp before we do anything definite."[58] Once again external realities could not be avoided in responding to farmers' demands. The man who might be expected to have had the clearest understanding of those external realities, Professor MacGibbon, was sympathetic to the desire of farmers for better credit conditions but he considered the proposition to create a provincial bank of issue "legally insuperable" and economically unsound. Not only was monetary policy a federal prerogative but in any case a provincial bank would be a small local bank in an era when only large banks were surviving. Then too there was bound to be the danger of political considerations interfering with its administration.[59] Complex interests obviously blocked a simple solution.

The government's argument was enough for Henry Wise Wood. Although his editorials on the virtues of close co-ordination with the U.F.A. of all farmer enterprises had graced the front page of most issues of *The U.F.A.* in 1922, he was never keen to interfere in the workings of government, which he had always understood to involve much more than simple attention to farmers' whims. Now he decided that the provincial bank had been debated long enough and should not survive another annual convention.[60] At the same time the government tabled Professor MacGibbon's report on March 1 and felt no need for action at the provincial level. The federal House of Commons was debating the revision of the Bank Act that spring and Greenfield in telegrams and letters attempted unsuccessfully to have Premiers Bracken of Manitoba and Dunning of Saskatchewan join him in appointing a common counsel to present the western provinces' case. Finally Greenfield simply forwarded to Prime Minister King a resolution of the Alberta legislature expressing the desire for a thorough investigation into agricultural credit conditions in the prairie provinces before final revision of the Bank Act.[61] The crusade for a provincial bank ceased, to the dismay of its faithful proponents.[62] Crusader Bevington, hitherto a tireless campaigner on behalf of the scheme, found in 1924 that his efforts to have the U.F.A. back educational programs on monetary reform were blocked: his committee, he was told, was to investigate monetary matters but not to promote particular solutions without the sanction of the board.[63]

V

By 1924, it must be kept in mind, economic conditions were generally improving for Alberta farmers (though not spectacularly) and successful pool operations were claiming the attentions of large numbers of farmers. The proportion of farmers with reason to complain no doubt dwindled. In combination with these favorable developments, opposition within the U.F.A. to the dominant position of the cabinet was considerably muted. It was symbolic at this point that the farmer premier, Greenfield, lost the confidence of his U.F.A. supporters in the legislature. Originally reluctant to assume the premiership, Greenfield gradually slipped into the shadow of his attorney-general, John Edward Brownlee. The only lawyer on the government side of the legislature, Brownlee was by far the most prominent U.F.A. speaker, especially after the start of the 1923 session, during much of which Greenfield was ill and absent, leaving Brownlee to act as house leader. Newspapers gave greater coverage to Brownlee's addresses than they did to Greenfield's and Brownlee came to be recognized as the chief U.F.A. spokesman in debate. W.M. Davidson, M.L.A., of the *Calgary Morning Albertan,* judged the highlight of the relatively uneventful 1924 legislative session to be "the eclipse of Premier Greenfield, who lost the confidence of the house and even of his own followers." Greenfield was too frequently absent during debates, and gave little support to his supporters. Borwnlee, on the other hand, impressed Davidson as the "strong man in the party" who exercised such amazing influence over U.F.A. votes as to warrant comparison with former Premier A.L. Sifton.[64] Brownlee's, not Greenfield's speech in the 1925 budget debate stirred the admiration of the *Edmonton Journal,* which considered Brownlee "one of the few eloquent speakers on the government side of the house."[65]

Brownlee apparently did not share the growing dissatisfaction of the "rank and file" with Greenfield, persistently resisting approaches from those supporting his elevation to the premier's position. Only when he could be sure that Greenfield bore him no animosity did Brownlee relent. On November 23, 1925, Greenfield tendered his resignation to Lieutenant-Governor Egbert with the recommendation that Brownlee be asked to form a government.[66]

This change was popular within the U.F.A. organization as well as among U.F.A. representatives in the legislature, even though Greenfield personally was still well liked. It was clear that the representatives had come to prefer the highly competent leadership which Brownlee could offer to the farmer leadership which had been Greenfield's principal appeal.[67] It was another indication that Alberta farmers had relinquished their 1921 campaign drive for farmer ascendancy in government. Following 1921 many agrarian proposals had been rejected by the government on the basis that the U.F.A. had not the superior sources of information or expertise available to the government with respect to variables beyond mere local matters. As a result farmers had by 1925 ceased to petition the government with hastily conceived panaceas for their dilemmas. Simultaneously much of their economic interest had shifted away from the U.F.A. to the co-operative marketing pools while economic conditions generally improved. New causes were not easily found to replace the old U.F.A. grounding in complaints about other sectors of the urban network. Alberta farmers were now to experience an era of competent government administration under Brownlee's direction at the same time as U.F.A.

activities stagnated.

The changes which had occurred in the first few years after the United Farmers' achievement of political power in Alberta proved to be crucial after the depression struck in 1929, eliminating general prosperity as well as the hope of the pools. Again a great proportion of farmers perceived no advantage in the system of specialists into which they were locked. But when Alberta farmers looked for solutions during the 1930s they could not regard the U.F.A. in the same way as before 1921, for the idea of farmers controlling their collective destiny by the flexing of direct muscle through the U.F.A. had proven a delusion. During the early years of the depression, to be sure, individuals and groups briefly renewed their demands of the early 1920s. As formerly, however, these were repeatedly judged by the government to be either impossible in the light of complex realities or valueless.[68]

When the opportunity arose, many Alberta farmers were thus well prepared to feel a strong sense of identification with William Aberhart, who insisted on the value of an attractive provincial monetary scheme rejected by the leadership of both the U.F.A. and the government, not to mention assorted economists. Political scientist Donald Smiley once professed to find at the core of Social Credit political appeal in Alberta and British Columbia a basic anti-institutionalism. Social Credit leaders, he argued, have always pursued the voters' support "in a most direct and uninhibited way without the deference to centres of influence and the complex balancing of group interests which is characteristic of other politicians;" Social Credit leaders identified closely with voters' attitudes "particularly as these attitudes embody resentments against the existing order...."[69] Professor Smiley's theory is particularly interesting in connection with the preliminary historical experience of Alberta farmers, a majority of whom in 1921 supported politically an organization claiming devotion exclusively to their wishes; the government which resulted, however, soon dedicated itself to the very "balancing of interests" said by Professor Smiley to be absent from Social Credit priorities. The first to suffer was not the government, but the original U.F.A. organization, for it had failed to fulfil its political promise. The frustrations kindled by the U.F.A. government's attitude were temporarily minimized by relative prosperity; they required the attendant strain of a major depression to stimulate absolute rejection. But when that time came, the experiences of the early 1920s may have determined the nature of both the solution and the advocate Alberta farmers would appreciate: those apparently impervious to criticisms by the government or any other urban institution.

Notes

Lewis Gwynne Thomas

1. L.G. Thomas, "The Umbrella and the Mosaic: The French-English Presence and the Settlement of the Canadian Prairie West" in J.A. Carroll, ed., *Reflections of Western Historians* (Topeka, 1969), p. 148.
2. L.G. Thomas, "The Ranching Period in Southern Alberta," unpublished M.A. Thesis, University of Alberta, 1935, p. 121.
3. *Ibid.*, pp. 148-49.
4. Minutes of the Faculty of Arts and Science, October 8, 1947.
5. *Ibid.*
6. Correspondence between President Newton and Professor Long, February 1945, in Robert Newton Papers "Department of History," University of Alberta Archives.
7. Undated report (probably 1941) of G.M. Smith on the Department of History: see Department of History minutes, p. 100.
8. *University of Alberta Calendar, 1949-50*, pp. 141.
9. Minutes of the Department of History, January 30, 1942, pp. 71-72.
10. Published by the University of Alberta in 1948, p. 70.
11. L.G. Thomas, "English Missionary Records and the History of the Canadian West," Canadian Historical Association, *Annual Report, 1954*, pp. 45-51.
12. S.D. Clark, "Foreword," in L.G. Thomas, *The Liberal Party in Alberta: A History of Politics in the Province of Alberta 1905-1921* (Toronto, 1959), pp. v-vi.
13. *Canadian Journal of Economics and Political Science*, Vol. XXVI, No. 3 (1960), p. 494.
14. *Pacific Northwest Quarterly*, Vol. 49, No. 2, pp. 55-60.
15. *Journal of the Canadian Church Historical Society*, Vol. III, No. 1, January 1956, pp. 1-11.
16. Minutes of the Department of History, November 5, 1963, p. 145.
17. *Ibid.*, p. 59.
18. *A History of the Canadian West to 1870-71* by Arthur S. Morton, 2nd ed. Edited by Lewis G. Thomas (Toronto, 1973), p. xxvi.
19. *Ibid.*, p. xxviii.
20. L.G. Thomas, "Churches and Church Records in the History of the Canadian West," *The Newsletter*, Vol. 3, No. 1 (1959).
21. *The New Trail*, Vol. XXIV, No. 3 (Winter, 1966-67).
22. L.G. Thomas, "Historiography of the Fur Trade," *Alberta Historical Review*, Vol. 17, No. 1 (1969), pp. 21-27.
23. L.G. Thomas, "The Rancher and the City: Calgary and the Cattlemen, 1883-1914," *Transactions of the Royal Society of Canada*, Vol. VI, Series IV: June 1968, Section II, pp. 203-15.
24. L.G. Thomas, "The Umbrella and the Mosaic." See note 1 above.
25. Canadian Historical Association, *Historical Papers 1973*, pp. 1-12.

The Diary of a Young Fur Trader: the 1789-1790 Journal of Thomas Staynor

1. Based on scattered references in the Hudson's Bay Company Archives. H.B.C.A., A1/46-47, A11/117, B42/a/110, and B121/a/5.
2. H.B.C.A., A11/117, Philip Turnor to the Governor and Committee in London, June 9, 1790.
3. H.B.C.A., B121/a/5, November 1, 1789.
4. *Ibid.*, November 1, 1789.
5. *Ibid.*, October 14, 1789.
6. William Tomison was an Orkneyman who had started with the Hudson's Bay Company as a laborer in 1790. Rising rapidly through the ranks he had been named inland master in 1778 and chief officer of York Factory in 1786 with the right to reside inland. Although it was to prove only temporary he had returned to England with the intention of retiring in the fall of 1789. J.B. Tyrrell, *Journals of Hearne and Turnor* (Toronto, 1934), pp. 581-91.
7. William Folster had joined the company as a laborer in 1772 and appears to have gone inland for the first time in 1780. He served at Hudson House and Manchester House gaining the reputation of being a "very steady man and a careful servant." E.E. Rich, ed., *Cumberland House Journals and Inland Journals, 1775-82,* Second Series, 1779-82 (London, 1952), 118n4; and H.B.C.A., B239/f/1.
8. H.B.C.A., B121/a/5.
9. *Ibid.*
10. *Ibid.*, November 14, 1789.
11. James Tate was an experienced servant from the parish of Orphir in Orkney who signed on in 1778 as a laborer. He had worked inland since 1779, mainly at Hudson House and Manchester House. Tate acted as master at South Branch House in the summer of 1788 and Walker had appointed him to go up to Manchester House as master in the fall of 1789 "till further orders from the Honourable Board Knowing him to be the properest person and the most steady." Rich, *Cumberland House Journals and Inland Journals, 1775-82,* Second Series, 15n1; H.B.C.A., B239/f/1; and B121/a/4, letter from William Walker to Malcholm Ross, September 20, 1789.
12. Peter Pangman was a Yankee of German extraction who had a lengthy experience in the fur trade. As early as 1767 he was trading on the Mississippi in partnership with James Finlay who the following year pioneered in the expansion of the Canadian trade network to the Saskatchewan. In 1771 Pangman moved to the Assiniboine River and in 1774 he also moved to the Saskatchewan. It was while he was trading on the Assiniboine that he went to York Fort with a canoe load of furs hoping to make arrangements to ship them from there at a considerable saving. For his pains the furs were seized leaving him only with a feeling of bitterness towards the Hudson's Bay Company. On the Saskatchewan River he appears to have been frequently at odds with the other Canadian traders, being excluded from the North West Company until 1787 when he was taken in as one of the major partners of the McLeod-Gregory concern. W.S. Wallace, *Documents Relating to the North West Company* (Toronto, 1934), pp. 490-491; and J.S. Nicks, "The Pine Island Posts, 1786-1794: A Study of Competition in the Fur Trade" (M.A. thesis, University of Alberta, 1975), pp. 53-54.
13. H.B.C.A., B121/a/5, December 12, 1789.
14. *Ibid.*, December 8, 1789.
15. *Ibid.*, December 13, 1789.
16. *Ibid.*, December 23, 1789.
17. *Ibid.*, December 25, 1789.
18. James Spence, who came from the Orkney parish of Birsay, had joined the Company as a laborer in 1773. Since 1775 he had been employed at the inland posts gaining experience at Cumberland House, Hudson House, and now at Manchester House. He had wintered on the plains for the first time in the winter of 1777-78 and had frequently stayed inland during the summers. He was married *a la facon du pays* to Nestichio, daughter of Isaac Batt and had several children. He was 36 years old in 1789 and was regarded as a capable steersman and a steady servant. Alice M. Johnson, ed., *Saskatchewan Journal and Correspondence* (London, 1967), 17n.
19. H.B.C.A., B121/a/5.
20. The four men were George Ross, an employee of the Company since 1772; William Rich, first hired in 1785; John Kirkness, who had been engaged in 1782 and James Johnston whose fur trade career began in 1781. All were therefore experienced men and their assignment to this duty suggests that it was probably regarded as a better assignment than doing the necessary chores within the fort. H.B.C.A., B239/f/1, and B121/a/5, December 26, 1789.

21. This encampment was located northeast of Manchester House near the northern edge of the grassland, east of the present town of Turtleford, Saskatchewan.

22. H.B.C.A., B239/f/1, 1789.

23. H.B.C.A., B121/a/5, January 4, 1790.

24. *Ibid.*, January 9, 1790.

25. H.B.C.A., B121/a/4, January 20, 1790.

26. H.B.C.A., B121/a/5, January 9, 1790.

27. H.M. Robinson, *The Great Fur Land* (New York, 1879), pp. 283-85.

28. H.B.C.A., B121/a/5, January 18, 1790.

29. *Ibid.*, February 1, 1790.

30. *Ibid.*, January 16, 1790.

31. J.S. Nicks, *op. cit.*, 205.

32. H.B.C.A., B121/a/5, February 3, 1790.

33. *Ibid.*, February 10, 1790.

34. *Ibid.*, February 11, 1790.

35. *Ibid.*

36. *Ibid.*, February 13 and January 25, 1790.

37. *Ibid.*, March 6, 1790.

38. *Ibid.*, February 16, 1790.

39. *Ibid.*, March 15, 1790 and H.B.C.A., B121/a/4, March 13 and 16, 1790.

40. J.S. Nicks, *op. cit.*, pp. 224-25.

41. Glyndwr Williams, ed., *Andrew Graham's Observations on Hudson's Bay* (London: 1969), pp. 279.

42. H.B.C.A., B121/a/4, March 18-31, 1790.

43. It seems likely that the bags had been made by the women living at the encampments out on the plains as was the practice a few years later. H.B.C.A., B49/a/27B, March 6, 1797.

44. Magnus Twatt had joined the Company in 1771 as a laborer when he was about 20 years old. From the Orkney parish at Orphir, he soon earned a reputation as a "brisk young handy man" with particular skill as a carpenter and canoe builder. He came inland to Cumberland House in 1776 and in subsequent years served also at Hudson House, South Branch House, and Manchester House. H.B.C.A., B239/f/1, York Factory Lists of Servants; and E.E. Rich, ed., *Cumberland House and Inland Journals. First Series 1775-79* (London, 1951), p. 143.

45. H.B.C.A., B121/a/5, May 20, 1790.

46. H.B.C.A., B121/a/4, April 19, 1790.

47. *Ibid.*, March 29, 30, April 2, 11, and 14, 1790.

48. H.B.C.A., B121/a/5, April 15, 1790.

49. A.J. Ray, *Indians in the Fur Trade: their role as trappers, hunters, and middlemen in the lands southwest of Hudson Bay 1660-1870* (Toronto, 1974), p. 102.

50. H.B.C.A., B121/a/4, September 17, 1789 and April 19, 1790.

51. H.B.C.A., B121/a/5, March 26-27, 1790.

52. Robert Garson or Gartson joined the Company in 1787 and this was only his second year at an inland post. He had proved to be "not fitt for the Journey up & down by reason of being Short Winded" but was considered to be "a valuable servant at the House, and taking care of the horses" and invariably stayed inland for the summer. Johnson, *Saskatchewan Journals and Correspondence*, 24n.; and H.B.C.A., B49/f/1, #47. Hugh Beakie of Bakey had been recruited one year earlier and was also considered a good servant but unfit for hard labor. H.B.C.A., B49/f/1, #11; and B239/f/1.

53. *Ibid.*, April 19, 1790.

54. *Ibid.*, April 23, 1790.

55. *Ibid.*, May 8, 1790.

56. *Ibid.*, May 13, 1790.

57. *Ibid.*, May 24, 1790.

58. H.B.C.A., B121/a/4, May 28, 1970.

59. H.B.C.A., A11/117, Philip Turnor to the Governor and Committee in London, June 9, 1790, and Thomas Staynor to the Governor and Committee in London, July 22, 1790.

The Struggle for the Athabasca

1. H.A. Innis, *Peter Pond, Fur Trader and Adventurer* (Toronto, 1930), pp. 122-31.

2. J.B. Tyrell (ed.), *Journals of Samuel Hearne and Philip Turnor* (Toronto, 1934), p. 398.

3. The Hudson's Bay Company had the buildings dismantled in 1939. Old-timers recall how the old journals and accounts were burned in a big bonfire on the beach.

4. C. Camsell and M. Wyatt, "The Mackenzie River Basin," Geological Survey of Canada, Memoir, 108, No. 92, Geological Series (Ottawa, 1919), p. 1.

5. Gordon C. Davidson, *The North West Company* (Berkley, 1918) Appendix J, p. 280. Later, in 1823, Mackenzie River became a separate district under the Hudson's Bay Company.

6. W.S. Wallace, *The Pedlars from Quebec* (Toronto, 1954), p. 15.

7. A.S. Morton, *A History of the Canadian West to 1870-1871*, 2nd edition, L.G. Thomas (ed.) (Toronto, 1973), p. 319.

8. J.B. Tyrell (ed.), *Hearne and Turnor Journals*, p. 56.

9. J. Richardson, *Arctic Searching Expedition* (London, 1851), Vol. 1, p. 111.

10. G. Back, *Narrative*, p. 70.

11. I.e. "provisions" was a term used by fur traders to describe food supplies.

12. J.B. Tyrell (ed.), *Hearne and Turnor Journals*, p. 394.

13. Guy H. Blanchet, "Emporium of the North," *The Beaver* (March 1946), p. 32.

14. I am indebted to Mr. Victor Mercredi and Mr. Horace Wylie of Fort Chipewyan for this information. Mr. Victor Mercredi's grandfather was post factor at Fond Du Lac during the 1850-90 period and Mr. Horace Wylie's grandfather was fort carpenter, 1862-1911.

15. J.B. Tyrell (ed.), *Hearne and Turnor Journals*, p. 455.

16. A.S. Morton, *History*, p. 295.

17. Quoted in L.H. Burpee, *The Search for the Western Sea: The Story of the Exploration of Northwestern America* (Toronto, 1908), p. 583.

18. H.A. Innis, *Peter Pond*, p. 82.

19. Letter from Alexander Mackenzie to agents of the Norht West Company, dated February 1, 1788, at Ila-la-Crosse, "Reminiscences" by Roderick McKenzie in L.R. Masson, *Les Bourgeois de la Compagnie du Nord-Quest* (Quebec, 1889), Vol. 1, p. 24.

20. *Ibid.*, p. 29.

21. Fort Chipewyan Report on District, 1820-1921, Hudson's Bay Company Archives [H.B.C.A.] B 39/e/3, p. 8. Fort Chipewyan Post Journals, 1831-1834, H.B.C.A., B 39/a/29, January 19, 1833.

22. R. Glover (ed.), *David Thompson's Narrative* (Toronto, 1962), p. 94.

23. Journal of James Mackenzie, Public Archives of Canada [P.A.C.], December 4, 1799.

24. G. Back, *Narrative*, p. 465, May 23, 1834.

25. V. Stefansson, *The Fat of the Land* (New York, 1956), p. 180.

26. *Ibid.*, p. 196.

27. R. Glover (ed.), *Thompson's Narrative*, p. 312.

28. J.B. Tyrell (ed.), *Hearne and Turnor Journals*, p. 452.

29. It is not suggested, however, that plentiful provisions were the rule. There were many reasons for shortages—climate, lack of hunters, shortage of ammunition, failure of fisheries—and the Post journals record these occurrences.

30. Nottingham House, XY Fort, Fort Wedderburn, and Fort Chipewyan.

31. The Bennett Dam on the Peace River now affects the flood levels.

32. J.B. Tyrell (ed.), *Hearne and Turnor Journals*, pp. 448-49.

33. Journal of James Mackenzie, P.A.C., April 16, 1800. See also James M. Parker "The Fur Trade of Fort Chipewyan and Lake Athabasca, 1778-1835" (unpublished M.A. thesis, University of Alberta, 1967), pp. 38-41.

34. The North Canoe measured 32 feet in length, 4 feet 5 inches in width, and 2 feet in depth. They carried 25 pieces plus eight men and equipment and took about two months travelling time in brigade. Fort Chipewyan Report on District, 1822-1823, H.B.C.A., B 39/e/5, p. 7.

35. E. Rich (ed.), *Colin Robertson's Correspondence Book, September 1817 to September 1822* (London, 1939), p. CXVIII.

36. Fort Chipewyan Report on District 1823-1824, H.B.C.A., B 39/e/5, pp. 7, 13.

37. E. Rich, *Hudson's Bay Company* (London, 1959), Vol. 2, p. 189.
38. E. Rich, "Trade Habits and Economic Motivation Among the Indians of North America," *The Canadian Journal of Economic and Political Science*, Vol. 26, No. 1 (February 1960), pp. 35-53.
39. *Ibid.*, p. 53.
40. R. Glover (ed.), *A Journey from Prince of Wales's Fort in Hudson's Bay to the Northern Ocean, 1769, 1770, 1771, 1772. By Samuel Hearne* (Toronto, 1958), p. 52.
41. Diamond Jenness, "The Indian Background of Canadian History," National Museum of Canada, Bulletin No. 86, p. 36.
42. A.S. Morton, *History*, p. 12.
43. Fort Chipewyan Report on District, 1824-1825, H.B.C.A., B 39/e/8, p. 6.
44. E. Rich (ed.), *Journal of Occurrences in the Athabasca Department by George Simpson, 1820 and 1821, and Report* (London, 1938), pp. 355-56.
45. R. Glover (ed.), *Hearne's Journeys*, p. 69.
46. *Ibid.*, p. 170.
47. W.K. Lamb (ed.), *The Journals and Letters of Sir Alexander Mackenzie* (Toronto, 1970), p. 151.
48. "An Account of the Athabasca Indians by a Partner of the North West Company" [Manuscript], McGill University Library, p. 7. See also Journal of James Mackenzie, P.A.C., April 9, 1800.
49. E. Rich, *Simpson's Athabasca Journal*, pp. 395-96.
50. R. Glover (ed.), *Hearne's Journeys*, p. 186.
51. Fort Chipewyan Report on District, 1824-1825, H.B.C.A., B 39/e/8, p. 30.
52. J. Richardson, *Arctic Searching Expedition*, Vol. 2, p. 27.
53. Fort Chipewyan Journal, Provincial Archives of Alberta, May 26, 1823.
54. W.K. Lamb (ed.), *Mackenzie's Journals and Letters*, p. 153.
55. J.B. Tyrrell (ed.), *Hearne and Turnor Journals*, p. 452.
56. Journal of John Porter, P.A.C., June 12, 1800.
57. J.B. Tyrrell (ed.), *Hearne and Turnor Journals*, p. 458. May 10, 1792.
58. Journal of John Porter, P.A.C., June 13, 1800.
59. R. Fleming (ed.), *Minutes of Council Northern Department, 1821-1831* (Toronto, 1940), p. 168.
60. John Richardson, *Arctic Searching Expedition*, Vol. 2, p. 31.
61. R. Glover (ed.), *Hearne's Journeys*, pp. 198-199.
62. Nottingham House Journals, 1802-1803, H.B.C.A., B 39/a/1, October 4, 1802.
63. E. Rich, *Hudson's Bay Company*, Vol. 2, p. 316.
64. Selkirk papers, P.A.C., M.C. 19E 1(1), Vol. 30, 9130. John McGillivray to McGillis and Stewart, dated Dunvegan, December 15, 1815.
65. E. Rich (ed.), *Simpson's Athabasca Journal*, p. 358.
66. *Ibid.*, p. 73.
67. Fort Chipewan Report on District, 1825-1826, H.B.C.A., B 39/e/9, p. 6.

"The Custom of the Country": An Examination of Fur Trade Marriage Practices

1. Variations of this phrase, which means "after the fashion of the country," are also found such as *en facon du nord* and "after the fashion of the North West."
2. E.E. Rich, ed., *Copy-Book of Letters Outward, 1680-1687* (Toronto: Champlain Society, Vol. XI, 1948), pp. 40-41.
3. In the 1680s, a governor at Albany had been allowed to bring out his wife and her companion. They proved such a nuisance, however, that the London Committee soon withdrew this privilege and ordered all captains to make sure that no women were aboard its ships when they departed from Gravesend.
4. E.E. Rich, ed., *James Isham's Observations and Notes, 1743-1749* (London: Hudson's Bay Record Society, Vol. XII, 1949), p. 79.
5. Hudson's Bay Company Archives, *Report from the Committee, appointed to inquire into the State and Condition of the Countries Adjoining to Hudson's Bay and of the Trade carried on there*, 24 April 1749, p. 219.
6. Samuel Hearne, *A Journey to the Northern Ocean, 1769, 1770, 1771, 1772*, ed. by Richard Glover (Toronto, 1958), p. 82; W. Kaye Lamb, ed., *The Journals and*

Letters of Sir Alexander Mackenzie (Cambridge, England, 1970), p. 134.

7. Rich, *Isham's Observations*, p. 101: "When a Young Man has a mind for a Wife, they do not make Long tedious Ceremony's nor yet use much formalities."; Glyndwr Williams, ed., *Andrew Graham's Observations on Hudson's Bay, 1767-1791* (London: H.B.R.S., Vol. XXVII, 1969), p. 153: "I cannot with propriety rank fornication and adultery (though very frequent amongst them) among their vices as they think no harm in either.

8. Rich, *Isham's Observations*, p. 95; Hearne, *Journey to Northern Ocean*, pp. 83-84; Williams, *Graham's Observations*, pp. 57-58. It was usually the failure of the white man to respect Indian mores, even though they were much more lenient than his own, which led to hostility.

9. H.B.C.A., Churchill Journal, November 27, 1750, B.42/a/36, f. 23. For a summation of the important economic role played by native women in the fur trade, see Sylvia Van Kirk, "Women and the Fur Trade," *The Beaver*, Winter 1972, p. 4.

10. J.B. Tyrrell, ed., *Documents relating to the Early History of Hudson's Bay* (Toronto: Champlain Society, Vol. XXVIII, 1931), pp. 229-30. See also Joseph Robson, *An Account of Six Years Residence in Hudson's Bay from 1733 to 1736, and 1744 to 1747* (London, 1752), p. 52.

11. H.B.C.A., Albany Journal, January 24, 1771, B.3/a/63, f. 18d.

12. H.B.C.A., Moose Journal, March 4, 1744, B.135/a/14, f. 32.

13. *Parliamentary Report, 1749*, p. 224; Rich, *Isham's Observations*, pp. 322, 325.

14. H.B.C.A., London Committee to R. Pilgrim, May 6, 1747, A.6/7, f. 110d.

15. Hearne, *Journey to Northern Ocean*, pp. 39-40.

16. Williams, *Graham's Observations*, p. 248.

17. H.B.C.A., T. Mitchell to G. Spence, February 3, 1745, B.3/b/2, f. 12; Moose Journal, May 16, 1742, B.135/a/11, f. 64.

18. Albany Journal, January 18-24, 1771, B.3/a/63, fos. 18-18d. Marten eventually succeeded in sending his son to England, having implored the London Committee to make an exception to the ruling passed in 1751 that no person of Indian or part-Indian extraction be allowed passage to Britain.

19. H.B.C.A., York Journal, September 22-24, 1762, B.239/a/50, f. 5-5d.

20. Numerous examples could be cited. Part of Samuel Hearne's hatred for Moses Norton undoubtedly stemmed from the fact that Norton went to great lengths to prevent any of his subordinates from having any dealings with Indian women (Hearne, *Journey to Northern Ocean*, pp. 39-40). A servant at Moose Fort in the 1740s, Augustin Frost, became very refractory when the tyrannical James Duffield cut him off from his Indian family (Moose Journal, May 16-18, 1742, B.135/a/11, fos. 64-66). Indian resentment at being barred from Henley House while their women were kept there by the master resulted in an attack on the post in 1755 (George Rushworth to London Committee, September 8, 1755, A.11/2, fos. 173-74).

21. Williams, *Graham's Observations*, p. 248; H.B.C.A., Churchill Journal, November 2-4, 1751, B.42/a/38, fos. 13-15.

22. W.S. Wallace, ed., *Documents relating to the North West Company* (Toronto: Champlain Society, Vol. XX, 1934), p. 211.

23. J.B. Tyrrell, ed., *Journals of Samuel Hearne and Philip Turnor, 1774-1792* (Toronto: Champlain Society, Vol. XXI, 1934), pp. 252-53.

24. "Connolly vs. Woolrich, Superior Court, 9 July 1867," *Lower Canada Jurist*, Vol. XI, p. 228; hereafter cited as "Connolly Case, 1867."

25. Toronto Public Library, George Nelson Papers, Journal 1810-11, pp. 41-42. This phenomenon is also seen among the Chinooks, Frederick Merk, ed., *Fur Trade and Empire: George Simpson's Journal, 1824-25* (Cambridge, Massachusetts, 1931), p. 99.

26. L.R. Masson, ed., *Les Bourgeois de la Compagnie du Nord-Ouest* (New York, 1960 [reprint]), pp. 251-52; Richard Glover, ed., *David Thompson's Narrative, 1784-1812* (Toronto: Champlain Society, Vol. XL, 1962), pp. 82, 255; Lamb, *Journals of Mackenzie*, pp. 151-52.

27. "Johnstone et al. vs. Connolly, Appeal Court, 7 Sept. 1869," *La Revue Legale*, Vol. I, pp. 280-81; hereafter cited as "Connolly Appeal Case, 1869."

28. W. Kaye Lamb, ed., *Sixteen Years in the Indian Country: The Journal of Daniel Williams Harmon, 1800-1816* (Toronto, 1957), p. 53.

29. Elliot Coues, ed., *New Light on the Early History of the Greater Northwest: The Manuscript Journals of Alexander Henry and of David Thompson, 1799-1814* (Minneapolis, Minnesota, 1965 [reprint]), Vol. 1, p. 228.

30. *Ibid.*, Vol. 11, p. 901.

31. Ross Cox, *The Columbia River*, ed. by Edgar and Jane Stewart (Norman, Oklahoma, 1957), pp. 209-11; Lamb, *Harmon's Journal*, pp. 28-29.

32. "Connolly Appeal Case, 1869," 280-82: "Une homme engage respectait la femme d'un bourgeois comme si elle eute ete la premiere femme dans ce pays."

33. Glover, *Thompson's Narrative*, p. 82.

34. Lamb, *Harmon's Journal*, p. 53.

35. Coues, *New Light on the Greater Northwest*, Vol. 1, p. 211.

36. "Connolly Case, 1867," p. 239: "I never heard of any of the men keeping two women at a time, it was not customary. A man could only have one wife at a time."

37. Tyrell, *Journals of Hearne and Turnor*, p. 275.

38. Public Record Office, England, Will of Robert Pilgrim, November 23, 1750, Prob. 11/784, f. 396.

39. Sailing Orders, May 16, 1751, A.6/8, f. 54d. See also Williams, *Graham's Observations*, p. 145.

40. Cox, *Columbia River*, p. 224.

41. Numerous examples of early bourgeois who followed this course of action could be cited, i.e. Roderick Mackenzie of Terrebonne, Patrick Small, William McGillivray, Charles Chaboillez and Nicholas Montour. For an account of the feting of the retired Nor'Wester by eastern society, see Cox, *Columbia River*, pp. 361-62.

42. The exception to this general statement would be the action of old N.W.C. engages who became "freemen" rather than leave their Indian families. They, however, had little prospect of returning to a comfortable life in eastern Canada and were the only group prepared to live a semi-nomadic life akin to that of the Indians. In the early 1800s, the North West Company had developed a plan for a settlement at Rainy Lake for superannuated engages and their families, but this came to naught owing to the bitter trade struggle (Lamb, *Harmon's Journal*, pp. 5-6).

43. Thomas Thomas to George Gladman, March 3, 1813, B.3/b/49a, f, 10d.

44. H.B.C.A., *Andrew Graham's Observations, 1771*, E.2/7, f. 5d; Williams, *Graham's Observations*, p. 145.

45. P.R.O., England, Will of John Favell, February 19, 1784, Prob. 11/1785, f. 551. The London Committee, which had received similar requests before, readily complied with Favell's wish. In fact, the administration of annuities for native families was to become a regular duty of the Company secretary in London. Many other examples could be cited of H.B.C. men who left detailed instructions in their wills for the care of their native families, i.e. William Bolland, Robert Goodwin, Matthew Cocking, and James Spence.

46. Alexander Henry, *Travels and Adventures in Canada and the Indian Territories, 1760-1776* (Edmonton, 1969 [reprint]), p. 248.

47. The continuing support given to the families of N.W.C. servants, plus the growth of a body of "freemen," helps to account for the fact that the mixed-blood progeny of the Nor'-Westers were early identifiable as a group distinct from the Indians. It took much longer for the mixed-blood offspring of H.B.C. men to become a recognizable group because they were absorbed directly into Indian society. In the eighteenth century, no distinction was made between "half-breed" and "Indian," and it appears that many of the "Home" Indians around H.B.C. posts were actually first or second generation mixed-bloods. This phenomenon has been elaborated by anthropologist Jennifer Brown in an unpublished manuscript entitled "Halfbreeds": The Entrenchment of a Racial Category in the Canadian Northwest Fur Trade," University of Chicago, 1973.

48. Cox, *Columbia River*, p. 361; "Connolly Appeal Case, 1869," p. 289: "L'habitude de quitter les femmes est tres-commune dans les pays sauvages, et j'ai meme connu des personnes qui donnaient de l'argent a d'autres pour prendre ces femmes comme leurs propres personnes, et aussi les charger le leur soutien et de leur famille."

49. Lamb, *Harmon's Journal*, p. 98.

50. Graham's Observations, 1771, E.2/7, f. 27.

51. P.R.O., England, Will of Matthew Cocking, January 27, 1797, Prob. 11/1322, f. 256; H.B.C.A., W.H. Cook to R. Miles, May 25, 1825, B.239/c/1, f. 201.

52. H.B.C.A., Will of James Spence, November 6, 1795, A.36/12.

53. Cox, *Columbia River*, p. 306. This is an important aspect of the pattern of intermarriage which developed among the Nor-Westers; a long list of officers who married metis women could be cited such as Peter and John Warren Dease, Colin Robertson, Francis Heron, William McIntosh, and Thomas McMurray.

54. Lamb, *Harmon's Journal*, p. 98. See also John Franklin, *Narrative of a Journey to the Shores of the Polar Sea, 1819-22* (London, 1824), p. 86: "The girls at the forts, particularly the daughters of Canadians, are given in marriage very young; they are very frequently wives at 12 years of age, and mothers at 14."

55. E.E. Rich, ed., *Simpson's Athabasca Journal and Report, 1821-22* (London: H.B.R.S., Vol. I, 1938), p. 245: Simpson was anxious to secure a match between one of his clerks and the daughter of an old voyageur Cayenne Grogne because she spoke French, Cree, and Mountainy [Chipewyan] fluently.

56. Charles Wilkes, *Narrative of the United States Exploring Expedition, 1838-1842*, 5 vols. (Philadelphia, 1845), Vol. 4, pp. 396-97.

57. By the late eighteenth century, the Nor'Westers on Lake Athabasca appear to have built up a nefarious traffic in Chipewyan women. When finally in 1800, a delegation of Chipewyan begged the bourgeois James Mackenzie that no more women should be traded "on any account," they received the curt reply that "it was not their business to prescribe rules to us." (Masson, *Les Bourgeois,* Vol. 11, pp. 387-88). See also Tyrell, *Journals of Hearne and Turnor,* pp. 446, 449.

58. Alexander Ross, *The Fur Hunters of the Far West,* ed. by Kenneth Spaulding (Norman, Oklahoma, 1956), p. 191.

59. Williams, *Graham's Observations,* p. 145.

60. H.B.C.A., A. Graham to London Committee, August 26, 1772, A.11/115, f. 144d; London Committee to J. Hodgson, May 25, 1803, A.6/16, fos. 159d-160.

61. Wallace, *NWC Documents,* p. 211. A change in attitude can also be noted on the part of H.B.C. officers, partly because of the coming of settlement: "As the Colony is at length set on foot and there is a prospect of Civilization diffusing itself among Us in a few years I would not advise you for the sake of the rising Generation to consent to either Officers or Men contracting Matrimonial Connections unless with the Daughters of Englishmen." (W.H. Cook to J. Swain, December 17, 1811, B.239/a/82, fos. 9d-10.)

62. "Connolly Appeal Case, 1869," pp. 286-87.

63. *Ibid.,* pp. 284-85. Marois' testimony was corroborated by another engage, Amable Dupras, p. 282.

64. *Ibid.,* p. 284.

65. George Nelson, Journal 1808, Fort Dauphine: "we were obliged to leave off and prepare for a dance . . . in honour to Mr. Seraphim's wedding—Mr. McDonald played the violin for us"; Coues, *New Light on the Greater Northwest,* Vol. 1, p. 571: "My neighbour [H.B.C. at Fort Vermilion] gave a dance in honor of the wedding of his eldest daughter to one of his men."

66. H.B.C.A., George Barnston to James Hargrave, February 1, 1823, B.235/c/1, fos, 3d-4.

67. H.B.C.A., G. Simpson to J.G. McTavish, January 7, 1824, B.239/c/1, f. 134.

68. H.B.C.A., Eastmain Register, 1806-1826, B.59/z/1.

69. P.R.O., England, Will of George Gladman, March 25, 1820, Prob. 11, 1663, f. 585.

70. Lamb, *Harmon's Journal,* pp. 194-95. Other Nor-Westers who took their mixed-blood wives to eastern Canada in the early 1800s were David Thompson, John "Le Pretre" Macdonell, and John "Le Borgne" McDonald. According to Ross Cox, those with means on coming to Canada with their families "purchase estates, on which they live in a kind of half-Indian, half-civilized manner, constantly smoking their calumet and railing at the fashionable frivolities of the great world," p. 361.

71. "Connolly Appeal Case, 1869," p. 287.

72. *Ibid.,* pp. 285-87.

73. Lamb, *Harmon's Journal,* pp. 62-63, 93-99; Coues, *New Light on the Greater Northwest,* Vol. 1, pp. 58, 162, 211; George Nelson, Journal 1803-04, p. 51 and Reminiscences, Part 5, pp. 206-207.

74. G.P. de T. Glazebrook, ed., *The Hargrave Correspondence, 1821-1843* (Toronto: Champlain Society, Vol. XXIV, 1938), p. 381.

75. Ross Cox tells the story of Francoise Boucher, the daughter of a Canadian, who was married at 14 to an interpreter. After he died, she was taken by a bourgeois in the Athabasca country, but when he left the district, she was handed on to his successor with whom she remained permanently, pp. 363-64. Although in a minority, one witness at the Connolly appeal case declared: "It was very common to change women in the Indian country. The French Canadians, in the North-West Company's employ and the English, did it too.," p. 287.

76. E.E. Rich, ed., *Minutes of Council of the Northern Department of Rupert's Land, 1821-31* (London: H.B.R.S., Vol. III, 1940), pp. 94-95.

77. John West, *The Substance of a Journal during a residence at the Red River Colony, 1820-23* (London, 1827), pp. 51-52.

78. West, *Red River Journal,* p. 26: ". . . having frequently enforced the moral and social obligation of marriage . . ."

79. H.B.C.A., Red River Register, E.4/1b, f. 195d; Nicholas Garry, *Diary of . . .* (Ottawa: Transactions of the Royal Society of Canada, Series 2, Vol. 6, 1900), p. 137: "Mr. West has done much good in persuading these Gentlemen to marry."

80. Church Missionary Society Archives, England, David Jones to Rev. Pratt, July 24, 1824, CC1/039.

81. C.M.S.A., William Cockran, Journal, March 3, 1829, CC1/018, Vol. 3.

82. C.M.S.A., Jones, Journal, August 25, 1828, CC1/039, f. 35; CC1/018, Marriage Register.

83. C.M.S.A., Jones, Journal, June 9, 1835, CC1/039.
84. B.C. Provincial Archives, Arch. McDonald to Edward Ermatinger, April 1, 1836, AB40 M142A.
85. *Ibid*. My emphasis.
86. B.C.A., Thomas Simpson to Donald Ross, February 20, 1836, AE R73 Si5.
87. Merk, *Fur Trade and Empire*, p. 108.
88. Thomas E. Jessett, ed., *Reports and Letters of Herbert Beaver, 1836-38* (Portland, Oregon, 1959), p. 2.
89. *Ibid.*, p. 86.
90. For details of McLoughlin's family life, see T.C. Elliott, "Margeurite Wadin McKay McLoughlin," *Oregon Historical Quarterly*, Vol. 36, 1935, pp. 338-47.
91. Jessett, *Beaver's Reports and Letters*, p. 141.
92. C.M. Drury, *First white women over the Rockies . . .*, 3 vols. (Glendale, California, 1963), Vol. 1, p. 111.
93. Jessett, *Beaver's Reports and Letters*, p. 58.
94. *Ibid.*, p. 77. Marriage by a Justice of the Peace had, in fact, been made legal by a law of 1836 in Canada and England, pp. xxi, 46, 116.
95. Jessett, *Beaver's Reports and Letters*, p. 93.
96. *Ibid.*, pp. 48-50.
97. *Ibid.*, pp. 50-51.
98. H.B.C.A., A.C. Anderson to H. Beaver, 1838, B.223/b/20, fos. 62-66d. It is significant that in Scotland it was possible for a legal marriage to be contracted without the sanction of either civil or religious authority, see F.P. Walton, *Scottish Marriages, regular and irregular* (Edinburgh, 1893). The fact that most of the fur traders were of Scottish origin may, therefore, help to explain their acceptance of "the custom of the country."
99. B.223/b/20, fos. 62-66d; H.B.C.A., Company Secretary to Rev. W. Hamilton of Orkney, March 17, 1823, A.5/7, fos. 78d-79: It was the opinion of "one of the Highest Dignitaries of the Church of England" that "the Custom of living together in Hudson's Bay be to all intents and purposes a valid marriage."
100. Marion B. Smith, "The Lady Nobody Knows," *British Columbia; a Centennial Anthology* (Vancouver, 1958), pp. 473-75; "Cathedral of the Pioneers," *The Beaver*, December 1940, p. 12.
101. Jessett, *Beaver's Reports and Letters*. p. 35.
102. *Ibid.*, pp. 120, 143-45.
103. West, *Red River Journal*, pp. 75-76; C.M.S.A., CC1/039, Jones, Journal, September 13, 1824, f. 11.
104. For numerous examples, see M.L.W. Warner and H.D. Munnick, eds., *Catholic Church Records of the Pacific Northwest* (St. Paul, Oregon, 1972).
105. *Ibid.*, Vancouver, Vol. 11, pp. 5, 6, and 7.
106. H.B.C.A., Marriage contract between Magnus Harper and Peggy La Pierre, Oxford House, August 18, 1830, B.156/z/1, f. 96. As has been seen, those with commissions as J.P.s were allowed to perform marriages in accordance with the law of Lower Canada that "a civil contract of marriage, executed before competent witnesses, and in the presence of a J.P., shall be perfectly valid in all respects, if no clergyman within 10 French leagues" (B.223/b/20, fos. 62-66d).
107. H.B.C.A., Minutes of Council, June 7, 1845, B.239/k/2, f. 183d.
108. Van Kirk, "Women and the Fur Trade," p. 11.
109. "Connolly Appeal Case, 1869," p. 288.
110. For a more detailed account of the story of Simpson and McTavish and their country wives, see Van Kirk, "Women and the Fur Trade," pp. 11-18.
111. H.B.C.A., J. Stuart to J.G. McTavish, August 16, 1830, E.24/4.
112. Glazebrook, *Hargrave Correspondence*, p. 311.
113. Public Archives of Canada, James Hargrave to Charles Ross, December 1, 1830, MG19 A21(1), Vol. 21.
114. P.A.C., Thomas Simpson to J. Hargrave, January 27, 1839, MG19 A21(1), Vol. 7, p. 1574; J. Hargrave to Cuthbert Grant, November 30, 1828, Vol. 21.
115. P.A.C., Wm. Cockran to J. Hargrave, August 8, 1835, MG19 A21(1), Vol. 5, p. 1078. According to Hargrave, while there were still some young gentlemen who married daughters of officers for money or perhaps "Kinder Motives," "a different tone of feeling on these matters had gradually come around." (Hargrave to Letitia Mactavish, July 24, 1838, MG19 A21(1), Vol. 21.
116. Jessett, *Beaver's Reports and Letters*, p. 57.
117. *Ibid.*, pp. 147-48.
118. Cox, *Columbia River*, p. 359.
119. Jessett, *Beaver's Reports and Letters*, p. 141.
120. C.M.S.A., Wm. Cockran to London Secretary, July 30, 1827, CC1/018, Vol. 1; G. Simpson to D. Jones, July 14, 1832, CC1/039.

121. Margaret A. Macleod, ed., *The Letters of Letitia Hargrave* (Toronto: Champlain Society, Vol. XXVIII, 1947), pp. 177-78.
122. W.S. Wallace, "Lefroy's Journey to the North-West" (Ottawa: T.R.S.C., Sec. 11, Vol. XXXII, 1938), p. 93.
123. *Catholic Church Records,* Vanc., Vol. 1, 8th and 9th pages.
124. H.B.C.A., John Rowand to George Simpson, September 14, 1849, D.5/25, f. 82d.
125. "Indian Women Rise to Social Eminence," December 14, 1913, Spokane, Wash. (newspaper clipping courtesy of Mrs. Jean Cole, Peterborough, Ontario); see also Archie Binns, *Peter Skene Ogden: Fur Trader* (Portland, Oregon, 1967), p. 355.
126. The following account has been constructed from the testimony given in the original case of 1867 and the appeal case of 1869, see *Lower Canada Jurist,* Vol. XI, pp. 197-265 and *La Revue Legale,* Vol. I, pp. 253-400.
127. "Connolly Case, 1867," p. 231.
128. H.B.C.A., G. Simpson to J.G. McTavish, December 2, 1832, B.135/c/2, f. 96.
129. "Connolly Case, 1867," pp. 230, 248.
130. *Ibid.,* p. 257. The decision was appealed by the associates of Julia Woolrich who had died in the interim before 1869. Four of the five appeal judges upheld the original decision. Plans were then made for an appeal to the Privy Council, but the parties ultimately settled out of court.

The Origins of the Mixed Bloods in the Canadian West

1. See W.L. Morton, "The Canadian Metis," *The Beaver,* September 1950. As an appreciation of Marcel Giraud's *Le Metis Canadien* (Paris, L'Institut d'Ethnologie), 1945, Morton accepts the dominant theme in Giraud's study.
2. James W. St. G. Walker, "The Indian in Canadian Historical Writing," *Historical Papers, Canadian Historical Association,* 1971, offers criticism equally appropriate to the historians' treatment of the Mixed Blood.
3. Such assessment, of course, begins with Alexander Ross, *The Red River Settlement* (Edmonton, 1972). Subsequent historians have done little to question the assessment.
4. G.F.G. Stanley, *The Birth of Western Canada* (Toronto, 1963), pp. 8 and 9.
5. W.L. Morton, *Manitoba, A History* (Toronto, 1957), p. 67. "Not all their children chose the ways of civilization; even these fortunate families were not free from the halfbreed's inevitable choice of the life of one parent or the other." This theme, arising with Ross, has remained unchallenged.
6. Both an "Indian" perspective and the variety of Indian perspectives have been ignored by historians.
7. In the Canadian context famous Indian leaders with a European progenitor include Joseph Brant of the Mohawk and Poundmaker of the Plains Cree.
8. One of the best examples in the context of Rupert's Land was A.K. Isbister, son of an Hudson's Bay Company officer, who established a name for himself in London as a scholar and schoolmaster. See W.L. Morton, *Manitoba, . . .,* p. 76.
9. Perhaps one man, Cuthbert Grant, reflected this heritage more clearly than any other individual in the course of his life. See M.A. MacLeod and W.L. Morton, *Cuthbert Grant of Grantown* (Toronto, 1974).
10. To date the most satisfactory scholarly treatment is found in W.L. Morton's "Introduction" in E.E. Rich, ed., *London Correspondence Inward From Eden Colvile, 1849-1852* (London, 1956).
11. Giraud, p. 473, recognizes metis canadiens and metis ecossais. His subsequent treatment, however, minimizes particular distinctions.
12. See Stanley, p. 9, and W.L. Morton, *Manitoba, . . .,* p. 67.
13. Provincial Archives of Manitoba, Red River Settlement, Red River Correspondence, 1845-47, James Sinclair, et al., to Governor Alexander Christie, August 29, 1845.
14. P.A.M., P.R.S., G.H. Gunn, ed., "The Journal of Peter Garrioch," unpublished manuscript, no date, pp. 309, 317, 319.
15. Public Archives of Canada, M.G. 19, E 6, Vol. I, Thomas Cook to Rev. John Smithurst, January 30, 1853.
16. P.A.C., M.G. 17, B 1, D 13, Society for the Propagation of the Gospel, Rupert's Land, 1850-59, Rev. D.T. Anderson to Rev. E. Hawkins, 24 November, 1852:

In allusion to my other letter I wished to explain that Mr. McDonald was born in this Country but is European on his Father's side and partly European on his Mother's—He does not therefore come under the same category as Mr. Budd, but is *Country-born [sic]*, not an Indian.—I state this because often the other idea gets abroad, and the Ch. Miss. Soc.Y in their Intelligencer speak of one Catechist as an Indian, to whom I had to explain the circumstance or he might naturally have been offended.

17. Governor Henry Sergeant's "parcell of Women," his wife and her companion, at Moose Factory from 1683 to 1686 were the only known exception. See E.E. Rich, *The History of The Hudson's Bay Company,* 1670-1870 (London, 1958), Vol. I, pp. 148, 215.

18. Glyndwr Williams, ed., *Andrew Graham's Observations on Hudson's Bay, 1767-91* (London, 1969), Introduction by Richard Glover, p. 248.

19. *Ibid.*

20. In some instances of course the relationship would fit the European definition of prostitution with the Indian husband receiving a bottle of brandy. See Hudson's Bay Company Archives, E 2/4 (1768-69) "The Observations of Andrew Graham," p. 16, as contained in Giraud, p. 412, fn. 8.

21. A.S. Morton, *A History of the Canadian West to 1870-71* (Toronto, 1973), L.G. Thomas, ed., pp. 129, 253.

22. Church Missionary Society Archives, North West America Missions, Incoming Correspondence, Rev. W. Cockran to The Secretaries, July 25, 1833.

23. Williams, p. 248.

24. The fact that promotion from the ranks became a fairly common practice in the Company during the eighteenth century, would lend support to this statement. Former servants who became officers had Home Guard families. It seems likely that such families began previous to the promotion to officer's rank. See H.B.C.A., A. 36/1A, "Officers and Servants Wills, 1763-1863," the will of William Thomas died November 27, 1818 in which his wife is identified as the daughter of John Best.

25. Williams, p. 158.

26. *Ibid.,* p. 248.

27. See H.B.C.A., A. 36/A, Officers and Servants Wills, 1763-1863."

28. Charles A. Bishop, "Ojibwa, Cree, and The Hudson's Bay Company in Northern Ontario: Culture and Conflict in the Eighteenth Century," in A.W. Rasporich, ed., *Western Canada Past and Present* (Calgary, 1975), p. 154.

29. Williams, pp. 192, 193, remains the best account of the Home Guard Cree.

30. A.J. Ray, *The Indians in the Fur Trade, 1660-1870* (Toronto, 1974), pp. 81, 85.

31. Many comments of British observers suggest a negative impact of the fur trade upon the Home Guard Cree. See Williams, pp. 152, 155, 156, 192. Yet no source suggests the Home Guard Cree would agree. With respect to the use of liquor, see Richard Glover's comment in *Ibid.,* xxxix.

32. *Ibid.,* p. 167.

33. *Ibid.*

34. *Ibid.*

35. *Ibid.,* p. 168.

36. *Ibid.,* pp. 155, 156.

37. *Ibid.,* pp. 150, 153, 157, 158, 175, 176.

38. *Ibid.,* p. 145.

39. Richard Glover, "The Difficulties of the Hudson's Bay Company's Penetration of the West," *Canadian Historical Review,* XXIX, 3, 1948, p. 240.

40. *Ibid.,* p. 241.

41. H.B.C.A., A. 30/1-10, "Lists of Servants in Hudson's Bay." The surnames were those of older men currently serving in the Company's service.

42. *Ibid.*

43. Williams, p. 192, denotes earlier practices.

44. The question of educating the young in this society occupied the attention of the officers. See H.B.C.A., A. 11/118, General Letter to the Governor and Committee, September 15, 1807. Also see E.E. Rich, *The History of the Hudson's Bay Company, 1670-1870* (London, 1959), Vol. II, p. 296.

45. The question remains as to the sophistication of the Mixed Bloods in English. See particularly Rev. John West, *Substance of a Journal* (London, 1824), p. 26.

46. Needless to say this remark is most appropriate in terms of those sons educated in Great Britain. See particularly the sons of Chief Factor William Sinclair, senior.

47. Williams, pp. 159, 167, 207.

48. *Ibid.,* pp. 282-84, 295-300.

49. *Ibid.,* p. 282.

50. Excellent examples from a somewhat later period are H.B.C.A., B.

22/a/10, Brandon House Journals, May 23, 1803, and *Ibid.*, B. 22/a/18a, Brandon House Journals, February 24, 1811.
    51.   The camaraderie of adult males was a significant feature of trading post society throughout the history of the fur trade. "Outsiders" were not welcome. See *Ibid.*, A. 11/118, William Auld to the Governor and Committee, September 26, 1811, for a particular example.
    52.   For an example see *Ibid.*, A. 36/1B, "Officers' and Servants' Wills, 1816-1873," the will of George Atkinson Sr. Geneologies of leading fur trade families, were they available, would be most helpful.
    53.   For an example see *Ibid.*, B. 22/a/10, Brandon House Journals, May 23, 1803.
    54.   Two excellent examples are *Ibid.*, B. 22/a/19-20, Brandon House Journals, February 26, 1816 and August 12, 1817.
    55.   *Ibid.*
    56.   An excellent example is *Ibid.*, B. 22/a/18b, Brandon House Journals, April 16, 1812.
    57.   See the "affair of the heart" involving young Charles Fidler, *Ibid.*, B. 22/a/21, Brandon House Journals, pp. 12, 13, 18, April 27, 1819.
    58.   The circumstances enjoyed by the officer-in-charge are most graphically illustrated in Williams, pp. 243, 248, 296, 297.
    59.   H.B.C.A., A. 11/118, Auld to the Governor and Committee, September 26, 1811.
    60.   Rich, I, p. 145, notes the "by fayre and gentle means" directive.
    61.   See Peter Laslett, *The World We Have Lost* (London, 1971), Chapter 1. His concept of the patriarchal household is particularly useful.
    62.   Williams, pp. 296, 297.
    63.   *Ibid.*, p. 243.
    64.   H.B.C.A., A. 6/20, Governor and Committee to Governor George Simpson, March 8, 1822.
    65.   *Ibid.*
    66.   *Ibid.* Also see C.M.S.A., N.W.A.M., Outgoing Correspondence, Rev. Josiah Pratt to Rev. John West, February 13, 1821.
    67.   Ross, pp. 110-11, 193-202.
    68.   *Ibid.*, pp. 156-57.
    69.   C.M.S.A., N.W.A.M., I.C., Journal of Rev. David T. Jones, December 20, 1823.
    70.   *Ibid.*, Rev. William Cockran to The Secretary, July 29, 1826.
    71.   A most interesting letter in this regard is *Ibid.*, Joseph Cook to The Lay Secretary, July 29, 1846.
    72.   Note particularly the role of James Sinclair as it appears in P.A.M., P.R.S., Red River Correspondence, 1845-47. Also see *Ibid.*, Gunn, ed.
    73.   The interests of Louis Riel pere and Rev. Georges Belcourt seemed to mirror those of James Sinclair and Andrew McDermot in the Red River Settlement during the 1840s. Yet the dramatic increase in the population of the Metis coupled with the Company's relatively constant demand in the market place and its rule of dealing only with "recognized hunters" may well offer a more substantial explanation.
    74.   Laslett, Chapter 1.
    75.   The question, of course, is whether such families would constitute "Home Guard" Indians.
    76.   Sylvia Van Kirk, "Women and the Fur Trade," *The Beaver*, Winter, 1972, p. 4.
    77.   To date I have not been able to identify Mixed-Bloods, other than Iroquois from the Montreal region, serving in the ranks of the voyageurs.
    78.   Ray, pp. 101-04, and Bishop, p. 160.
    79.   Bishop, pp. 152, 160.
    80.   Harold Hickerson, *The Chippewa and Their Neighbors: A Study in Ethnohistory* (Toronto, 1970), pp. 74-75.
    81.   Harold Hickerson, "The Genesis of A Trading Post Band: The Pembina Chippewa," *Ethnohistory*, III, 4, 1956, pp. 289-90, 294, 307.
    82.   *Ibid.*, p. 305.
    83.   Giraud, p. 366.
    84.   A.S. Morton, "The New Nation, The Metis," *Transactions of the Royal Society of Canada*, Series III, Section II, 1939.
    85.   Giraud, p. 619.
    86.   Ross, p. 246.
    87.   Giraud, pp. 669-72.
    88.   J.M.S. Careless, "Frontierism, Metropolitanism and Canadian History," *C.H.R.*, XXXV, March 1, 1954.

89. The most noted attempt in this context was J.P. Pritchett, *The Red River Valley* (Toronto, 1942).

A Probe into the Demographic Structure of Nineteenth Century Red River

The work for the demographic study, still uncompleted, was financed by a Canada Council grant. The author is particularly thankful to Mr. and Mrs. Leo Sabulsky of Grindrod, British Columbia, who contributed much to the paper as my research assistants during the summer of 1975. The author also wishes to thank the Hudson's Bay Company for permission to use their archives.

1. E.E. Rich, ed., *London Correspondence Inward from Eden Colville, 1849-1852*, intro. by W.L. Morton, Vol. XIX (London: The Hudson's Bay Record Society, 1956), pp. xxiii-xxiv.

2. John Foster, "The Country-born in the Red River Settlement: 1820-1850" (unpublished Ph.D. thesis, University of Alberta, 1972) contains the best description of the early life of the settlement.

3. These figures are based on an analysis of the 1832, 1838, 1843, 1847, and 1849 censuses using the Statistical Package for the Social Sciences (S.P.S.S.). See Appendix VII.

4. In 1815 Cook wrote that he had 10 children (Hudson's Bay Company Archives, E.8/5, fos. 126-9). In 1820 when he was first listed as an "annuitant" in the "H.B.C. Account Book" (H.B.C.A., B.235d, fo. 35) only eight children remained. The ages of the male children were calculated from the 1849 census in the Provincial Archives of Manitoba. For other information on the Cook family see H.B.C.A., A.30/6, fo. 6, H.B.C.A., E.8/5, fos. 126-9, and H.B.C.A. Land Register B, Lot 155 and Lot 578.

5. For material relating to the Bird Family see H.B.C.A., B235d, fo. 7, Hudson's Bay Company Account Book; H.B.C.A., A.36/1b. fos. 46-7, The Probated Will of James Bird, and P.A.M., St. John's Baptisms, 1813-1828, 87, P.A.M., St. John's Marriages, 1820-35, 19, and P.A.M., Kildonan Correspondence, M.G. 2.55, p. 49.

6. For information relating to the Corrigal family see P.A.M., 1832 Census; P.A.M., St. John's Marriages 1820-1835, 62; H.B.C.A., A.36/6, fo. 6; P.A.M., St. John's Baptisms, 1813-1828, 269; P.A.M., Peter Corrigal Collection, photograph; and H.B.C.A., Land Register B, Lot 136 and 562.

7. H.B.C.A., Land Register B, Lot 493.

8. H.B.C.A., B.235d./35, fo. 1; H.B.C.A., A.30/1, fo. 35d; P.A.M., St. John's Baptisms, 1813-1828, 64; P.A.M., 1832 Census; H.B.C.A., Land Register B, Lot 107.

9. H.B.C.A., A.30/1, fos. 62, 31; P.A.M., St. John's Baptisms, 1813-1828, fos. 415-8. The ages of the children were calculated from P.A.M. 1832 Census. H.B.C.A., Land Register B, Lot 225 and 226.

10. P.A.M., St. John's Marriages, 1820-1835, 22; St. John's Baptisms, 1813-1828, 113-7, 391, 562. H.B.C.A., Land Register B, Lot 577, Lot 138.

11. William Flett should not be confused with George Flett, a distant relative. H.B.C.A., A.30/16, fos. 9d-10; P.A.M., 1849 Census. H.B.C.A., A.36/1b, fo. 1; H.B.C.A., A.44/2, fo. 151.

12. H.B.C.A., Land Register B, Lot 165, 225, 226, H.B.C.A., A.36/1b, fos. 46-7.

13. Appendix II.

14. Appendix II.

15. P.A.M., St. John's Baptisms, 1828-1879, 91, 232, 449.

16. P.A.M., St. John's Baptisms, 1813-1828, 659; 1828-1879, 292.

17. P.A.M., St. John's Baptisms, 1828-1879, 59, 221, 429, and 632.

18. P.A.M., St. John's Baptisms, 1828-1849, 48.

19. P.A.M., St. John's Baptisms, 1828-1879, 59.

20. P.A.M., St. John's Burials, 1821-75, 103, 109; P.A.M., St. John's Baptisms, 1821-75, 573.

21. P.A.M., St. John's Burials, 1822-1875, 79, 1204, 1206.

22. P.A.M., St. John's Burials, 1822-1875, 1879, 223, 375, 1032, 973, and 1223.

23. Mrs. Sabulsky suggests that the change from a predominantly hunting to a more agricultural life in the 1830s contributed to a state of transitory malnutrition especially amongst the mixed-bloods. Apparently the body requires a few years to produce the amino acids needed to digest plant carbohydrates after being accustomed to a high protein meat diet.

24. Alexander Ross, *The Red River Settlement* (London: Smith, Elder and Company, 1856), p. 135.

25. Appendix I.

26. Appendix I. It is of course not valid to label all Scots as Kildonans but when a random sample of Kildonans were extracted and analyzed there was no statistical difference from the more general sample.

27. Glenbow Archives, Sutherland Correspondence, James to John Sutherland, August 10, 1840.

28. H.B.C.A., A.34/1, fo. 57.

29. P.A.M., Peter Garrioch Diary, p. 1.

30. P.A.M., Archibald Collection, 18.

31. P.A.M., Red River Collection, James Bird to Alexander Christie, March 31, 1846.

32. P.A.M., Peter Garrioch Diary, p. 34.

33. P.A.M., Peter Garrioch Diary, p. 11.

34. P.A.M., Red River Collection, James Bird to Alexander Christie, March 31, 1846.

35. Public Archives of Canada, Church Missionary Society Archives, Rev. William Cockran, Journal, August 3, 1833, p. 570.

36. H.B.C.A., Land Register B, Lot 115, 578.

37. H.B.C.A., Land Register B, Lot 225, 226.

38. H.B.C.A., William H. Cook's Will and Probate.

39. H.B.C.A., Land Register B, Lot 225, 226, 1388.

40. P.A.M., R.R.C., James Bird to Alexander Christie, March 31, 1846.

41. Appendix I.

42. These men may have married Indian women outside of Red River although there is not evidence to suggest such.

43. P.A.M., St. Andrew's Marriages, 1825-1860, 100.

44. P.A.M., St. Andrew's Burials, 1835-1870, 154; P.A.M., St. Andrew's Marriages, 1835-1870, 154.

45. P.A.M., St. Paul's Baptisms, 1850-1878, 3.

46. P.A.M., 1849 Census.

47. P.A.M., 1849 Census.

48. The most recent study of the events of 1849 that includes an examination of the social factors is John Foster, "The Country-born in Red River 1820-1850," Chapter V.

49. A preliminary investigation of the economic indicators given in the censuses, such as the number of livestock, agricultural implements, and cultivated land per family indicates that agriculture began to stagnate in the late 1830s, primarily, one can perhaps assume, because there was no longer any room for expansion.

50. For an examination of the role of the churches in the social structure of Red River and for a general indication of the leadership of the churches see F. Pannekoek, "The Churches and the Social Structure in the Red River Area 1818-1870" (unpublished Ph.D. thesis, Queen's University, 1973). The principal argument of the thesis is that the churches were a primary contributor to the social disintegration of Red River.

Canadianizing the West: The North-West Mounted Police as Agents of the National Policy, 1873-1905

1. R.C. Brown, *Canada's National Policy, 1883-1900: A Study in Canadian-American Relations* (Princeton, 1964), p. 12.

2. Medicine Hat *Times*, May 28, 1887, quoted in C.G. Edwards, "The National Policy as Seen by the Editors of the Medicine Hat Newspapers: A Western Opinion, 1885-1896" (unpublished M.A. thesis, University of Alberta, 1969), p. 81.

3. S.W. Horrall, "Sir John A. Macdonald and the Mounted Police Force for the Northwest Territories," *Canadian Historical Review*, LIII, 1972, pp. 179-200. There are indications that Macdonald was thinking about the problems even before Confederation. The following passage appears in a letter from Governor-General Monck in 1865: "I return Mr. McMicken's letter which appears satisfactory as regards the state of the West. I think the suggestion as to the appointment of Police as a good one." Public Archives of Canada, Macdonald Papers, Vol. 74, Monck to Macdonald, n.d. 1865.

4. Marjorie Freeman Campbell, *A Century of Crime: The Development of Crime Detection Methods in Canada* (Toronto, 1970) and Desmond Morton, "Aid to the Civil Power: The Canadian Militia in Support of Social Order, 1867-1914," *Canadian Historical Review*, LI, 1970, pp. 407-25.

5.　When Lt.-Gov. A.G. Archibald reported serious election riots at Red River in 1872, Macdonald replied that they were regrettable but, ". . . not of a more serious character than we have seen in older communities. . . ." Public Archives of Manitoba, Alexander Morris Papers, Macdonald to Archibald, October 7, 1872. See also Michael S. Cross, "The Shiner's War: Social Violence in the Ottawa Valley in the 1830s," *Canadian Historical Review*, LIV, 1973, pp. 1-26.

6.　Dale and Lee Gibson, *Substantial Justice: Law and Lawyers in Manitoba, 1670-1970* (Winnipeg, 1972) and Roy St. George Stubbs, *Four Recorders of Rupert's Land* (Winnipeg, 1967).

7.　P.A.C., Macdonald Papers, Vol. 210, Indian Agent T.P. Wadsworth to Indian Commissioner E.T. Galt, July 25, 1881.

8.　P.A.C., R.C.M.P. Records (RG 18), Comptroller's Office Official Correspondence Series (A-1), Vol. 103, file No. 63, Father J. Hugonnard to Indian Commissioner, December 19, 1894 and Inspector Constantine to Superintendent A. Bowen Perry, January 8, 1895.

9.　In 1888 a constable by the name of Simons was accused of giving some iodine to an Indian woman who drank it and died from the effects. Superintendent P.R. Neale reported, ". . . I do not think any Western jury will convict him." P.A.C., RG 18, A-1, Vol. 24, No. 667, Neale to Commissioner L.W. Herchmer, July 17, 1888. See also Public Archives of Saskatchewan, Diary of William Wallace Clarke, 1875 and P.A.C., Diary of Constable R.N. Wilson.

10.　P.A.C., RG 18, A-1, Vol. 26, No. 43, correspondence between the Commissioner and High River Branch, Alberta Stock Growers' Association, November 1888-January 1889.

11.　P.A.C., RG 18, Commissioner's Office, Orders and Regulations, 1880-1954 (B-1), Vol. 8, General Order No. 901 (Old Series), 1883.

12.　In the early days, for example, Commissioner Macleod had ruled that the Sun Dance was to be respected and no arrests were to be made during the ceremony, on the analogy of a church. By the 1890s the police were actively engaged in efforts to eradicate the Sun Dance as a relic of barbarism. P.A.C., RG 18, A-1, Vol. 36, No. 817, Superintendent S. Steele to Commissioner L.W. Herchmer, August 12, 1889 and Vol. 55, No. 586, Steele to Herchmer, June 23, 1891. See also Hugh A. Dempsey, *Crowfoot: Chief of the Blackfeet* (Edmonton, 1972).

13.　S.B. Steele, *Forty Years in Canada* (Toronto, 1915), pp. 196-200. For the strikebreaking incident see P.A.C., Diary of Superintendent R. Burton Deane.

14.　The best examples of this kind of police work are to be found in the reports of Inspector G.E. Sanders concerning his supervision of construction on the Crowsnest Pass Branch. P.A.C., RG 18, A-1, Vol. 145, No. 56.

15.　See, for example, P.A.C., RG 18, A-1, Vol. 42, No. 495, Calgary Patrol Reports, April-June, 1890.

16.　For the churches see G.N. Emery, "Methodism on the Canadian Prairies, 1896 to 1914: The Dynamics of an Institution in a New Environment" (unpublished Ph.D. thesis, University of British Columbia, 1970); for the schools see Neil Gerard McDonald, "The School as an Agent of Nationalism in the North-West Territories, 1884-1905" (unpublished M.Ed. thesis, University of Alberta, 1971).

17.　This applied to such American immigrant groups as the Mormons as well as to Europeans.

18.　P.A.C., RG 18, A-1, Vol. 96, No. 413 and Vol. 100, No. 886.

19.　P.A.C., RG 18, A-1, Vol. 22, No. 413 and Vol. 117, No. 76.

20.　*Canadian Military Gazette*, March 1, 1894.

21.　Ottawa *Free Press*, February 16, 1888.

22.　P.A.C., RG 18, A-1, Vol. 205, No. 110, and Vol. 269, No. 763.

23.　P.A.C., RG 18, A-1, Vol. 134, No. 163, Commissioner L.W. Herchmer to Comptroller F. White, February 4, 1897 and Laurier Papers, Vol. 186, J.M. Skelton to Laurier, February 1, 1901.

24.　See, for example, Glenbow-Alberta Institute Archives, Frederick A. Bagley Papers and Diary, A.C. Bury Diary and Reminiscences, Sergeant S. Hetherington Diary; P.A.C., Constable James Finlayson Diary, Constable R.N. Wilson Diary.

25.　Glenbow-Alberta Institute Archives, William John Redmond, "History of the Southwestern Saskatchewan Old-Timers' Association" (unpublished manuscript, 1932).

26.　P.A.C., RG 18, A-1, Vol. 74, No. 68, Herchmer to White, January 13, 1893.

27.　P.A.C., RG 18, A-1, Vol. 126, No. 6, Vol. 165, No. 193, Vol. 167, No. 224, and Vol. 257, No. 512.

28.　P.A.C., RG 18, A-1, Vol. 97, No. 587, Starr to T.M. Daly, July 17, 1894.

29. *Ibid.,* Superintendent J.H. McIlree to White, August 16, 1894.
30. P.A.C., RG 18, A-1, Vol. 172, No. 438, Oliver to White, June 1 and 8, 1899.
31. *Ibid.,* Inspector Wilson to Superintendent Griesbach, June 21, 1899.
32. P.A.C., RG 18, A-1, Vol. 285, No. 24, Commissioner A. Bowen Perry to Superintendent Griesbach, May 11, 1903.
33. P.A.C., RG 18, A-1, Vol. 274, No. 353, Perry to White, October 17, 1903.
34. P.A.C., RG 18, A-1, Vol. 168, No. 241, Sergeant Byrne to Superintendent J. Howe, March 12, 1899.
35. P.A.C., RG 18, A-1, Vol. 76, No. 161, Regina Monthly Report for August 1893.
36. P.A.C., RG 18, A-1, Vol. 253, No. 304, Wilson to Assistant Commissioner McIlree, February 28, 1903.
37. P.A.C., RG 18, A-1, Vol. 250, No. 177, Lethbridge Monthly Report for October 1903.
38. P.A.C., RG 18, A-1, Vol. 8, No. 29, Major-General Selby-Smyth's Report, p. 8.
39. P.A.C., Macdonald Papers, Vol. 229, pp. 98707-8, Vol. 263, pp. 119719-20, Vol. 395, pp. 189133-5, Vol. 405, pp. 195420-1, Vol. 417, pp. 202381-3, 202511-13, 2022663-4, Vol. 430, pp. 210880-2, Vol. 442, pp. 219466-7. See also R. Burton Deane, *Mounted Police Life in Canada: A Record of Thirty-One Years' Service* (London, 1916), pp. 64-6.
40. P.A.C., Laurier Papers, Vol. 39, Memo by Comptroller White, March 5, 1897.
41. P.A.C., Laurier Papers, Vol. 45, Frank Oliver to Laurier, May 12, 1897; Vol. 65, Oliver to Laurier, February 5, 1898; Vol. 105, J.M. Douglas to Laurier, March 27, 1899. P.A.C., RG 18, A-1, Vol. 136, No. 268, T.O. Davis to White, March 31, 1897, and Vol. 168, No. 269, J.M. Douglas to White, January 28, 1899.
42. P.A.C., RG 18, A-1, Vol. 528, No. 108, Laurier to Premiers Walter Scott and A.C. Rutherford, February 7, 1906.

Contracting for the Canadian Pacific Railway

1. The best books dealing with the construction of the Canadian Pacific Railway include: H.A. Innis, *A History of the Canadian Pacific Railway* (Toronto: University of Toronto Press, 1971) (reprint); Pierre Burton, *The Last Spike: The Great Railway, 1881-1885* (Toronto: McClelland and Stewart, 1971); P. Turner Bone, *When the Steel Went Through* (Toronto: Macmillan, 1947); J.H.E. Secretan, *Canada's Great Highway: From the First Stake to the Last Spike* (London, 1924); Walter Vaughan, *The Life and Work of Sir William Van Horne* (New York, 1920).
2. The information in this section is drawn from the Correspondence Files, Registers, and Letterbooks of the Chief Engineer's Office, Department of Railways and Canals, and from the Correspondence, Files, and Letterbooks of the Deputy Minister's and Minister's Offices, Department of Railways and Canals, Public Archives of Canada, Record Group 43. (New filing systems were begun in this department in 1859, 1879, and 1901. Material relating to the C.P.R. can be found in all these series since much of the material was brought forward from one filing system to the next.) All the early contracts were approved by the federal cabinet, and copies of contracts, together with supporting materials, are available with the records of the Privy Council (P.A.C. Record Group 2) and the Department of Finance (P.A.C. Record Group 19). The records of the Superintendent of Immigration (P.A.C. Record Group 76) contain much detailed information on working conditions in the construction camps. These files do not cover the period of the 1880s, but they do refer frequently to conditions prevalent in the C.P.R. construction camps in the 1880s. The C.P.R. records at the Glenbow-Alberta Institute, Calgary, have some original contracts, specifications, correspondence, and diaries of people who worked in the C.P.R. camps in the 1880s. In addition Glenbow-Alberta also has original copies of some still unpublished reminiscences of early railway men, the most useful of which for this study was William McCardell, "Reminiscences of a Western Pioneer." Interesting and useful information was also found in W.G. Sloan "Construction Methods and Equipment of Railways," *The Canadian Engineer,* Vol. 29, (December 23, 1915), pp. 706-09.
3. Department of Railways and Canals file 8317 "C.P.R. Cost of Construction, British Columbia," file 834 "Agreement re original construction," and file 6727, "Taking over railway Port Moody to Savona's Ferry." P.A.C. Record Group 43.
4. A copy of this contract was tabled in the House of Commons and published as CANADA. *Sessional Paper, No. 31,* 1884, pp. 73-86. A detailed review of the

work done by Langdon and Shepherd is given in *The Montreal Herald and Daily Commercial Gazette*, November 3, 1885.

5. Pierre Burton, *The Last Spike: The Great Railway, 1881-1885*, p. 26 *passim*, provides more detailed information about Stickney's departure.

6. C.P.R. Corporate Archives, Ross Correspondence File, contains a number of scathing remarks about Egan's attempts to interfere in matters relating to construction.

7. See particularly Pierre Berton, *The Last Spike*, and Walter Vaughan, *The Life and Work of Sir William Van Horne*.

8. Very few records and letters have been discovered which show in detail the relations between Langdon and Shepherd and Van Horne. J.H.E. Secretan, *Canada's Great Highway: From First Stake to the Last Spike*, speaks very favorably of the work done by Langdon and Shepherd, and his interpretation has been widely accepted. Secretan has very little to say about the later construction managers. The reason for this is very simple. Secretan was one of the first to lose his job with the Canadian Pacific Railway when James Ross and Herbert Holt took over responsibility for construction on the western section. The first letters and reports filed by these two men, particularly Holt, clearly indicate that Secretan was quite mistaken when he said Langdon and Shepherd's organization "was almost perfect."

9. CANADA. *House of Commons Debates, 1883*, pp. 778-79.

10. CANADA. *Sessional Papers No. 31, 1884*, pp. 52-61.

11. There is some ambiguity about the name and, to some extent, the true functions of this contracting company. Officially it was The North American Railway Contracting Company, but the letterheads used by Herbert Holt were those of The North American Contracting Company, and those of The North American Railway Contracting Company. The Company was also known as The North American Construction Company, the latter reference being common on a contract held by the company in New Brunswick. James Ross generally used Canadian Pacific Railway, Construction Department, letterheads. In the correspondence both Holt and Ross are addressed as 'Manager of Construction,' N.A.C.Co.

12. CANADA. *Sessional Paper No. 31, 1884*, pp. 52-61.

13. The financial arrangements are discussed in detail in H.A. Innis, *A History of the Canadian Pacific Railway*.

14. All these details are taken from CANADA. *Sessional Paper No. 31, 1884*, pp. 52-61, and from the *Annual Reports of the Canadian Pacific Railway Company, 1883 and 1884*.

15. P. Turner Bone, *When the Steel Went Through: Reminiscences of a Railroad Pioneer* (Toronto: Macmillan, 1947). C.P.R. Corporate Archives, Correspondence folders containing Ross letters, Holt letters, Miscellaneous Correspondence. These are separate folders which, while not complete, give a very good indication of the work done by Ross and Holt.

16. P. Turner Bone, *When the Steel Went Through*, p. 43.

17. For a time some of these Ontario contractors and their Ontario equipment seemed out of place in the Rockies, but many completed contracts to the satisfaction of the managers. D.B. Hanna, *Trains of Recollection* (Toronto: Macmillan, 1923), tells the story of William Mackenzie and his Ontario "Farmer's outfit."

18. Holt's contract, the prices paid, and the difficulties encountered in completing it are outlined in some detail in letters from James Ross to Van Horne, particularly a letter dated October 20, 1884. C.P.R. Corporate Archives, Ross Correspondence.

19. C.P.R. Corporate Archives, *Shaughnessy Letterbook No. 21*, pp. 336 and 343. See also *Ibid.*, No. 8, pp. 928-29 and 547. These letters by Shaughnessy to Donald Mann, William Mackenzie, Herbert Holt, and James Ross show clearly the very high regard of the senior C.P.R. administrators for their Canadian contractors. James Ross reported on a number of occasions on his various contractors, repeatedly referring to ,some of the Canadian contractors as "good stuff."

20. Testimony and Evidence given by Thomas Oakes in litigation arising out of the Northern Pacific Railroad Receivership; Baker Library, Harvard, *Villard Papers*, Folder entitled, "Northern Pacific and Manitoba Railway Company Testimony." A copy of the transcript of this testimony is also available at Minnesota State Historical Society, Records of the Northern Pacific Railroad Company, Secretary's Office Code 0003, Box 3, File 26.

21. R.M. Hamilton, compiler. *Canadian Quotations and Phrases, Literary and Historical* (Toronto: McClelland and Stewart, 1965), p. 228.

The Northern Saskatchewan River Settlement Claims 1883-1884

1.   J.P. James Campbell to Edgar Dewdney, November 13, 1883; Dewdney to Macdonald, November 13, 1883, *Macdonald Papers* (Public Archives of Canada), 89951.

2.   Macdonald to Macpherson, July 7, 1882, *Macdonald Papers* (P.A.C.), 112194.

3.   *Macdonald Papers* (P.A.C.), 61427; *William Pearce Letter Books: P.A. Claims* (University of Alberta Archives), pp. 37 and following.

4.   One of the major concerns of the settlers was to obtain the right to pre-date their homestead applications to the date they took up the land. By 1883 many had already met homestead requirements and were eligible for patents. Failure to secure this right would mean a further three years residence before gaining title. This no doubt was one of the principal reasons so few applied for patents in 1882 and 1883, pending the government's decision on this matter.

5.   *Interior Records* (P.A.C.), 65366, A memorandum to the Privy Council, October 18, 1883.

6.   Pearce to Walsh, February 14, 1884, *W.P.L.B. P.A. Claims.*

7.   William Pearce, "Half-breed and Indian Outbreak, 1885; Causes of and Suppression of Same." An address to the Alberta Military Institute, October 16, 1923, *William Pearce Papers* (University of Alberta Archives).

8.   Pearce had earlier authorized Evans to perform the duties of a Homestead Inspector in view of the shortage of qualified men. Pearce to Duck, August 22, 1884, *W.P.L.B. P.A. Claims.*

9.   Evidence on the Van Luven case, *W.P.L.B. P.A. Claims*, pp. 3-12, 125-57, 168-69, 182, 193-200, 218-33, 235-41, 275-80.

10.   Pearce to Walsh, September 12, 1883, *Department of the Interior Records* (P.A.C.), 65366.

11.   Pearce to Walsh, February 5, 1884, *W.P.L.B. P.A. Claims.*

12.   Pearce to the Minister of the Interior, January 19, 1884, *W.P.L.B. P.A. Claims.*

13.   Duck to the Surveyor-General, March 11, 1882; Burgess to Duck, September 22, 1882; Duck to the Secretary of the Department of the Interior, December 17, 1883; A memorandum on the visit of Nolin and Vegreville to Pearce, January 22, 1884, *W.P.L.B. P.A. Claims*; Pearce to Macdonald, January 17, 1884, *Macdonald Papers* (P.A.C.), 42201.

14.   Pearce to H.H. Smith, November 7, 1885; Burgess to Macpherson, May 31, 1885, *Interior Records* (P.A.C.), 57904 and 163849.

15.   Michael Canny had applied to make entry onto lands in the sectional grid but could not get his neighbors to witness his affidavits. Pearce to Macpherson, January 22, 1884, *W.P.L.B. P.A. Claims*, p. 271.

16.   *Macdonald Papers* (P.A.C.), 42352.

17.   William Pearce, "History of Manitoba, Saskatchewan, and Alberta" (manuscript), *William Pearce Papers*, file 19.12.

18.   The Edmonton Land claims, *W.P.L.B. P.A. Claims, passim.*, pp. 538-58. The 3,000 acre Hudson's Bay Company Reserve had been surveyed in 1873 by W.S. Gore along prescribed north-south lines. Today this area is bounded by 101 Street on the east, 121 Street on the west and lies between the North Saskatchewan River and 127 Avenue.

19.   Walter was the owner of a blacksmith shop and wagon making establishment and had large timber interest. McDonald and Garneau were freighters.

20.   *The Edmonton South Bank Dispute*

	Claim	Buildings	Breaking	Fences	Total
L. Garneau	Lot 7	$ 250	$175	$200	$ 625
John Walter	Lot 9	$1,260	$100	$150	$1,510
Joseph McDoanald	Lot 11	$ 355	$ 40	$100	$ 495

W.P.L.B. P.A. Claims, p. 619.

21.   A signed affidavit giving the history of the claims dated September 8, 1882, *W.P.L.B. P.A. Claims,* p. 619.

22.   Gavreau was Duck's assistant at Prince Albert during Pearce's investigation there and had since been transferred to the Edmonton Lands Office as the Lands Agent.

23.   Report on the Battleford claims, August 16, 1884, *W.P.L.B. P.A. Claims,* p. 748, *passim.*

The Mounted Police at Battleford had been unable to take a favorable crop of hay from the sandy soils about their post. Their failure led to a dispersal of settlement.

24. Unfortunately in 1884 no one knew where the telegraph office had been located at the time of the reserves being established and therefore Pearce was never certain where the townsite boundaries actually were.
25. Pearce to Walsh, August 20, 1884, *W.P.L.B. P.A. Claims*.
26. Pearce to W. Scott Robertson, September 3, 1884, *W.P.L.B. P.A. Claims*.
27. William S. Waddell, "The Honourable Frank Oliver," unpublished M.A. thesis, University of Alberta, 1950, p. 13.
28. Pearce to Oliver, September 8, 1884; Pearce to Walsh, September 9, 1884. *W.P.L.B. P.A. Claims*.
29. Pearce to Burgess, July 27, 1884, *W.P.L.B. Private, 1883*.
30. *W.P.L.B. P.A. Claims*, pp. 909-28.
31. Macdonald to Smith, April 25, June 17, and June 30, 1884, *H.H. Smith Papers* (P.A.C.).

The Turner Thesis and the Canadian West: A Closer Look at the Ranching Frontier

1. Frederick Jackson Turner, "The Significance of the Frontier in American History," in *The Frontier in American History* (New York: Henry Holt and Company, 1920), p. 38.
2. See, for example, Walter Sage, "Some Aspects of the Frontier in Canadian History," *Canadian Historical Association Annual Report* (1928), pp. 67-72; A.L. Burt, "The Frontier in the History of New France," *Canadian Historical Association Annual Report* (1940), pp. 93-99; F. Landon, *Western Ontario and the American Frontier* (Toronto: McClelland and Stewart, 1967); S.D. Clark, *Movements of Political Protest in Canada* (Toronto: University of Toronto Press, 1959); A.R.M. Lower, *Canada, Canadians in the Making* (Toronto: Longmans Canada Ltd., 1968).
3. Lower, p. 367.
4. Clark; S.M. Lipset, *Agrarian Socialism: The Cooperative Commonwealth Federation in Saskatchewan* (Berkeley: University of California Press, 1967).
5. G.F.G. Stanley, "Western Canada and the Frontier Thesis," *Canadian Historical Association Annual Report* (1940), pp. 104-14. J.E. Foster, "The Country Born of the Red River Settlement, 1800-1875 (unpublished Ph.D. dissertation, University of Alberta, 1972).
6. W.S. MacNutt, "The 1880s" in *The Canadians 1867-1967*, ed. J.M.S. Carless and R. Craig Brown (Toronto: Macmillan of Canada, 1967), pp. 83-84.
7. C.A. Dawson and E.R. Young, *Pioneering in the Prairie Provinces: The Social Side of the Settlement Process*, Vol. VIII of *Canadian Frontiers of Settlement*, ed. W.A. Mackintosh and W.L.G. Joerg (Toronto: Macmillan Co. of Canada Ltd., 1930), p. 12.
8. *Ibid.*, pp. 21-23. In presenting the social ethos of the Canadian ranch country the authors adopt and quote at length the detailed character assessment by the distinguished American Turnerian, W.P. Webb in his classic, *The Great Plains*. The historiography of the ranching frontier in Canada is very limited and interpretation for the most part is consistent. See also, R.W. Murchie, *Agricultural Progress on the Prairie Frontier*, Vol. V of *Canadian Frontiers of Settlement*, ed. W.A. Mackintosh and W.L.G. Joerg (Toronto: Macmillan Co. of Canada Ltd., 1936), p. 53. A.S. Morton and Chester Martin, *History of Prairie Settlement and "Dominion Lands" Policy*, Vol. II of *Canadian Frontiers of Settlement*, ed. W.A. Mackintosh and W.L.G. Joerg (Toronto: Macmillan Co. of Canada Ltd., 1938), p. 91. The revisionist possibilities implicit in the excellent work on the border country by Paul F. Sharp in *Whoop-Up Country: The Canadian-American West, 1865-1885* (2nd ed.; Helena: Historical Society of Montana, 1960), have not gained the attention warranted.
9. G. MacEwan, *Between the Red and the Rockies* (Toronto: University of Toronto Press, 1952), p. 116.
10. *Ibid.*, p. 150.
11. Turner, p. 9.
12. The extent to which the Canadian range was patrolled is suggested by the more than 2,000 mounted patrols performed in 1889 by the Calgary Division, one of the five police divisions serving the ranch country. John P. Turner, *The North-West Mounted Police, 1873-1893* (Ottawa: King's Printer, 1950), II, pp. 425-29.
13. D.H. Breen, "Plain Talk from Plain Western Men: Cattle Baron v. Sodbuster, 1885," *Alberta Historical Review*, XVIII (Summer, 1970), pp. 4-13.
14. *Fort Macleod Gazette*, February 3, 1883; March 9, 1886; Glenbow Alberta Institute, Calgary (hereafter G.A.I.), Western Stock Growers Association Papers, B1,

F3, Minute Book, p. 163, December 7, 1905; G.A.I., A.E. Cross Papers, B58, F463, G. Lane to A.E. Cross, February 5, 1906 and F 464, M.S. McCarthy to A.E. Cross, March 19, 1906.

15.   E.C. Morgan, "The North-West Mounted Police, 1873-1888" (unpublished M.A. thesis, University of Saskatchewan, 1970), p. 174.

16.   *Fort Macleod Gazette*, December 6, 1895. A few cowboys, usually Americans, wore six-guns and the practice continued in the Cypress Hills country until after the turn of the century. The carrying of side arms, however, was actively discouraged by the police and in the foothill region, where the practice had been very limited from the outset, was almost totally unknown by the middle 1890s.

17.   Canada, *Sessional Papers*, No. 13 (1890), Appen. CC, 164.

18.   See, for example, *Calgary Herald*, November 12, 1884; *Fort Macleod Gazette*, February 21, 1885; April 11, 1885; August 18, 1893. It should not be construed, as it is so often in Canadian settlement literature, that social tension was largely unknown. Tensions are in fact readily apparent; the point that should be made is simply that the strength of established institutions assured that such anxieties would be very effectively contained.

19.   Turner, "The Problem of the West," p. 211.

20.   Turner, "The Ohio Valley in American History," p. 170.

21.   Thomas Le Duc, "History and Appraisal of U.S. Land Policy to 1862," in *Land Use Policy and Problems in the United States*, ed. Howard W. Ottoson (Lincoln: University of Nebraska Press, 1963), pp. 6-14.

22.   E.S. Osgood, *The Day of the Cattlemen* (Chicago: The University of Chicago Press, 1968), pp. 182-84. Osgood cites a typical newspaper claim advertisement. "I, the undersigned, do hereby notify the public that I claim the valley, branching off the Glendive Creek, four miles east of Allard, and extending to its source on the South side of the Northern Pacific Railroad as a stock range—Chas. S. Johnson. *Glendive Times* (Glendive, Montana), April 12, 1884.

23.   Chester Martin, *"Dominion Lands" Policy*, ed. Lewis H. Thomas (Toronto: McClelland and Stewart Ltd., 1973), p. 140.

24.   Canada, *Sessional Papers*, No. 13 (1885), 31-32. Herds found grazing on public land were liable to seizure. Public Archives of Canada (hereafter P.A.C.), RG 18, B2a, Vol. 23, 192192, W. Pearce to the Secretary of the Interior, January 25, 1890.

25.   For a more expanded discussion of the contest between rancher and farmer see, D.H. Breen, "The Canadian Prairie West and the 'Harmonious' Settlement Interpretation," *Agricultural History*, XLVII (January 1973), pp. 63-75. In 1887, for example, the federal government posted notices warning: "Whereas it is stated that squatting to some extent is being done on the lands under lease to the British American Ranch Company, situated on both sides of the Bow River west of Calgary, the public are hereby notified that the Government will in no way recognize such squatting. . . ." *Calgary Herald*, August 26, 1887.

26.   Lewis H. Thomas in introduction to Chester Martin, *'Dominion Lands' Policy*, p. xiv.

27.   D.H. Breen, "The Canadian West and the Ranching Frontier, 1875-1922" (unpublished Ph.D. dissertation, University of Alberta, 1972), pp. 69-71. One can identify a few key individuals from south of the border who contributed a great measure of practical experience to the developing range cattle industry, but contrary to popular belief, the actual direction of the larger ranches was not generally in the hands of Americans. The evidence would seem to suggest also that from the late 1870s the percentage of American ranchers was declining and that through the 1880s there was even an absolute decline. The established cattle compact was largely successful, through parliamentary legislation, in keeping most American ranchers away from the Alberta range.

28.   For a thorough analysis of the N.W.M.P. as a social-cultural force in the west see R. C. Macleod, "The North-West Mounted Police 1873-1905: Law Enforcement and the Social Order in the Canadian North-West" (unpublished Ph.D. dissertation, Duke University, 1972); and R.C. Macleod, "Crime and Class: Some Aspects of Law Enforcement in the Canadian North-West, 1885-1905" (paper read before the Eleventh Annual Conference of the Western History Association, at Santa Fe, October 1971).

29.   For additional comment on the social milieu of the ranching frontier in Canada see Breen, "The Canadian West and the Ranching Frontier, 1875-1922," Chapters I-III.

30.   An example of the traditional contrary assertion is, W.S. Macnutt, "The 1880s," pp. 83-84. "Macleod could produce Canada's best version of a wild west. The famous Camoose House, kept by an ex-trader, ex-preacher, and squawman, was the resort of all the whisky vendors, bull-whackers, and mule-skinners of the region who called themselves ranchers." With upwards of 100 police stationed in the town, the Fort Macleod version of the "wild west" must have been very tame indeed.

31.   Alexander Begg, "Stock Raising in the Bow River District Compared with Montana," in *Manitoba and the Great North West*, ed. J. Macown (Guelph: The World Publishing Co., 1882), pp. 273-77, quoting Prof. W. Brown.

32. Lewis G. Thomas, "The Rancher and the City: Calgary and the Cattlemen, 1883-1914," *Transactions of the Royal Society of Canada*, VI, Ser. IV (June 1968), pp. 213-14.

33. It is apparent that the region and the industry were dominated by a relatively few individuals and companies with herds over 400 head, who were in turn superseded by a closely knit "compact" of eighteen individuals and companies with herds over 1,000 (1889 figures). Of the estimated 110,516 head of cattle on the Canadian range in 1889, approximately 96,793 or 87 per cent were owned by the "large" operators having 400 head or more. About 68 per cent of the cattle were owned by ranchers with herds of 1,000 or more. A herd of 400 cattle, the minimum herd size from which the "large" stockmen have been arbitrarily ranked, represented a conservatively estimated investment of $10,000. In the 1880s and 1890s this was no small amount, especially relative to the farmer or squatter whose assets were usually valued in the hundreds of dollars. The cattlemen, even at the lower end of the range hierarchy, enjoyed an economic status vastly superior to their few farm neighbors. Breen, "The Canadian West and the Ranching Frontier, 1875-1922," pp. 138-39.

34. Breen, "The Canadian Prairie West and the 'Harmonious' Settlement Interpretation," p. 65; P.A.C., RG 15, B2a, Vols. 2-20.

35. *Calgary Herald*, September 10, 1895. Prospective "gentlemen" farmers were repeatedly warned by the press of the notable failures of others of their class in such endeavors.

36. Isabelle Randall, *A Lady's Ranch Life in Montana* (London: W.H. Allen, 1887), p. 19.

37. Saskatchewan Archives, "Matador Land and Cattle Company," MacBain to R.L. Lair, November 3, 1914.

38. This strong identification with the Empire before World War I was by no means peculiar only to the cattlemen. See, C. Berger, *The Sense of Power: Studies in the Ideas of Canadian Imperialism 1867-1914* (Toronto: University of Toronto Press, 1970).

39. Breen, "The Canadian West and the Ranching Frontier, 1875-1922," pp. 459-61.

40. P.A.C., RG 15, B2a, Vols. 2-20; Department of Consumer and Corporate Affairs, Documents of Incorporation.

41. Breen, "The Canadian Prairie West and the 'Harmonious' Settlement Interpretation," pp. 72-73.

42. *Calgary Herald*, June 29, 1891; *Tribune* (Calgary), February 6, 1891; G.A.I., W.S.G.A. Papers, B1, F3, Minute Book, 161, May 11, 1905.

43. The ranch community's loyalty to the Conservative party is well illustrated in the returns of the region's first federal election in 1887. The Liberal party, identified as the "farmers" party, received only three of the 301 votes cast in the ranching communities of Fort Macleod and Pincher Creek. *Fort Macleod Gazette*, March 22, 1887.

44. Marcus Lee Hansen, *The Immigrant in American History* (Cambridge: Harvard University Press, 1948), p. 190. The confident attitude of this new population is well illustrated in William R. Stewart, "The Americanization of the Canadian Northwest," *The Cosmopolitan*, XXXIV (April 1903), pp. 603-04.

45. *Lethbridge Herald*, March 12, 1912.

46. See, for example, G.A.I., Walrond Ranch Papers, D. McEachran to Sir John Walrond-Walrond, October 21, 1905. ". . . I would prefer when we go out of business that British people reap the benefits of our struggles and anxieties instead of as may happen it may be given over to the Mormon Church as American speculators. . . ." or Cross Papers, B113, F909, A.E. Cross to Captain Balfour, April 12, 1911. Cross expressed his preference ". . . to have good British people as neighbors rather than inferior, moving Americans. . . ." also University of Alberta, Pearce Papers, 14B12, L.O. Garnett to W. Pearce, March 14, 1899; L.E. Roberts, ed. *Alberta Homestead: Chronicle of a Pioneer Family* (Austin: University of Texas Press, 1968), pp. 25-26.

47. G.A.I., Cross Papers, B56, F457, "General Idea of Proposed Ranch School" (1904).

48. The Bradfield College Ranch, extended challenge: "Though no one ought to grudge our American cousins their enterprise, foresight and progressive sagacity, yet it would appear the bounden duty to the British Empire of those in positions of trust and influence in England to act as pioneers in encouraging the best of our sons to people and control the immense tracts of our great Dominions." Library of the Royal Commonwealth Society (London), H.B. Gray, *The Bradfield College Ranch for Bradfield Boys Near Calgary* (Reading: Blackwell and Gutch, 1909), p. 8.

49. It would be totally wrong to imply that change was largely forestalled in the cattle country. There was indeed vast change after the turn of the century but this essentially was demographically rather than environmentally inspired. The ranchers eventually retreated in face of higher land costs that came when dry-land farming technology advanced to the point that the per acre return for wheat promised greater profits than beef. This economically inspired attrition, coupled with the social decapitation suffered by the ranch

community through war losses, brought an end to the old social order. The vast majority of the new settlers were Americans of different temperament and class background and they soon made the rural areas of southern Alberta, apart from the political system, not much different from the western farm states to the south. It is perhaps observation of this latter group and the failure to appreciate the significant population shift, that has led to the "popular" acceptance of the "American" stereotype.

The Emergence and Role of the Elite in the Franco-Albertan Community to 1914

1. Marcel Giraud, *Le Metis Canadien* (Paris: Institut d'Ethnologie, 1945), pp. 1034-35.
2. Oblate Archives, "Registre des Baptemes et Marriages faits dans les Missions des Forts des Prairies 1842-50."
3. Raymond A. Maclean, "The History of the Roman Catholic Church in Edmonton" (unpublished M.A. thesis, University of Alberta, 1958), p. 13.
4. *Census of the Three Provisional Districts of the North-West Territories 1884-85*, pp. 10-11.
5. Souvenir pamphlet of Saint Joachim's parish published on its centenary (1959), p. 12; Maclean, pp. 99-100.
6. A.I. Silver, "French Canada and the Prairie Frontier 1870-1890," *Canadian Historical Review*, 50 (January 1969), pp. 15-18.
7. Canada, Department of the Interior, *Annual Report, 1894*, Part III, "Report of the Colonization work by Rev. Father Morin," p. 81.
8. *L'Ouest Canadien*, 22 juin, 1899.
9. *Ibid.*, 28 septembre, 1899.
10. Jean-C. Falardeau, "Evolution Des Structures Sociales Des Elites Au Canada Francais," in *Structures Sociales du Canada francais*, ed. by Guy Sylvestre (n.p: University of Toronto Press, 1966), p. 11.
11. *Edmonton Bulletin*, June 25, 1894.
12. *Statutes of Canada*, 38 Vict., c. 49, s. 11 and 40 Vict., c. 7, s. 11; *Ordinances of the N.W.T.*, 1884, No. 5.
13. *L'Ouest Canadien*, 30 juin, 1898.
14. *Ordinances of the N.W.T.*, 1901, c. 29, s. 8 and s. 136.
15. C. Cecil Lingard, *Territorial Government in Canada—The Autonomy Question in the Old North-West Territories* (Toronto: University of Toronto Press, 1946), pp. 134-35.
16. Personal interviews with community members, 1970.
17. *Le Patriote de l'Ouest*, 23 decembre, 1925 and 28 juillet, 1926; Personal interview with Georges Bugnet, September 28, 1970.
18. *Le Courrier de l'Ouest*, 7 mai, 1908.
19. *Ibid.*, 16 mars, 1911.
20. *Census of the Prairie Provinces*, 1916, p. 222.
21. L.G. Thomas, *The Liberal Party in Alberta* (Toronto: University of Toronto Press, 1959), p. 143; *Le Courrier de l'Ouest*, 5 aout, 1913.
22. *Le Courrier de l'Ouest*, 3 mars, 1910.
23. *Ibid.*, 18 juin, 1914.
24. *Ibid.*, 2 octobre, 1913; The monetary pledges of many leading community members were made on the eve of a severe economic recession yet most of them stood by the pledges even at the price of the very real hardship involved in meeting them.

Farm Politics in an Urban Age: The Decline of the United Farmers of Alberta after 1921

1. J.M.S. Careless, "Somewhat Narrower Horizons," Canadian Historical Association *Historical Papers*, 1968, pp. 1-10 and "'Limited Identities' in Canada," *Canadian Historical Review*, Vol. 50 (1969), pp. 1-10; A.R.M. Lower, "The Metropolitan and the Provincial," *Queen's Quarterly*, Vol. 76 (Winter 1969), pp. 577-90 and "Townsman and Countryman: Two Ways of Life," *Dalhousie Review*, Vol. 50 (1970-71), pp. 480-87 and "Metropolis and Hinterland," *South Atlantic Quarterly*, Vol. 70 (1971), pp. 386-403. Careless has since postulated that metropolitan development involves passage through not only the

hinterland but also, prior to that, the frontier stages: "Metropolitan Reflections on "Great Britain's Woodyard'," *Acadiensis,* Vol. 3, No. 1 (Autumn 1973), pp. 103-09 and "Urban Development in Canada," *Urban History Review,* No. 1-74 (June 1974), pp. 9-14.

2. See Eric E. Lampard, "The History of Cities in the Economically Advanced Areas," in *Economic Development and Cultural Change,* Vol. III (University of Chicago Research Center in Edmonton Development and Cultural Change, 1955), pp. 90-119; Leo F. Schnore, "The City as a Social Organism," *Urban Affairs Quarterly,* Vol. 1 (1966), 58-69; and Richard D. Brown, "The Emergence of Urban Society in Rural Massachusetts, 1760-1820," *Journal of American History,* Vol. 61, No. 1 (June 1974), pp. 29-51. Brown discusses the development of various heterogeneities and communication networks other than merely the economic as characteristics of urbanization: the key point in the transition of a community to the urban condition seems for him to be transcendance of the "corporate insularity" which he associates with homogeneity in early Massachusetts society.

3. C.B. Macpherson, *Democracy in Alberta* (Toronto, University of Toronto Press, 1953), pp. 62-92 and 142-43; W.L. Morton, "The Western Progressive Movement and Cabinet Domination," *Canadian Journal of Economics and Political Science,* Vol. 12 (1946), pp. 136-43 and "The Social Philosophy of Henry Wise Wood," *Agricultural History,* Vol. 22 (1948), pp. 120-23.

4. John A. Irving, *The Social Credit Movement in Alberta* (Toronto, University of Toronto Press, 1959), p. 158.

5. *Grain Growers' Guide* (hereafter referred to as *G.G.G.*), January 31, 1917, p. 7 and following and September 10, 1917, p. 10; Morton, "The Social Philosophy," especially pp. 118-19. For Wood's application of his concept (tensions among specialists stimulating cooperation) to the educational complex, see *Edmonton Bulletin,* April 1, 1921, p. 11.

6. W.K. Rolph, *Henry Wise Wood of Alberta* (Toronto, University of Toronto Press, 1950), pp. 68-72. The U.F.A. had maintained representation in the Canadian Council of Agriculture since 1909.

7. *G.G.G.,* May 7, 1919, p. 7. E.J. Garland, prominent U.F.A. leader of the time and later U.F.A. Member of Parliament, always remembered the fervor with which Wood believed economic reasons to be the sole lasting basis for group loyalty. See taped interview with E.J. Garland by Una Maclean, 1961, Glenbow-Alberta Institute, Calgary (hereafter referred to as "G.A.I.").

8. Carl Betke, "The United Farmers of Alberta, 1921-1935: The Relationship between the Agricultural Organization and the Government of Alberta" (unpublished M.A. thesis, University of Alberta, 1971), pp. 25-30; Rolph, *Henry Wise Wood,* pp. 79-86. Wood came to be regarded as the living embodiment of the U.F.A., with an uncanny knack for putting into words what farmers were thinking. See E.J. Garland interview, *op. cit.;* taped interview with Milton McCool by Una Maclean Evans, 1961, G.A.I.; copy of an article by Randolph Patton, *Saskatoon Star, ca.* November 14, 1921, entitled "W.H. Wood on Federal Election Prospects 1921," found in G.A.I., Walter Norman Smith papers, File 102.

9. *G.G.G.,* January 26, 1921, p. 10 and July 6, 1921, p. 12.

10. Betke, "The United Farmers," pp. 30-35.

11. U.F.A. "Declaration of Principles," 1921, G.A.I., U.F.A. Papers, File 18.

12. Morton, "The Western Progressive Movement," p. 140.

13. List of U.F.A. materials distributed during 1921 elections, G.A.I., Walter Norman Smith papers, File 50.

14. *Edmonton Bulletin,* July 2 and 13, 1921.

15. Quotations from the *Lethbridge Herald* and the *Vegreville Observer* were found in the *Edmonton Bulletin,* July 2, 9, and 13, 1921.

16. *Edmonton Journal,* July 9, 1921.

17. U.F.A. pamphlet, "Group Organization and Cooperation Between Groups," 1921, G.A.I., U.F.A. Papers, File 18; *Western Farmer and Weekly Albertan,* July 13, 1921. Pages 6 and 7 of this publication were regularly contributed by the Western Independent Publishing Company, Donald Cameron (of the U.F.A.), President.

18. *Western Farmer and Weekly Albertan,* July 13, 1921.

19. G.A.I., George Cloakey collection of official provincial election returns for Alberta, 1905-1963.

20. *Census of Canada, 1921,* Vol. IV, pp. 292-317.

21. The new attorney-general, John E. Brownlee, much later remembered no great conviction in Wood that group government should be initiated: not only were the practical difficulties overwhelming, but the government should carry on, Wood felt, free of U.F.A. interference. Taped interview with Brownlee by Una Maclean, 1961, G.A.I. See also Garland interview, *op. cit.;* the transcript of an interview with R.G. Reid by Mrs. E. Kreisel and J.E. Cool, 1969, and a taped interview with Henry G. Young by J.E. Cook and F.A. Johnson, 1971, Provincial Archives of Alberta, Edmonton (hereafter referred to as "P.A.A.").

22. See H.W. Wood's presidential addresses to the U.F.A. annual

convention in 1923 and 1928, *The U.F.A.,* February 1, 1923 and February 1, 1928.
   23.   Betke, "The United Farmers," pp. 10-13.
   24.   Membership never exceeded 16,000 after 1922 except in 1930. See reports in the appropriate editions of the *Canadian Annual Review* or *The U.F.A.* For a summary of membership totals for 1909-1927 see *The U.F.A.,* February 1, 1928, p. 9. These figures include members of the United Farm Women of Alberta and of the junior branch.
   25.   Letter, David Christie, Secretary-Treasurer, Haig U.F.A. Local, to Greenfield, July 30, 1921, P.A.A., Premiers' Papers, File 1-600-9.
   26.   Letter, H. Higginbotham, U.F.A. Secretary, forwarding a July 25 Executive resolution to Greenfield, August 22, 1921, P.A.A., Premiers' Papers, File 1-600-9.
   27.   Telegram, A. Allenbach, Mannville, to Greenfield, August 18, 1921, P.A.A., Premiers' Papers, File 1-600-9.
   28.   Address by Samuel Brown (U.F.A.—High River) during the Throne Speech debate, 1922. *Edmonton Bulletin,* February 11.
   29.   *Edmonton Bulletin,* February 3, 1922.
   30.   *Edmonton Bulletin,* February 18, 1922; *Edmonton Journal,* March 3, 1922.
   31.   Brownlee interview, *op. cit.; Journal of the Legislative Assembly of the Province of Alberta* (1922), 97-98; *Edmonton Bulletin,* March 11, 1922; *Calgary Albertan,* March 11 and 13, 1922.
   32.   Brownlee interview, *op. cit.;* taped interview with Russell Love by Una Maclean Evans, 1962, G.A.I.
   33.   Address by Nelson S. Smith in the Legislature, 1922 session, *Edmonton Journal,* February 8, 1922.
   34.   *Edmonton Journal,* February 14, 1922.
   35.   Letter, Greenfield to the Lieutenant-Governor-in-Council, September 2, 1921, P.A.A., Premiers' Papers, File 1-100-6. See also in the same file a memorandum of relief requirements in northern Alberta prepared for H. Stutchbury, Provincial Director of Relief.
   36.   Letters, J.P. Watson, Secretary-Treasurer, Chinook U.F.A. Local, to Greenfield, September 12, 1921, enclosing a Local resolution of September 3, and John Egger, Sullivan Lake, to Greenfield, September 18, 1921, P.A.A., Premiers' Papers, File 1-100-6.
   37.   Letter, W.C. Smith to R.G. Reid, October 23, 1921, P.A.A., Premiers' Papers, File 1-100-6.
   38.   Telegram, E.G. Gardiner, Coronation, to Greenfield, January 9, 1922, P.A.A., Premiers' Papers, File 1-100-6.
   39.   Letter, Greenfield to Captain T.S. Acheson, General Agricultural Agent, C.P.R., Winnipeg, August 18, 1921, P.A.A., Premiers' Papers, File 1-100-6.
   40.   Letters, Greenfield to James Fletcher, Kingman, December 16, 1921, to T.W. Harris, Taber, September 16, 1921, to J.P. Watson, Chinook, September 19, 1921, and to W.A. Reid, Silverdale Rural Credit Society, Consort, November 10, 1921, P.A.A., Premiers' Papers, File 1-100-6.
   41.   "Memorandum of Agreement between the Honourable Sir James Lougheed, Minister of the Department of the Interior, on behalf of the Government of the Dominion of Canada, and the Honourable Herbert Greenfield, Premier, on behalf ot the Government of the Province of Alberta, entered into this 27th day of October, 1921." P.A.A., Premiers' Papers, File 1-100-6.
   42.   Letter, Greenfield to A. Walker, Travers, September 19, 1921, P.A.A., Premiers' Papers, File 1-100-6; Province of Alberta, Report of the Survey Board for Southern Alberta (January 1922) as well as preliminary memoranda collated by Arthur Woolley, P.A.A., Premiers' Papers, File 1-100-40.
   43.   Correspondence, October 1922 to January 1923, between Greenfield and each of R. Johnson, Secretary-Treasurer, Blue Grass U.F.A. Local; P.H. Wedderburn, Chinook; R.L. Cross, Secretary-Treasurer, Naco U.F.A. Local (Wiste); R.N. Mangles, Secretary, Youngstown District U.F.A. Cooperative Association; Harry Jewsbury, President, Armada U.F.A. Local, P.A.A., Premiers' Papers, File 1-100-40.
   44.   *Statutes of Alberta,* 1922, Chap. 29: "An Act to Provide for the Temporary Partial Suspension of the Tax Recovery Act"; Chap. 65: "The Seed Grain Act"; Chap. 66: "The Provincial Relief Act, 1922"; Chap. 43: "The Drought Area Relief Act."
   45.   *Edmonton Bulletin,* March 25, 1922.
   46.   Letter, J.M. Roebuck, Whitla, to Greenfield, July 6, 1922, P.A.A., Premiers' Papers, File 1-100-6; Letter, J.R. Johnson, Secretary-Treasurer, Blue Grass U.F.A. Local, to Greenfield, July 1922, P.A.A., Premiers' Papers, File 1-100-32.
   47.   Report of inspection of the area south of Hanna by Medicine Hat District, Agriculturist James Murray to Deputy Minister of Agriculture H.A. Craig, n.d. (August 1922), P.A.A., Premiers' Papers, File 1-100-6.
   48.   Telegram, Greenfield to Matt O'Reilly, Sunnybrook, August 1, 1922, and Letter, Greenfield to W.A. Hague, Mizpah, August 3, 1922, P.A.A., Premiers' Papers, File 1-100-6; Telegrams between Greenfield and Federal Minister of the Interior Charles Stewart, late

September, 1922, P.A.A., Premiers' Papers, File 1-100-32.
    49. Letter, Greenfield to W.J. Oakford, Elmworth, September 3, 1922, P.A.A., Premiers' Papers, File 1-100-6.
    50. *Edmonton Journal,* February 17, 1923; *The U.F.A.,* February 15, 1923, p. 12; U.F.A. Annual Convention resolutions presented to the government, 1923, P.A.A., Premiers' Papers, File 1-600-9.
    51. U.F.A. Annual Convention resolutions presented to the government, 1922, and a letter, W.N. Smith, Editor, *The U.F.A.,* to Greenfield, August 7, 1922, P.A.A., Premiers' Papers, File 1-600-9.
    52. Letter, Greenfield to E.R. Briggs, Excel, April 4, 1922, P.A.A., Premiers' Papers, File 1-1600-10.
    53. Memorandum, Greenfield to Brownlee, May 20, 1922, P.A.A., Premiers' Papers, File 1-1600-10.
    54. While H.W. Wood appears not to have had much time to look at Douglas's proposals, he permitted the editor of *The U.F.A.,* W. Norman Smith, to advertise relevant material. Smith's attitude to the subject was one of ambivalent fascination. See letters, Smith to Henry Spencer, U.F.A. M.P., July 18, 1922, Wood to Charles A. Bowman, Editor, *Ottawa Citizen,* September 16, 1921, and Smith to Bowman, February 25, 1922, G.A.I., Walter Norman Smith Papers, Files 5 and 102.
    55. Paraphrased account of Brownlee's statement to a U.F.A. executive meeting, Calgary, June 16, 1922, G.A.I., Microfilm of U.F.A. Executive Board and Committee Minutes, 1917-1935.
    56. Memorandum of government replies to 1922 U.F.A. Annual Convention resolutions, submitted to the U.F.A. executive by Greenfield on December 16, 1922, P.A.A., Premiers' Papers, File 1-600-9.
    57. *The U.F.A.,* February 15, 1923, pp. 4, 10, 11.
    58. Minutes, meeting of U.F.A. executive members and Cabinet members, Edmonton, February 3, 1923, P.A.A., Premiers' Papers, File 1-600-9.
    59. D.A. MacGibbon, *Report of the Commissioner on Banking and Credit with respect to the Industry of Agriculture in the Province of Alberta,* submitted to Attorney-General Brownlee, November 4, 1922, P.A.A., Premiers' Papers, File 1-1600-10.
    60. Brownlee interview, *op. cit.;* Reid interview, *op. cit.*
    61. *Edmonton Journal,* March 1, 1923; Letters and telegrams among Greenfield, Bracken, Dunning, and King, February to May 1923, P.A.A., Premiers' Papers, File 1-1600-10.
    62. Letter, protesting government disregard for the U.F.A. convention resolution in favor of a provincial bank, A.F. Aitken, President, Battle River U.F.A. Political Association, to Greenfield, August 20, 1923, P.A.A., Premiers' Papers, File 1-600-9; Minutes, U.F.A. Annual Convention, Edmonton, January 15-18, 1924, G.A.I., Microfilm of U.F.A. Annual Convention Reports and Minutes, 1917-1935.
    63. Minutes, U.F.A. executive meeting, February 15-16, 1924 and U.F.A. board meeting, July 10, 1924, G.A.I., Microfilm of U.F.A. Executive Board and Committee Minutes, 1917-1935.
    64. *Calgary Morning Albertan,* April 16, 1924.
    65. *Edmonton Journal,* March 4, 1925.
    66. Brownlee interview, *op. cit.; Calgary Morning Albertan,* November 24, 1925; *The U.F.A.,* December 1, 1925, including a quotation from the *Red Deer Advocate,* late November 1925.
    67. Transcript, interview with Hugh Allen by Una Maclean, 1961, G.A.I.
    68. Betke, "The United Farmers," pp. 104-30.
    69. Donald V. Smiley, "Canada's Poujadists: A New Look at Social Credit," *The Canadian Forum,* Vol. 42 (September 1962), pp. 121-123. One of the earliest U.F.A. politicians has also noted the anti-elite nature of the 1921 U.F.A. campaign: taped interview with Lorne Proudfoot by J.E. Cook and F.A. Johnson, 1972, P.A.A.